BEAUTY OF THE BEASTS

BEAUTY OF THE BEASTS
Rethinking Nature's Least Loved Animals

Jo Wimpenny

BLOOMSBURY WILDLIFE
LONDON · OXFORD · NEW YORK · NEW DELHI · SYDNEY

BLOOMSBURY WILDLIFE
Bloomsbury Publishing Plc
50 Bedford Square, London, WC1B 3DP, UK
Bloomsbury Publishing Ireland Limited,
29 Earlsfort Terrace, Dublin 2, D02 AY28, Ireland

BLOOMSBURY, BLOOMSBURY WILDLIFE and the
Diana logo are trademarks of Bloomsbury Publishing Plc

First published in the United Kingdom 2026

Text copyright © Jo Wimpenny, 2026
Cover and chapter illustrations © Abby Cook, 2026

Jo Wimpenny has asserted her right under the Copyright,
Designs and Patents Act, 1988, to be identified as Author of this work.

For legal purposes the Acknowledgements on p. 307
constitute an extension of this copyright page.

All rights reserved. No part of this publication may be: i) reproduced or transmitted in any form, electronic or mechanical, including photocopying, recording or by means of any information storage or retrieval system without prior permission in writing from the publishers; or ii) used or reproduced in any way for the training, development or operation of artificial intelligence (AI) technologies, including generative AI technologies. The rights holders expressly reserve this publication from the text and data mining exception as per Article 4(3) of the Digital Single Market Directive (EU) 2019/790.

Bloomsbury Publishing Plc does not have any control over, or responsibility for, any third-party websites referred to or in this book. All internet addresses given in this book were correct at the time of going to press. The author and publisher regret any inconvenience caused if addresses have changed or sites have ceased to exist, but can accept no responsibility for any such changes.

No responsibility for loss, injury or illness caused to any individual
or organization acting on or refraining from action as a result of material
in this publication can be accepted by Bloomsbury Publishing Plc or the author.

A catalogue record for this book is available from the British Library.

Library of Congress Cataloguing-in-Publication data has been applied for.

ISBN: HB: 978-1-3994-1761-7; Audio edition: 978-1-3994-1762-4;
ePub: 978-1-3994-1760-0; ePDF: 978-1-3994-1758-7

2 4 6 8 10 9 7 5 3 1

Typeset in Bembo Std by Lumina Datamatics Ltd
Printed and bound in Great Britain by Clays Ltd, Elcograf S.p.A.

To find out more about our authors and books visit www.bloomsbury.com
and sign up for our newsletters.

For product safety related questions contact productsafety@bloomsbury.com.

For Ross and Josh, with hope that you'll stop killing wasps.

Contents

Preface	9
Chapter 1: All animals aren't equal	13
Chapter 2: An awfulness of teeth and claws	31
Chapter 3: Snake in the grass	75
Chapter 4: To make flesh creep	113
Chapter 5: Keep calm and carrion	157
Chapter 6: Easy on the aye-aye	195
Chapter 7: Naughty neighbours	233
Chapter 8: The good, the bad and the animal	277
Epilogue	301
Acknowledgements	307
Selected bibliography	309
Index	315

Preface

It was 2010, in our rental house in Sheffield, and I'd just made a coffee. Settling onto the hard orange sofa I heard the letterbox snap and spotted the cheery red of the postman as he moved off down the road. A moment later my housemate, Charlie, entered the room carrying a letter and, on top of the letter, a Worldwide Fund for Nature (WWF) flyer seeking donations for threatened Bengal tigers. As typical for such flyers, it depicted a stunning animal, staring directly at the camera, as if to implore people to do something. *Help me.* Charlie glanced at it, uttered the depressing words, 'Who cares?' and threw it in the bin. Catching my expression, he shrugged. 'Why should I care if there are tigers in India? It doesn't matter to me, it's not going to impact my life.'

Oof. I still remember my shock. And outrage. This was not an opinion I was familiar with and I didn't know how to react. Slack-jawed, I think my first response was, 'What's wrong with you?' I'm pathologically non-confrontational but inside my head I was raging. Why couldn't he see the beauty of the tiger? Why didn't he appreciate that we had a responsibility to protect this animal? Why wasn't he as moved by the natural world as everybody *should* be?

It was sometime later before I realised something else. Charlie was right. Why *should* he care about tigers in India?

That encounter was significant, because for the first time, probably ever, I realised that not everybody cares about the wild world. That will sound stupidly obvious, but it had never hit me so hard before. I, like so many of us, had been living in a little echo chamber, surrounded by people who shared my views about nature and conservation, and I was unprepared for this radical, alternative perspective. Community is important, and it feels good to be part of a group with a common set of values, which might extend from the people we call up to go to the pub to our virtual communities, and our preferred news sites. But as we cultivate these group memberships, we prune away those with dissenting voices, and it becomes easy to ignore, even forget, that our common ground within these echo chambers is not *the* common ground. It's good to poke our heads out of the bubble from time to time and tune in to what other people think, especially when those thoughts fly in the face of what you consider to be important. Renting a room in a house of complete strangers is a good way to do this. I was shocked by Charlie's disregard for tiger conservation, and it was a good lesson for my younger self.

With the shattering of my idealistic naïvety came a second, important, discovery. It was the realisation that I couldn't just lecture Charlie into caring more. I waded into that argument, armed with my degrees in zoology, with the arrogant assumption that I knew better than him. Turns out, that's a terrible way to change minds. Charlie and I differed on one fundamental belief – that animals have an intrinsic right to exist – and as much as I tried, blaming and shaming him into agreeing with that was never going to work. Nobody likes to be told that they're wrong or, worse, stupid. I needed to understand where Charlie was coming from and that meant approaching the conversation with an open mind. He, like many people, wasn't moved by the beautiful imagery and emotional content of the tiger leaflet. But rather than try to bend Charlie to fit the messaging, I realised that the messaging needed to be bent to fit Charlie. We needed to answer his question: why *should* people care?

Tigers, it should be acknowledged, are an easier proposition than many animals. If Charlie can't see the value of a charismatic, culturally significant apex predator like the tiger, what hope is there that he'll appreciate snakes, cockroaches or wasps? They are neither cute nor charismatic, and the popular press demonises them at every opportunity. People are never going to be comfortable around spiders if, every autumn, the newspapers shout about 'killer' spiders 'invading' our homes (as they do in the UK).

Bookshops are already full of the 'good' stuff. There are shelves upon shelves of books about dogs and cats, great apes, dolphins, honeybees, elephants and more. And that's for good reason: there are many fascinating things to learn about these creatures. But we're missing an awful lot of the natural world. It makes sense, of course – why would we want to learn about vulgar vultures, creepy cockroaches, or horrible wasps, when they make us feel scared or grossed out? Why would anybody write a book about the creatures that people don't like? That'd never sell.

Well, reader, I did just that. I wrote this book to shine a light on the creatures that are hated, reviled, scorned or simply overlooked. It's a love letter to the underdogs, and I did it because I want to convince you that we've got them wrong.

It's a two-pronged approach, because I want to capture hearts and minds. Prong one is aimed at your brains. Using the latest findings from an array of scientific fields, my aim is to convince you that even the most unappealing creatures play important roles in our lives. It may not look like it (I'm looking at you, mosquitoes and cockroaches), but nature has spun a phenomenally tangled web of life, and we ignore its interconnectedness at our peril. Prong two is aimed at your hearts – I've pulled together the latest evidence on what goes on in the minds of these unloved beasts, and how that translates into a dazzlingly complex diversity of behaviour. I want you to connect with sharks, admire the social smarts of wasps, maybe even empathise with rats.

My aim is to challenge the knee-jerk responses that we all show towards certain animals. To create a bit of friction between the way that we may feel and the way that we may behave. I hope that by doing so, you feel inspired to go out and champion these beasts, to spread the word about their good points and fight for a world in which they're allowed to live. It might be a bit much to hope for universal adoration but that's

OK. I'm aiming for greater tolerance, whether that comes through recognising their right to life or recognising their importance to us. If we can achieve that and let these animals get on with their jobs, the world will be in a much better state.

In Chapter 1, I take an overarching look at the human–animal relationship, considering how nature and culture has shaped our views of other animals. Subsequent chapters focus on a different aspect of the relationship, arranged according to the emotional response that is triggered: from fear for life to disgust to annoyance. Thus, Chapters 2 and 3 deal with large predators and venomous snakes, respectively; while Chapters 4 and 5 cover the emotion of disgust – from animals that may spread disease to animals that are defined by their association with death. Chapter 6 looks at the aesthetically challenged, while Chapter 7 tackles pests.

Chapter 8 flips everything on its head, with a focus not on the least loved but the widely adored, asking whether their positively anthropomorphised characters deserve their reputation. Shocking accounts of violence, gang rape, infanticide and necrophilia in otters, dolphins, lions and penguins will be presented as evidence that even 'good' animals have a dark side.

To help me convey these messages, I've spoken with a lot of different experts in academia, conservation and industry, many of whom are themselves outspoken champions for the species with which they work. There will always be more people I could have spoken to, more studies I could have referenced, and more animals that could (perhaps should?) have been included. I can guarantee that as you're reading this, you will think of other stories concerning scary or unpleasant animal encounters that might have fit well here. You might even have your own! And I will take this as a win, because above all else, I want this book to stimulate thought.

I hope that you enjoy discovering the beauty of our least loved beasts as much as I've enjoyed writing about them. It's time they had a bit of the limelight.

CHAPTER 1

All animals aren't equal

Everywhere the correcting hand and contriving brain of man are needed to eliminate the worthless and noxious productions, in which Nature is so fatally prolific.
Evans, *The Criminal Prosecution and Capital Punishment of Animals*, 1906

Human beings, i.e. the hominin species of ape called *Homo sapiens*, have existed for about 300,000 years, and for most of that time we have lived like animals.

We'll never truly know what life was like for our early ancestors, but other animals have undoubtedly held a special status for much of our history. Nowhere is this more apparent than cave art. From the people on the Indonesian island of Sulawesi, who 50,000 years ago painted scenes of hunters and giant pigs, to those who depicted lions in the Chauvet caves and bison in Altamira, early humans seemed fixated on creating representations of animals. It makes sense – our ancestors' lives were intimately and violently tied up with the lives of these beasts: as prey, competitors and predators. Early humans needed an expert awareness of animal form and they needed to recognise them in the dark or in dense undergrowth. Some have suggested that caves, with naturally lumpy, textured and contoured walls, may have given the illusion of animal shapes; it may not have been too big a step to mark some simple lines and join the features. The care and attention to these paintings also suggest that people had a reverence for the natural world, consistent with other evidence that our hunter-gatherer ancestors held animistic beliefs, i.e. that animals, plants and objects had a spiritual essence. Together with shamanism and the emergence of burial practices, these beliefs and rituals laid the foundations of the religions to come.

We are still animals, and we're still connected to nature, of course, but in recent millennia our relationship with the other beasts has gone somewhat awry. About 12,000 years ago, at the dawn of the neolithic era, our ancestors started to 'curate nature', developing the knowledge to grow crops and keep livestock. This marked an extraordinary change in how we lived and interacted with the world, spearheading a shift from nomadic life to permanent dwellings, complex societies and technological advances. People's lives became less entwined in the fluctuations and richness of the natural world, and the consequences of this separation were profound. Before that, humans had hunted, scavenged, foraged, and been hunted too – just like any other animal.

The agricultural revolution had other consequences, for as people started to work the land, they also started to categorise it – *this* bit of land was for growing maize, while *this* bit of land was where animals could graze. And all that other land, well, that was where the wild predators roamed, the ones that threatened lives and livestock. Setting ourselves apart from nature, we controlled the animals that we kept for food, and we constructed barriers and other ways to deter the animals that threatened us. As settlements grew, more people could keep watch for these creatures and more people could work together to defend themselves.

Social religions originated after this, likely as a way for an intellectually advancing people to make sense of the world, and many have animism at their core. This is especially true for religions of Asian origin, such as Hinduism, Jainism, Buddhism and Shintoism, whose followers have a deep connection with the natural world. That's in contrast to the Abrahamic religions, which taught a message of human superiority – according to these, God provided the living world as a resource, and while we had a role as stewards, we could subdue and exploit it as we saw fit. Accordingly, all life could be ordered on a huge scale, with the 'lower' forms at the bottom, and the divine at the top. Humans, being made in the image of God, naturally came just below the holiest forms of life.

The belief that other animals were put on the planet for our benefit really came to the fore during medieval times, a period of history that was fantastically creative in its depictions of animals but was also the era of animal criminal trials, one of the most bizarre examples of how much the human-animal relationship had changed.[1] The first recorded example was in 824 AD and concerned a group of moles (collectively known as a labour) that were excommunicated in the lush alpine Valle d'Aosta, in north-west Italy. The trial subsequently made its way into Edmund Evans' comprehensive monograph, *The Criminal Prosecution and Capital Punishment of Animals* (1906).[2] Evans provides no further details on the trial of the moles, so we don't know the specifics of their crime, although we could take a pretty good guess.

---

[1] This was the era of the bonnacon, the ox-like beast of legend that deterred its enemies with jets of fiery faeces!
[2] This includes around 200 cases, although Evans notes that this is very likely an underestimation.

Animals continued to be put on trial for their 'crimes' throughout the following centuries, and incredibly, all the way to the twentieth century. It was serious business – just as serious, in many cases, as for human criminals. As the man who killed another in a bar fight was hanged for murder, so was the ox who trampled a farmhand's son. Many other large livestock animals that were capable of inflicting harm on people were tried and punished. Animals were hanged, strangled, burned alive, buried alive, and some were even tortured on the rack, though to what end is unclear. You may have heard about the pig that was found guilty of murdering a child and was sentenced to be maimed and hanged in the town square. The animal was dressed in men's clothes.

It wasn't all about murder. Animals could be sentenced to death for other heretical things, like the poor pig who, in 1394, was hanged at Mortaign for having 'sacrilegiously eaten a consecrated wafer.' Or they could be caught up in the equally serious crime of bestiality, for which they and the human instigator were killed. Thus, we are told of the man and cow who, in 1546, were hanged and burned in Paris; and the man and mare who, in 1609, were executed and buried in a carrion pit at Niederrad.

Aosta's moles fit into a different category. They, like the locusts, slugs, termites and caterpillars that plagued crop fields, orchards and buildings, were a nuisance and, according to Evans, that required something different: 'the intervention of the Church and the exercise of its supernatural functions.' Cue the sprinkling of vast quantities of holy water, repeated threats of excommunication, and a dominant church that either took credit for the cessation of the pests or blamed the villagers for their sins until the problem stopped.[3]

---

[3] In one case Egbert, Bishop of Trier, anathematized the swallows for chattering during sermons and – what is likely the real reason – because they 'sacrilegiously defiled his head and vestments with their droppings, when he was officiating at the altar'.

What seems absurd by today's standards needs to be interpreted in the cultural context of medieval Europe. Take the following detail from a nine-month trial of weevils, accused of ravaging vineyards in the sixteenth century. The weevils' advocate, Pierre Rembaud, argued that:

> ... it was their legitimate right to be able to eat, since in the book of Genesis it is written that 'to every thing that creepeth upon the earth, wherein there is life, I have given every green herb for meat'.

The prosecution's response summed up the dominant position of the time:

> [Animals] were intended to be subordinate to him and subservient to his use, and that this was, indeed, the reason of their prior creation. They have no raison d'etre except as they minister to man, who was made to have dominion over them.

There's a bizarre paradox at play here. On the one hand, animals were not afforded moral rights, because according to the dominant religion they were put on Earth to be subordinate and subservient to man. From that perspective, they were clearly set apart from people and could not be expected to have the same kinds of minds. On the other, convicted animal 'murderers' were treated the same as human murderers. Evans presents itemised costs for the incarceration and execution of a pig, covering her board in the prison (the same cost as for a human), the wage of the executioner, the cost of a carriage to take her to the place of execution, and the costs of cords and gloves for binding her.

Thinking about animals as 'criminals' isn't totally confined to the history books. Little more than a century ago, people were still executing animals, like Topsy, an Indian elephant who trampled a man and was publicly electrocuted at the grand opening of Luna Park, on Coney Island in 1903. Or Mary, another Indian elephant, who in 1916 was publicly hanged from a crane after throwing and killing her inexperienced handler when he hit her with a metal hook.

Even these aren't the most recent animal criminal convictions, although thankfully the punishments in more recent years are far less brutal. For example, in 2004, a female brown bear named Ekaterina (or Katya) was imprisoned on a life sentence in the notorious penal colony of Kostanay, Kazakhstan.[4] She had been convicted of attacking two people at a campsite, a particularly harsh ruling given that she was in a cage at the time of the attacks. Then, in Macedonia in 2008, a bear was convicted *in absentia* of theft and damages for stealing honey. Beekeeper Zoran Kiseloski initially attempted to deter the bear with lights and loud music by the Serbian 'turbo-folk' star Ceca, which worked up until the generator ran out of power and the bear came back. The year-long case found the bear guilty, but since it had no owner and was a protected species, the punishment was directed to the state, ordering them to pay Kiseloski $3,500 in damages.

★★★

Our ease at slipping into the roles of judge, jury and executioner for other animals is only possible because we consider ourselves to be the superior animal; that is, when we accept that we are animal at all, which isn't always the case. It's called 'anthropic' thinking and it permeates almost every aspect of our lives – from the ways in which we see traces of human personalities in other animals (anthropomorphism), to the ways in which we interpret the world with the human race firmly at its centre (anthropocentrism), and to the ways

---

[4] She became a feature of the prison, beloved by many of the 730 or so other inmates who liked to bring her biscuits and fruit, and a statue of her was even erected outside. After 15 years, Katya was 'released' to a mini zoo, where she was promised greater freedom, and more natural conditions, presumably including conjugal visits, which she was not allowed whilst in prison.

in which we consider ourselves separate from and superior to the rest of the animal kingdom (human exceptionalism).

As philosopher Susana Monsó has written, superiority must be in comparison with something else, and that's where we run into a problem. We are only superior in certain things, and since other animal species are not quite like us, nor quite like each other, that means there's no fair comparison. In her words: 'humans are superior – by human standards.'

Monsó has proposed that a fairer metric to compare species superiority would be something that all species strive for, such as survival. And when we do that, we lose our crown. She points out that, at an individual level, tardigrades (tiny invertebrates also known as moss piglets) can survive for years without food or water, can endure temperatures between -272°C and 150°C, pressures of 7.5GPa and high levels of radiation, and can live for days in the vacuum of outer space. By comparison, we are nothing more than ravenous and fragile sacks of squishy stuff. But maybe that's not a fair comparison – tardigrades must be outliers, exceptions to the rule. Let's consider the survival of our lineage, the humans, which includes us and all extinct hominins. It's tempting to think that our big brains and exceptional technological and cultural capacities will help us to persist on this planet, but it seems highly unlikely that humans will come anywhere close to challenging the 500-million-year lineage of jellyfish, which includes surviving five major extinction events. As Monsó wrote in 2019: 'We have existed for barely 200,000 years and are already well on the way to creating the perfect conditions for our own species to become extinct.' She notes that using fairer standards to compare humans against other animals can be 'a humbling experience', and may help us to realise we are not as special as we like to think.

The big problem with exceptionalist thinking is that by elevating ourselves so far above the rest of the animal kingdom, we start to think that we exist independently of the natural world. There's a sense that the cultural changes that power human societies have so little to do with the natural world that nature has become a separate 'thing'; we might travel to see nature in an exotic country, national park or dedicated reserve, perhaps take a nice photo, and then return to our human worlds. The most obvious example of this is our very definition of 'nature'. It doesn't include humans, something I was stunned to discover when the campaign group, We Are Nature, published their open letter to UK publishers in April 2024, asking them to amend their dictionary's definitions. As they state on their website: 'We are a *part* of nature, not *apart* from it.' In their letter, they outlined their view that considering ourselves as exceptional rather than interdependent, 'is a root cause of our behaviour as a species towards our natural world.'

Exceptionalist thinking can translate into a lack of concern to support pro-environmental measures. If we believe that the natural world is nothing more than an optional 'other' that we can choose to engage with or not, we will be less likely to recognise any obligation towards protecting it, or only support pro-environmental actions when they benefit us. Indeed, research has found that American individuals with high exceptionalist scores are less likely to attribute damage from extreme weather events to global climate change and are more likely to believe that humans will survive the impacts of climate change, regardless of which other species survive. Higher levels of exceptionalist thinking also predict lower willingness to invest in environmental restoration or volunteer on restoration projects.

Exceptionalist thinking isn't inevitable. But studies have shown that it's far more common among children brought up in WEIRD populations (Western, Educated, Industrialised, Rich and Democratic) than Indigenous groups. To break free of it, especially regarding our attitudes towards other animals, we need to see the perspective of the beast. And that's a tough ask. It's difficult enough sometimes to see the perspective of friends or family, let alone a creature with whom you last shared a common ancestor potentially hundreds of millions of years ago. But it's essential to realise that while we are the centre of *our* worlds, we're not the centre of *the* world. As much as we impose ourselves onto the lives of other creatures, we need to realise that for most animals on this planet, what we do is irrelevant.

Human exceptionalism is a myth and a mistake. We can't simply decouple ourselves from nature and expect that everything will be OK. We may have developed ingenious solutions to solve many problems facing humanity, but even the most advanced technology won't fix the impacts of our disconnect from the planet.

★★★

Since medieval times, life has gotten better for animals in many ways. They are no longer routinely convicted of crimes and punished with their lives. Previously popular 'sports' using animals are far less acceptable than they once were. And there are many more people who care about the health and well-being of wildlife.

It's gotten considerably worse too. Between 50 and 70 per cent of Earth's land surface is currently modified for human use and that number will only continue to grow as we continue to spread into and consume from the wild lands. We need more space, we need more food, we need *more*. And as the world gets ever more crowded, it becomes a much more difficult place for wildlife to live: they have less space, less food, more pollution, more disease, and a higher chance of coming into contact (and conflict) with us.

What's left has been systematically damaged, weakened and destroyed, in some cases irrevocably, and it's happened in the blink of a geological eye. Earth has gone through five mass extinction events before, where the very face of the planet changed, and we're undeniably in the midst of the sixth — except this time it's not because of an asteroid or some swing in global temperatures that happened over thousands of years. Never has the natural world been forced to adapt to such extreme change over such a short period of time.

Many animals are doing very badly out of this, as you'd expect. Having evolved over tens or hundreds of millions of years in relatively stable environments, at least at a scale on which natural selection could operate, they cannot cope with rising temperatures, rising sea levels, or the increased unpredictability of global climates happening over a couple of centuries. Many of the more specialised species will go extinct, unless they are lucky enough to capture the attention of the public and policymakers and become the subject of a concerted conservation effort. Sadly, there aren't enough resources to do this for all creatures at risk — they can't all be pandas.

Other species are adapting, learning to live alongside us and make the most of the human world. That sounds like it should be a good thing, and it would be, were it not for the fact that as these creatures connect their lives more and more to ours, we are distancing ourselves more and more from them. Ironically, given the increased chances of encountering certain wild animals in our towns and cities, we are losing our connection with the natural world. We are living through an 'extinction of experience', a term first proposed by lepidopterist Robert M. Pyle, and popularised in 2016 by researchers Masashi Soga and Kevin Gaston. As we lose these joyful, emotive encounters with the natural world, what happens? Well, as with many things which we don't fully understand, without a direct, positive encounter we can develop negative, unfavourable attitudes. It's been termed 'biophobia' and it's the opposite of Edward O. Wilson's 'biophilia', the theory that humans have an innate affinity for the natural world. According to the biophilia theory, humans subconsciously seek connections with the rest of life. Biophobia, in contrast, predicts the opposite – without direct experience of the natural world people lose their understanding of it, and that turns to fear and avoidance.

No longer, in the Western world, are naughty animals thought to be possessed by the devil. But that doesn't mean they're not still demonised. It's just that this time, the sermons come not from the Church, but from popular culture. We propagate stories about animals that have their roots in long-past ancient civilisations, their animal characters immortalised in the modern equivalents of cartoons, films, and comics. And new stories are being created all the time, with new animal stars – like the crow who used a lid to sledge down a snowy roof or the cat who scared an aggressive dog away from a toddler. We have new animal villains too, and you don't need to look far in the popular press to find them. One moment there's a 'biblical plague of cannibal crabs!', while the next, 'terrorist gulls are squawking too loudly!' Clearly, nature is out to get us.

Language matters, and we have a real language problem when it comes to talking about other animals. They clearly aren't terrorists, but that word comes up time and time again. Animals aren't malicious either – they might be carnivores that hunt other animals for food, but that doesn't mean they are doing so in an intentionally cruel way. A lion can therefore legitimately be described as a creature that kills other animals, but a 'killer' lion conjures mental imagery of malevolence and violence. What, then, are we to make of a headline that shouts about '10 million killer spiders'? If its justification is that at least one person in the UK has died from complications caused by a false widow spider bite, then we should also describe lots of other things as 'killers' – refrigerators, for example, or falling coconuts. Don't get me started on how many people have died taking selfies for social media.

Often, our thoughts about animals come down to a feeling, a gut reaction, that we might have about them, rather than any rational consideration. This aspect of our decision-making process is governed by something called affect, which is the specific quality of 'goodness' or 'badness' that becomes associated with a 'thing'. Much of our thinking about animals is governed by such affective reasoning, and this accounts for a great deal of the over-reaction that we see towards certain species.

One key feature of affective reasoning is that the risks and benefits of an object, animal or idea often negatively correlate, rather than being considered in isolation. That's even if the nature of the benefits is completely different to the nature of the risks. For example, a group of people that fear spiders and therefore judge them to be high on risk, will likely consider them to be low on benefits, and vice versa, even though these two properties of spiders bear no relation to the other. Spiders are hugely beneficial animals, and that's independent of the specific properties of their venom that may also pose a risk to human health. Both can be true.

There's another property of affective reasoning that's particularly relevant, and it's to do with how much weight we give to different risks. On the whole, people tend to underestimate large risks such as diabetes or climate change, which we might all have some awareness of but which come across as mundane and non-threatening. Conversely, we greatly overestimate small risks such as shark attacks, terrorism or tornadoes, which are extremely rare but tend to be over-reported and sensationalised. We pay more attention to these risks because the potent imagery and emotional narratives associated with them have greater affect. These are the risks that therefore become encoded in our memories and to which we experience the strongest reactions.

★★★

Part of the problem is that, as a species, we really like categorising things. You might go as far as to say that we are obsessed with putting things into their metaphorical boxes. Black or white, right or wrong, good or evil. It's how our brains like us to process the world, because it keeps things nice and simple; categories help us to sort and make sense of everything. The problem is that most aspects of life, nature included, are not black and white, so classifying animals in this way often results in extremely simplistic and anthropomorphised dichotomies.

Worse, we hang these dichotomies over expectations of their behaviour that are built on human rules, propagating this further with misinformation or sensationalism in the popular press. We demonise spiders or foxes for entering our homes or gardens, even though these 'invaders' have no concept of the boundaries that they are supposed to respect. Then, hypocritically, we expect other animals to tolerate our disruptive presence in their territories, punishing them for acts of self-defence. It's a form of exceptionalist thinking that reaches its zenith when we look at an animal and ask, "What is even its point?"

In this human-dominated world, animals have taken on particular roles. In the most basic terms, they're either useful, problematic or redundant. Obvious examples of the former are the billions of domesticated animals that provide us with meat, milk, labour or other products, and the billions of domestic dogs, cats and other pets that provide companionship. Those aside, animals are often either problematic (because they're dangerous or a pest) or redundant. And that's a far more precarious place to be, because if we don't value them we won't care if they're pushed to extinction. Millions of years of exquisite evolutionary adaptation is being wiped out in the blink of an eye because we either blame creatures for crimes they don't know they're committing, or we don't know that they exist or, worse, we're aware of their existence but don't see the point of them.

Our blinkered and anthropomorphised views – enthusiastically reinforced by popular media – can prevent us from seeing the many and varied qualities of these animals. And in a time of catastrophic biodiversity loss, that is a true crime. We need to appreciate the nuances and subtleties that blunt the meaning of words like good and evil, right or wrong. File down the sharp corners of these words, allow the chalk outline to blur. We must do this, because nature is not built on sharp corners and distinctions, but on interconnections and overlapping.

This is a book about nuance, because it's all a lot more complicated than that. We don't like nuance, we don't really want it in our lives, it makes thoughts and decisions harder. But it should be clear that black-and-white thinking doesn't work. Anthropomorphic thinking is linked to this, because when we see animals as 'good' or 'bad', we can't help but see traces of ourselves in their behaviour. We endow 'good' or 'nice' animals with positive, social traits, such as the capacities for love, friendship, generosity and altruism. But what strikes me as remarkable is that for the animals that are 'bad', we don't just view them as incapable of the good stuff (in the words of the late, great ethologist Frans de Waal, 'anthropodenial'). No. What we do is much worse. We travel down that continuum of moral character, and we go right to the other extreme. These animals, which scare, disgust, or infuriate us, are bestowed with equally impressive cognitive abilities, but of the malevolent, psychopathic kind. As villains, they are assumed to be immoral.

Much has been written about the perils and pitfalls of anthropomorphism, and while it's good to be aware of the overall risks of attributing human intentions, beliefs and emotions to other animals, it's not something that we can just turn off. As the late entomologist John S. Kennedy set out in his 1992 book, *The New Anthropomorphism*, our tendency to draw on human characteristics to explain what animals do is an inbuilt trait: 'We could not abandon it even if we wished to.' What we can do is exhibit some caution around it, recognise that animals are not little people, and keep reminding ourselves that we live in a more-than-human world.

Animal villainisation is at the heart of this book, and it's something that really bothers me. Mainly, because it's biologically absurd. A villain is a person who has committed a crime or been malevolent in some way – this is completely inappropriate to use for an animal. When we use terms like 'invading,' 'terrorist', or 'evil', we're assuming that these animals are intentionally maligning us – not only that, but we're also casually ascribing them with complex cognitive abilities. Human villains achieve their nefarious means through mental feats like tactical deception, which involves an understanding of what the 'victim' is thinking and how your behaviour will influence them (i.e. theory of mind); future planning, which requires the ability to mentally project yourself into imagined future scenarios; and behavioural flexibility, in case things don't go to plan.

Armies of scientific experts are currently trying to determine whether any animal possesses these sorts of abilities, and as yet, even among the 'smartest' beasts like chimpanzees, the evidence is limited. There's no evidence that any other animal could pull off the mental feats needed to be a villain. How unfair, then, that in so many creatures, the public and popular media seem intent on underestimating the good stuff and overestimating the bad. I understand why it happens – we're a storytelling species, our stories often feature animals, and stories usually revolve around the actions of a hero and a villain. And that's fine for fictional tales, even those using animal characters, such as fables. Where it's not fine is when the villains of our childhood stories become the same villains of the cartoons and movies of our adulthood, and the same villains of newspapers and social media. Where it's not fine is when these villainous characters become one and the same as the real animals, because we then experience the same emotions towards them as towards their fictional personas. We'll never be able to shake our negative perceptions of some species when our cultures reinforce them at every turn.

I emailed eminent human-animal studies researcher, Hal Herzog, to ask what he thought about this. His book *Some We Love, Some We Hate, Some We Eat* provides a fantastic overview of the inconsistencies by which people think about and behave towards animals, and I wanted to know if he agreed with my hunch: do people attribute 'bad' cognition to 'bad' animals? 'I think you are onto something,' he wrote back, noting also that the topic is woefully understudied. 'There are thousands of studies on the attitudes and beliefs about the 'some we love' animals but many fewer on the 'some we hate' creatures … there are now lots of studies on factors related to the relative moral status of different creatures, but I can't think of anything directly related to the overestimation of cognition in creepy-crawlies, predators, etc.'

As a species, we have enacted the greatest changes to our world in a dizzyingly short period of time. That's cause for despair, but it should also be cause for hope. Because humans may be reckless, greedy and flawed in numerous ways, but we are also resilient, creative and compassionate, and we have the knowledge and the skills to fix this. We are fighters and when the things that we deeply care about are on the line, we can unite to stunning effect. The key here is that single verb: care. Unless we care about something, we're not going to alter our behaviour or do anything to further a cause. And in order to care about a given entity, we need to both know of its existence and have some opinion on its value.

Basing those opinions on how closely the animals resemble us, and thinking of them positively only when their behaviour aligns with our laws and preferences sets them up to fail, given our ever-expanding footprint on this planet. Instead, we need to appreciate them for the vital roles that they play in this world, as well as for the many adaptations that make them remarkable. Knowledge is power, and if we can understand more about why animals are doing things that we find scary or unpleasant, we give ourselves the tools to identify misinformation and choose how to respond to future encounters. At the heart of this is an important distinction: harm can happen when we encounter wild creatures but that does not mean that wild creatures mean us harm; it's subtle, but essential, because our own well-being may depend on us learning to love nature's most misunderstood beasts.

CHAPTER 2

An awfulness of teeth and claws

In this manner the crocodile seizes and destroys all animals, and is equally dreaded by all. There is no animal but man alone that can combat it with success.
Buffon, *Histoire Naturelle,* 1828

When Rajan Chaudhary was 19 years old, his oldest brother was killed by a tiger. The men, together with another brother, had been in the forests near their home of Khusalpatuwa, on the outskirts of Nepal's Bardiya National Park. Rajan did not witness the attack, but he saw something equally harrowing – the tiger returned to eat his brother's body. Now in his forties, Rajan still lives in the same village, where he works in conservation. He recently lost a close family member to a leopard attack and told me that between the pandemic in 2020 and when I spoke with him in January 2024, 19 people lost their lives to tigers in an area just 7km². 'Can you imagine?' he asks me, and I shake my head, dumbstruck.

In 2023, Australian Marcus McGowan was attacked by a crocodile while snorkelling off the north Queensland coast. In a statement released at the time by the Queensland Government hospital service, McGowan said the animal had attacked him from behind and clamped down on his head. Luckily, it was almost certainly a juvenile crocodile who didn't have the gargantuan bite force of a fully grown adult, and McGowan was able to prise the animal's jaws open and escape. Incredibly, he survived the attack with nothing more than minor injuries. In his statement, McGowan said that he was simply 'in the wrong place, at the wrong time', acknowledging that he was aware of the risks of entering the territory of potentially dangerous animals. His was the fifth crocodile attack in the region in less than six months.

Nearly 10,000 miles away, in the UK, shark-phobic Danni Perrot hasn't done more than paddle in the sea for more than 34 years, despite living on the coast and having never seen a shark in her life. Seeking help to deal with her severe phobia from TV therapists, The Speakmans, she tells the camera, 'I'm afraid of sharks in every situation,' describing how she feels nervous about entering the deep end of a swimming pool and how even an image of a shark on the internet causes her immediate anxiety. Danni's phobia is impacting her relationship with her daughter, who would love to go surfing. 'I just can't let her do it,' she says. Instead, she is on constant vigilance to protect her daughter from the sharks that haunt her imagination. 'They're out there', she says, gesturing out to the open water.

In July 2015, also in the UK, where our largest remaining native land carnivore is the European badger, a group of eight people barricaded themselves inside a

AN AWFULNESS OF TEETH AND CLAWS

village sports club for three hours after being 'terrorised' by a 'vicious' fox.

It's fair to say that our relationship with the predators of this world is complicated.

★★★

Most of this book is designed to alleviate concerns about animals, and to reassure you that animals that cause us harm aren't doing so intentionally. Venomous snakes, cockroaches, rats and wasps aren't out to get you. But we can't dismiss all animal encounters so easily. While we like to think that we've transcended the rest of the animal kingdom, certain beasts remind us that we're still part of the food chain.

This can be an unsettling reality. As a species, our embrace of technology over nature makes it easy to forget that for much of our evolutionary history, we were simply a source of meat for bigger, scarier animals. Our two-legged stance, strange 'fur' and unpredictable defence strategies make us peculiar prey, but to a hungry predator we're nothing special. That's a jarring thought. It's a challenge to human exceptionalism and it exposes another uncomfortable truth: that wealth and privilege don't matter. Nature really is the great equaliser, and there's surely something to respect about the tiger or crocodile that has zero respect for us, whether we're a multibillionaire tech entrepreneur, a budding writer, or a subsistence farmer.

Few people have experienced what it is like to be prey and lived to tell the tale. One who did was late Australian ecophilosopher Val Plumwood who, in 1985, became one of the few people to have survived a crocodile death roll. In fact, Plumwood survived three death rolls during her ordeal while kayaking in Kakadu National Park and incredibly, against all odds, she escaped. Perhaps more incredibly, given her horrendous experience and injuries, Plumwood resisted calls to kill the crocodile. 'I was the intruder,' she wrote in her 1995 essay 'Human Vulnerability and the Experience of Being Prey'. 'It is a humbling and cautionary tale ... about the need to acknowledge our own animality and ecological vulnerability.'

Despite Plumwood trying to minimise publicity after her attack, it was a media frenzy. Her story was stereotyped and sensationalised, hyped up to exaggerate the crocodile's size and her struggles, and framed around the myth of the crocodile as a 'monster'.[5] This is an age-old, persistent characterisation of our dangerous predators and it sits at the heart of our villainisation of them – it being that much easier to persecute a creature that you believe to have a less-than-human mind compared with one that behaves like us. Humanity has been trying to conquer the natural world, by which I mean rid it of her natural predators, for millennia. We're very good at it, too. But we've been labouring under false pretences. First, we've attributed these creatures with monstrous minds, and that has eroded public support. Second, we've historically assumed that they play a negligible role in the functioning of the natural world. Both led to the belief that predator eradication was necessary to create the most civilised version of society.

Both beliefs are demonstrably untrue. But before we start to unpick them, it's worth thinking about how we came to be in this position and that starts with one simple truth: you, and everybody on this planet, are a story of survival. You are only sitting here, reading this, because you represent a long line of survivors, your ancestors, who lived long enough to reproduce. And I'm not talking about

---

[5] It was also marred by sexist overtones, with some implying that the bush was no place for a woman. The film *Crocodile Dundee*, 'the most advanced expression of this masculinist mind-set,' according to Plumwood, was shot in Kakadu National Park not long after her encounter.

great grandmother Alice, or even your supposed link to Charlemagne. I'm going further back. Much further back.

★★★

The 300,000-year history of *Homo sapiens* has been filled with danger. A veritable menagerie of terrifying beasts stalked, slithered, scuttled and swam the lands and seas, from huge reptiles to giant hyenas, cave bears, and sabre-toothed cats. There were even giant killer kangaroos that pursued prey on all fours. Compared with today's biggest and baddest, these were predators with the steroid dial turned to max. It's hard to see how our ancestors stood a chance.

But they did. They survived for long enough to have sex and pass on their genes, and that's thanks to one powerful, primal emotion: fear.

Clearly, being hunted by other animals is not something specific to us or our ancient lineage. Most creatures that have ever lived have needed to address the risk of ending up as another's dinner, meaning that threat detection is one of the most ancient and well-conserved systems to have evolved in animals. The emotion of fear is part of that system, and it's best thought of in a functional way: as an internal state that accompanies the anticipation of a threat and which elicits particular changes in physiology or behaviour that help to avoid or cope with the threat. It's a dry (boring) way to think of it, but necessary to draw the distinction between the emotion of fear and the feeling of being afraid.

Feelings are different to emotions. A feeling that you might have of being scared (or happy, jealous, frustrated) is a personal, private state that is unique to you. It can't be measured by taking your pulse, a blood sample or even a brain scan. The only way that I can understand how you're feeling is if you tell me. Emotions, on the other hand, are externally broadcast and measurable – fear can be revealed in our physiology, with increased heart rate, blood pressure and hormone levels; and in our behaviour, through facial expressions, whimpering, or running away. We can talk about other animals having emotions because we are able to measure these things — whether they have feelings is a much trickier question.

Our fear response is an exquisitely fast and fine-tuned system; so good that it bypasses conscious thought so our bodies can respond instantaneously. It starts with our senses, primarily our eyes and ears, perceiving something in our environment which could signal danger. These sensory inputs are sent directly to a structure in the brain called the amygdala, which sends an instantaneous distress signal ('WARNING!') to another part of the brain, the hypothalamus. Taking charge, the hypothalamus sends messages all over the body, activating the fight-or-flight response and preparing the body for intense physical activity.[6] The heart starts pounding, ensuring that blood is being pushed to the muscles, heart and other vital organs. Breathing rate increases and tiny airways in the lungs open wider, ensuring that they can get as much oxygen as possible. Extra oxygen is sent to the brain to help with alertness, sharpening all the senses; while non-essential activities, like digestion, are slowed down. And the release of the hormone adrenaline stimulates the release of glucose and fats from the liver and other temporary storage sites, pumping the bloodstream full of fuel for the muscles. Thanks to this response, our ancestors stood a fighting chance against predators.

Fear is rooted in every one of us, to a greater or lesser extent. Yes, we need to learn what to be afraid of and we start to do so from the earliest age, but we aren't the blank slates that early psychologists believed. We have what is

---

[6] It was American physiologist Walter Bradford Cannon who, in 1915, introduced the term 'fight or flight' to describe how people tend to either confront threats or flee from them. 'Freeze' was latterly added to this as a third type of response, and recently 'fawn' and 'flop' have also been suggested.

termed an 'evolved fear system', meaning that we are predisposed to learn what is scary – specifically, things that might have threatened us in our long-distant past.

Modern life presents a paradox: our ancient fear circuits remain and yet four billion people (more than half the global population) now live in towns and cities, where the risk of large predator attacks is close to zero. Here, we're better off worrying about the much more significant risks posed by cars or cardiovascular disease. But we can't turn our fear circuits off. We are haunted by the ghosts of animals that we will never meet, conditioned by natural selection and popular culture to 'beware the beast,' so that the shadows of bears, lions and snakes still flicker in our brains. Our nervous systems are primed to respond to these threats, despite our rational brains knowing that, for those of us not living alongside any possible predators, they're not really threats at all.

In contrast, I was in the Masai Mara National Park several years ago, and got talking to some of the young Masai warriors about lions, because traditionally their initiation has included them killing a lion to demonstrate their bravery. I asked one of them whether he would find that scary and his response was unexpected. 'Oh no.' He grinned at me. 'I am not scared of lions. I respect the lion. I am scared of terrorists.' Context is everything, and for people like the Masai tribe, the lion is a persistent, but known, threat. Terrorism, in contrast, is an unknown, unpredictable and therefore far scarier proposition.

This ties in with another component of fear – the power of suggestion. There's a reason why *The Blair Witch Project* was hailed as truly terrifying, because it was a film in which we, the viewer, did all the mental heavy lifting. We didn't need to see the director's idea of what was scary; it was far more effective to let our imaginations run wild, drawing on our own worst fears. This is also why books are so powerful. We don't need to see the threat in its entirety, we can create monsters in our minds if the premise is plausible enough.

For scary movies to resonate, directors therefore tend to play into our inbuilt anxieties, rather than create novel worries around things that are rarely scary. As a result, stories typically tap into biologically relevant fears, often involving dangerous or unhinged people (our biggest threat), but also ferocious animals, infectious disease, darkness, confinement or isolation. These fear-inducers are so powerful that they can leave lasting imprints, and that's where we run into difficulties: a film about a killer kettle probably won't leave you worrying about going into the kitchen in the same way as *Jaws* did about going into the sea.

Jaws may have been based on a fictional story, but its success came down to its perceived realism – for many people, it may as well have been a natural history documentary. That's because, even if we have no experience with sharks and don't even go to the beach very often, the idea that a giant, bloodthirsty predator stalked the seas isn't implausible, and that makes it terrifying. The oceans are not our natural habitat – we can be literally and metaphorically out of our depth when we enter them – and we only know a fraction of what's beneath the surface: these facts alone make them scary propositions for some people. Add to that the facts that sharks are considered to be apex predators of the ocean, some (for example great whites) can be up to 6m long, they look scary, and they are known to attack people. The shark character of *Jaws* was easily assimilated into our minds, because our minds are already set up to pay attention to and remember dangerous beasts.

It did another thing too – it portrayed the shark as a vengeful killer with a taste for human flesh. As Chris Pepin-Neff, associate professor of public policy at the University of Sydney, has written, 'There is nothing scarier or more fascinating than the intelligent monster.' While we know that this is not how sharks operate (more later), the anthropomorphising of the shark in this way, as Plumwood experienced around her crocodile attack, also faced little friction from our brains. All this combined to make for a spectacularly scary and successful film, with the outcome that sharks became some of the world's most feared animals. Fifty years later, the fear is still being felt. The 2024 Chapman Survey of American Fears reported that 35 per cent of the 1,008 respondents reported being afraid or very afraid of sharks, which was the same as fear of heights and higher than fear of dying (32 per cent) or public speaking (29 per cent). Given the size of the US and the proportion of the population that live nowhere near the coast, that theoretically projects up to a huge, baffling number. But it's consistent with the research – Pepin-Neff has found that 'the idea of sharks can be more threatening than sharks themselves.'

We live in a time of great fear – of wars, terrorism, climate collapse, AI, pandemics, the list could go on and on. But in fact our world is so much safer for many of us than it once was. Lifespans have increased, child mortality has gone down, and yet, we are still so scared. Fears of war and disease are perfectly rational, of course, but there's another fear that has pervaded deep into many parts of human society, insidious in its spread and poisonous in its effects. It's the fear of nature, and of being part of nature. The fear of being 'just' an animal, as much as we try to hide that fact. And it's for this reason that we need, more urgently than ever, to examine the nature of human fear and to get a good grasp of the facts.

Ultimately, fear is a double-edged sword. It kept our ancestors alive, but today things have got muddled. In certain parts of the world, the fears evoked by dangerous animals are legitimate 'factual fears.' Elsewhere, aided by the fuel of online misinformation, popular culture, and historical perspectives about the place of predatory animals in refined society, people are influenced by monster tropes to develop irrational fears of animals that pose no direct threat. And that's a problem because these 'fictional fears' can fuel the persecution of animals that deserve our respect and protection.

But what's the truth to the monster myth? To answer that, we need to understand the data on both the number of fatalities caused by animal predators, and the inner workings of their minds. The former should be straightforward, though is made challenging in locations where attacks may go unreported, or where the cause of death is ambiguous. The latter is considerably harder, because historically these animals have not featured strongly in the pages of scientific research journals. Fortunately, as scientists gather more and more evidence about the natural behaviour of predators, their neurobiology and their capacity for thought and emotions, they're painting a picture of animals with a softer side, and that's helping to demolish many of the same, tired, old stereotypes. Let's take a look at two of the most wronged – crocodiles and sharks.

★★★

Conveniently located about half an hour's drive west of Oxford, surrounded by a patchwork of open farmland, is the UK's only crocodile zoo.[7] Crocodiles of the World has more than 100 individuals from 18 species of crocodilian, including Nile crocodiles, American alligators, black caiman and more, and I've come here to get a feel for them – not literally, I should add.

It's a cold, misty January day and stepping inside I curse myself for not realising that a down jacket, woolly hat and scarf would be completely redundant. It's obviously tropical. I'm met by Colin Stevenson, head of education, who takes me on the tour. An Australian expat, he's been 'somewhat obsessed' with crocodiles all his life, and it shows. He knows his stuff and he's passionate about overturning the

---

[7] Here, and throughout the chapter, unless a species name is given, 'crocodiles' is used in place of the scientific family name, crocodilians, which includes all 26 known species of crocodiles, alligators, caimans and gharials.

misconceptions surrounding these animals. But we'll get to those; let's start with the facts.

According to CrocAttack, the worldwide crocodilian attack database, nearly 5,000 crocodile attacks were reported between 2015 and 2024, half of which were fatal. Over a fifth of the attacks in that period were reported in Indonesia, mostly by saltwater crocodiles ('salties'), which, when under-reporting is accounted for, are estimated to kill 150–200 people annually. It's important to note that Indonesia is not the only global hotspot, and the salty is not the only dangerous crocodile. CrocAttack suggests that on the other side of the world, the Nile Crocodile is 'likely responsible for hundreds of deaths annually,' but severe underreporting in central and east Africa mean the data aren't there. An overall realistic estimate for crocodile attacks worldwide might therefore be 500 to 1,000 per year, largely attributed to these two species.

It probably doesn't matter if you smile at a crocodile, but what you really need to be careful about is entering waters where they're known to live – as Plumwood and McGowan experienced, these are undeniably dangerous predators, and the risk that they pose cannot be downplayed. Grahame Webb, one of the world's leading authorities on crocodiles, didn't sugarcoat this when he wrote in a 2012 article for news website The Conversation: 'If you dive off the Adelaide River bridge, 60 km east of Darwin's city centre, and start swimming, there is 100 per cent chance of being taken by a saltwater crocodile. It is not the same as swimming with sharks.'[8]

Good news for shark-o-phobes, but not for the increasing number of people who happen to live, and work, in and around crocodile habitat.

These are big animals and they're dangerous, Stevenson says, but they're also misunderstood. Many of the beliefs

---

[8] The full article is available online: Grahame Webb, Crocodile culls won't solve crocodile attacks. *The Conversation*, 9th December 2012.

we have about crocodiles come from natural history documentaries, and they are not always the most representative of the group. 'I can guarantee, if there's a show on crocodiles, they're going to show you the Nile croc and the great migration.' He shakes his head. 'I cannot watch that stuff anymore. That is something that happens in one part of Africa at one time of the year.' He explains that Nile crocodiles may only hunt wildebeest once a year, when the animals make their perilous river crossings, so what we see is 'weird, unusual, very uncommon, very rare behaviour.' Nonetheless, it's this footage, usually involving large crocodiles exploding out of the river and dragging hapless herbivores to their deaths, that most of us are familiar with, and that therefore becomes our mental model of 'crocodile'. In reality, Stevenson says, for most of the year these crocodiles prey on fish, birds and smaller mammals, which isn't quite as impactful.

It's also the case that documentaries preferentially show footage of the big, dangerous species like Nile crocodiles and salties but Stevenson says these are the exceptions in the group, and this therefore also skews the public's understanding. Most species, he tells me, aren't big enough to harm us in any serious way. Thinking for a moment, he then adds, 'I mean that in the wild – in captivity, crocodiles can cause you some serious injuries.' He's been bitten numerous times and has the scars to prove it, but is quick to highlight that this is always due to user error: 'If I was the sort of person to have tattoos, I should have a tattoo on each scar saying "idiot", because I've made a mistake. I put it in a situation where it was uncomfortable, I was too close or not paying attention.' Animals, Stevenson emphasises, don't lash out because they're malicious, but because they feel threatened.

If the typical representation of Nile crocodiles isn't representative of the group, what should our conception of crocodiles be – what are these animals really like?

One of the difficulties in answering this, according to behavioural researcher Vladimir Dinets, is that their behaviour is extremely difficult to see, especially in the wild. They tend to live in swamps and murky rivers in the tropics and if they're active at all, it's usually at night. When Dinets started researching crocodiles, for his PhD at the University of Miami, he 'expected them to be boring'. Crocodiles have a very different relationship with time to us. They spend a lot of it sitting still and quietly watching the world to save energy – for this reason, Dinets has previously referred to them as the 'Taoist sages' of the animal world. That's not a particularly attractive proposition for a research student who is eager to publish exciting new findings, meaning that many people interested in wild animal behaviour instead gravitate towards creatures that are easier to observe and more active. Oh, and that won't kill you either. Because when a crocodile decides that it's time to jump into action they can literally jump – at Crocodiles of the World, daily feedings show the explosive power of this when the reptiles launch themselves out of the water to grab a chunk of meat. Faced with these two extremes, it is perhaps understandable why many young researchers choose to study apes, crows or ants.

Crocodile research has also suffered from a fair dose of 'taxonomic chauvinism'. Scientists interested in reptile behaviour have historically needed to work harder to justify the importance of their work compared with those studying animals that are either more closely related to us, like primates, or of economic importance, like honeybees. That has meant that their findings have tended to be published in niche herpetology journals, rather than more widely read animal behaviour or life science publications. The outcome? Fewer people seeing them, less impact and fewer studies of reptile behaviour making it into animal behaviour and cognition textbooks.

Fortunately, Dinets was not easily put off, and once he'd spent enough time observing crocodiles the Taoist mask began to slip. As he writes to me, 'If you figure out how to be there when the animals become active and stuff happens, you can see a lot of amazing things in a few minutes or hours – that was a big surprise for me.'

One of those things was the discovery that American alligators place sticks on their snouts to apparently lure bird prey during the nest-building season, which was the first report of tool use in a reptile. Another is that they engage in courtship 'dances'. While this is a spectacle that has been observed by tourists in the Florida Everglades, it was only described scientifically in 2010, after Dinets made the decision to study the alligators' nocturnal behaviour. This involved him either watching from shore or paddling around in an inflatable kayak, using a headtorch with a red filter on moonless nights. From 380 hours of observations over three breeding seasons, he documented the fascinating interactions that these animals were having overnight. In essence, as he has described on social media, it was the alligators' equivalent of a night on the town: 'They gather in groups of up to a hundred, swim in circles, court, caress their prospective partners, and sometimes fight. Picture a dance night in a small town dance hall.' It's an amazing image and must have been exhilarating to observe, although gathering these data won't have been for the faint-hearted. Fortunately, as he wrote in his paper on the behaviour, the animals 'seemed remarkably indifferent' to his presence, 'often courting, bellowing or mating within 1–2m of the kayak.' Just the thought of it makes me a bit nervous, but Dinets is clearly in the right line of work: 'You have to be careful and cautious when working with wild animals, but you should never be afraid. Many of them can sense your fear.'

Back at Crocodiles of the World, we're watching two dwarf crocodiles in a tank, Stevenson using them to point out the difference in jaws and teeth between alligators and crocodiles. They're attractive little beasts, with dark, extremely tough-looking scaly skin. As we watch, the crocodile nearest the window moves towards the other and puts its arm on it, and Stevenson pauses. 'I wouldn't read anything into this behaviour,' he says, 'but certainly when they're mating the movement is extremely gentle, with lots of rubbing arms and snout rubbing, it's quite delicate and really the opposite of what people expect ...' He tails off as the instigator crocodile, which I learn is the male, continues stroking the other one and edging on top of it. 'He may actually be trying to get his leg over,' says Stevenson, as the male continues. He explains that the male will raise the female up and flip his tail under hers, and then bring their cloacas together and, as if guided by him, the dwarf crocodiles do exactly this.

'Well, it's not very often that visitors get to see that!' says Stevenson. I feel privileged to have such an insight into the way these animals bond. It seemed almost tender, and while I'm not sure what I ever expected from crocodiles mating, I don't think that would be it. The care doesn't stop there either, because once the female has constructed a nest and laid her eggs, she vigilantly guards it.

All species of crocodile show some form of parental care, which astonishes me: I had assumed that females simply laid their eggs and left them to fend for themselves, as with snakes or turtles. That's my own bias showing, but it was also the recognised 'truth' up until relatively recently. Not only were crocodile mothers not thought to care for their young, they were also thought to cannibalise them, which won't have helped with their reputation. That's because mothers were frequently seen carrying eggs or hatchlings away from the nest and into the water, never to be seen again. It was a fair assumption to make, but only until better observations could be made. Once that was possible, it was clear that rather than cannibalising their young, crocodile parents were giving them the start they needed in life – gently rolling the eggs in their mouths cracks them open, and they then help their hatchlings to emerge straight into the water where they can swim away.

Most of this parental care is woefully under-described. But, says Gordon Burghardt, professor emeritus at the

University of Tennessee, it has been known about for several decades: first reports date to the 1930s, and the behaviour was even mentioned in a book from the 1890s.

Burghardt is the world's leading authority on reptile minds, having studied and championed this group for more than 60 years. He's a self-confessed snake fanatic and these animals have been the thread that runs through his research career. More on that in the next chapter. But he has also conducted extensive research on parental care and tried to raise the profile of reptile brains among those interested in making comparative studies of cognition. In this, his life has been made harder by the 'triune brain' theory, which is the source of the popular notion of the 'reptile brain', an outdated belief that reptiles cannot possibly be capable of intelligence because they only have primitive brain structures. As he tells me: 'There are now many reports of parental care in many crocodilians, showing that moms stay with the babies for up to several years. And there are now scattered reports of postnatal and hatching parental care in lizards, snakes, and turtles, but crocodilians really showed that the whole triune brain idea was false.'

Perhaps the most striking example of this, Burghardt says, is the gharial – a large, Critically Endangered crocodilian living in northern India and Nepal, whose long, skinny snout is well-adapted for catching fish. Female gharials build nests together and lay their eggs communally, meaning that several hundred of the tiny, long-snouted babies may hatch together. The parents then show incredible parenting by defending the nests against birds, turtles or fish that would all consider these babies to be a tasty snack. Both sexes of parent protect the creche, and parents protect all the babies – not just their own, a clear example of cooperative care. In other crocodiles, parents carry their babies in their mouths for protection, but with so many to care for, gharial fathers have a different strategy. A male gharial, Burghardt says, 'protects and carries dozens of babies on his back, many of which may not actually be his own.' I don't have to go far to see an image of this — the cover of Burghardt, Dinets and Sean Doody's recently published book, *The Secret Social Lives of Reptiles*, features a beautiful photo of a big male with several dinky, very alert-looking miniature gharials riding on his back.

At Crocodiles of the World, I get my own glimpse of parental care when we move to a walkway looking down on the American alligator enclosure. One adult is floating in the water nearby, while another is further back, and four babies can be seen, mostly under a heat lamp at the back of the pool. 'That's Daisy,' says Stevenson, pointing to the nearest alligator, 'and that's Albert at the back.' Daisy lies still in the water, facing us and staring. There's a lot of staring with these animals. Stevenson says the parents are highly protective of their young (she's definitely keeping an eye on us), but more than that, they are also known to feed them, which is an advanced form of care. 'Say we're feeding Albert rats. He'll eat a few of them, but then he'll take one, swim over there,' Stevenson points towards the back, 'lift his head up and go *crunch, crunch*, and then drop it in the shallow water. The babies do come over, though there's not much they can do with a large rat. But he is quite clearly trying to help them.' That's astounding. It's one of a handful of such observations, several from American alligators, who seem to be dedicated parents. And it's observations like these that are showing the softer side to crocodiles.

I have one more question for Stevenson. People tend to go to zoos to see animals doing things, particularly children, who often rush past the motionless creatures, preferring instead to watch monkeys and meerkats and things that are actually, well, moving. How does it work at a zoo where their star animals may as well be plastic models for much of the day?

Stevenson says that this comes up a lot. 'And I always say to people, "When you're looking at a crocodile thinking it's weird for being so still, that crocodile is looking at you, thinking, "What an absolute weirdo. All you're doing is walking around feeding your face all the time." What we do makes no sense to them – we are, without question, a bunch of weirdos.'

It's hard to argue with that.

Moving out of the swamps and estuaries and into the ocean proper, we're also starting to learn some of the mysteries of those other feared predators. Let's find out why sharks aren't the monsters we think.

★★★

'Attack', 'bitten', 'terrifying'. These were the top three words identified by an analysis of Australian media outlets' posts about sharks on Facebook in 2016. The outlets also frequently incorporated words like 'mauled' and 'savaged' into these stories, and they usually focused on dangerous shark species. Such posts, by implying that incidents are more common than they are, and, by using emotionally charged language, would be more than enough to trigger anxieties about going into the ocean. The outcome? A maintenance of fear surrounding sharks, negative public attitudes, and lack of support for their conservation.

In 2024, there were 47 unprovoked shark bites around the world, four of which were fatal. Four. In the whole world. That's a few less than in 2023, but entirely in line with the five-year global annual average of six unprovoked fatalities per year. Those were the headline findings of the 2024 report from the Florida Museum's International Shark Attack File (ISAF), whose comprehensive records include more than 6,800 incidents stretching back to the early 1500s. ISAF data show that between 1960 and 2015, there were 2,060 unprovoked attacks across 14 countries. The US was the shark-attack capital, accounting for more than half of all attacks during that 55-year period, while Australia and South Africa followed.

Eighty-five per cent of those attacks were non-fatal. That still leaves a lot of people with bites and other life-changing injuries, as well as the psychological trauma of the incident, but importantly they're still alive. And that strongly suggests that sharks are perfectly capable of hunting humans, yet in most cases choose not to.

Nowhere is this more apparent than along the coast of southern California, where juvenile great white sharks (between 1.5m and 3m long) congregate in nurseries for several weeks or months. These waters are also prized by surfers, swimmers and paddle-boarders, and drone footage between January 2019 and March 2021 showed just how much sharks and people overlapped: daily human–shark co-occurrence was a staggering 97 per cent. The young sharks ranged from 2m offshore to over 700m, but averaged around 100m out – the same zone used by surfers and stand-up paddleboarders. In other words, sharks of a large-enough size to cause significant injury and death were encountering people multiple times every day. And yet, although millions of people use southern California's beaches and waters for leisure activities each year, only one potential unprovoked shark bite was reported over the study period.

Even when they attack us, it might not be because they're intending to kill. The 'mistaken identity' hypothesis suggests that the appearance of surfers and their boards from beneath might be too similar to the appearance of a seal or sea lion for a shark to tell the difference. Recent research seems to support this – video footage of two sea lions, one fur seal, human swimmers, and humans paddling surfboards was taken from the perspective of a great white shark swimming below, processed to imitate the shark's retina, and the different shapes were then compared. There was no real difference between them: the silhouettes of a swimmer or surfer paddling were not overly dissimilar to the silhouette of a swimming sea lion. An alternative hypothesis suggests that sharks simply bite things that are at the surface, taking a 'bite first, decide later' approach. Either way, it seems very possible that shark bites are often shark mistakes.

Why are sharks still so feared when the data tell such a different story? Surely all that shark conservationists need do is ensure that these statistics are front and centre of every campaign and in every aquarium, and people will soon lose their fear?

Sadly not, according to João Neves, head of education and conservation at Zoomarine Algarve, in Portugal. He says that the statistics should offer reassurance, but they shouldn't be the only tool used; and it can even be counter-productive for aquariums to focus their communications on them. I'm baffled and ask him to explain. 'It can be counter-productive to jump in really fast and try to deconstruct the whole idea of sharks, if it's culturally ingrained, because all the barriers to getting new information in will rise.' Neves elaborates that educators must consider the psychological phenomenon of cognitive dissonance, whereby people feel uncomfortable holding conflicting beliefs, values or attitudes. When it comes to sharks, 'if the new information is too dissonant to what they expect, that won't work.' If people hold deep beliefs about sharks being bloodthirsty monsters, then telling them that they have a greater risk of death from fireworks, or drowning, or heart disease just won't sink in, despite the risk of death caused by the latter being 1 in 5, compared with 1 in 4,332,817 for shark attack.[9]

Humans severely overestimate the risk posed by sharks, and combatting this involves first understanding why people hold such beliefs, and then working out how to communicate with them in the right way. Neves says that 10 years ago, he

---

[9] For more excellent statistics, please do visit the ISAF's very useful webpage, Risk of Death: 18 Things More Likely to Kill You Than Sharks.

would try hard to change people's incorrect beliefs about sharks when he spoke to them, but these days he's less dogmatic, saying, 'I think because I now understand that challenging people doesn't work.' What's needed, he says, is a better understanding of why most people's prototypical 'shark' is a great white. 'Even young children who haven't seen *Jaws* have this same prototype. Deconstructing this is the strategy.'

Challenging the stereotypes means shining a light on shark diversity, of which there is a great deal across the 548 known species. Only 13 of these are known to have bitten humans 10 or more times – notably great whites, bull and tiger sharks, meaning that most people's prototype is wildly misrepresentative. From peaceful plankton-feeding whale sharks, which at up to 17m long are the largest fish in the oceans, to 20cm dwarf lanternsharks, via the acrobatic spinner shark, there's so much more to this group. We also need to delve into their behaviour, because it's possible to identify commonalities that may resonate with us. 'Personally, I'm all in favour of using careful anthropomorphism in communications,' says Neves. That's not the same as humanising them, he explains, but when people learn about aspects of sharks' lives that may relate to their own, it can help to engage an audience.

Fortunately for Neves and others working in shark education, in recent years there has been an influx of new research into the shark's mind. And it's helping to overturn many of the myths about these animals being cold, cruel killers.

★★★

In 2003, late professor of marine science Arthur Myrberg was invited to speak on the topic of shark cognition at a conference in Germany. According to researchers Peter Klimley and Ila France Porcher, introducing a special issue of the journal *Behaviour* in 2023 that focused on cognition in sharks and rays (elasmobranchs), he wrote to all 15 people then studying elasmobranch behaviour for an update on the evidence. Unfortunately, none of them had seen anything that could 'even be speculated to be indicative of cognition.'

While the public fear the idea that sharks can be intelligent monsters, for scientists interested in understanding their minds, sharks have historically been uninteresting because they're 'just big fish', and fish have long been dismissed as non-starters for intelligence studies. After all, we all know that fish only have a three-second memory and if you can't remember things then you can't learn; and if you can't learn, then you can't be intelligent. Right?

Wrong. 'What's pretty obvious, for any animal, is that if they didn't have the capacity for learning and memory, they couldn't get by. That's the reality.' This is Culum Brown, head of the Fish Lab at Sydney's Macquarie University and an outspoken champion of fish intelligence. He tells me that when he gives talks, he often brings up Dory from *Finding Nemo*, because, 'Even little kids think that's hilarious, because it's obvious even to them that an animal that doesn't know her name, where she's going or where she's been, couldn't possibly exist in the real world.'

Sharks have been around for an astonishingly long time – close to half a billion years. Sharks, in fact, have not only been swimming the seas since before the earliest dinosaurs, but since before trees as well. That's an impressive pedigree, but for many people, sharks' ancient evolutionary history simply reinforces the view of them as 'living fossils', unchanged for hundreds of millions of years. Brown shakes his head. 'Most of the modern sharks that we see are no more ancient than humans. Sharks haven't been stuck as they were 450 million years ago – natural selection has still been rolling and rolling all that time.' Rather than being primitive beasts, a better way to think about sharks is that they've had a long time to evolve solutions, as Brown explains: 'They've had maybe a 400-million-year head start in terms of getting it right, because they've been constantly evolving and changing and updating. That's why I think they are so good at what they do. And to be fair, they also made it through a bunch of mass extinctions that many other animals didn't.'[10] Five mass extinction events, to be precise, which is a phenomenal survival record, and likely reflects both their deep-sea living and their spectacular diversity of forms – every time there was a major die-off, at least some shark species were able to persist.

So, we can throw away the notion that sharks are primitive, living fossils. Just look to the fantastically weird hammerhead sharks, which are thought to be the youngest group at only about 23 million years old. That's two million years after the first apes are thought to have evolved from their old-world monkey ancestor.

What about the idea that sharks are solitary, instinct-driven killers? Based on what Brown and others are finding, we can throw that one away too.

Brown's lab explores the cognition and ecology of a range of different fishes, including sharks. Most of their shark work is done using juvenile Port Jackson sharks ('PJs'), which have the advantage of hatching at a very convenient length, 15–20cm long, and being ready to go. Working with large adult sharks is just not practical, given their needs for space. And while Brown says that he only 'dabbles' in sharks, his team is finding some fascinating things. 'Fifteen years ago, we basically knew nothing about sharks in terms of their intelligence,' he says. 'We were coming from a very low baseline – the expectation that they're just mindless killing machines. And that's all changed, and it's down to technology.'

---

[10] Sharks made it through Earth's five mass-extinction events: End Ordovician event (444 million years ago) killed 86 per cent of species; Late Devonian event (360 mya) killed 75 per cent of all species and gave rise to the 'golden age of sharks', some 359 million years ago; End Permian (aka the 'great dying'; 252 mya), which saw around 96 per cent of all marine life eradicated; End Triassic (200 mya), killing 80 per cent of species; and the End Cretaceous (66 mya), which killed 76 per cent of species.

One of the big breakthroughs is that sharks are not, as typically assumed, solitary beasts. Back to that shortly. But the reason that technology has been so important is that it's provided researchers with invaluable alternative means to study their behaviour: previously, how they interacted with others could only be a best guess based on glimpses of behaviour above the waves or from limited dives. It's the same for reproduction, which remains one of the outstanding mysteries in shark lives.

Some of the earliest technological advances came from Klimley, aka Dr Hammerhead, who started studying wild sharks in the 1970s. On a trip to the Florida Keys, he heard people talking about sharks but noticed that nobody was going in the water to study them so, inspired by a *National Geographic* article on Dian Fossey's work with wild gorillas, Klimley decided he would. His supervisor, Donald Nelson, agreed, and told him that large schools of hammerhead sharks had been seen off a remote island in the Gulf of California, advising, 'If you really want to learn about sharks, you've got to dive with those sharks. But you know, the hammerheads are the third most dangerous of all sharks.'[11]

Undeterred, Klimley grabbed the opportunity, becoming one of the first scientists to free dive with sharks. A pioneer in the study of sharks' natural behaviour, Klimley conducted observations as he swam alongside groups of hundreds of scalloped hammerheads, using a purpose-built stereo camera and even attaching miniature compass sensors to some of them by hand. A key question, during the early research, was how the animals navigate, since they consistently travelled between the El Bajo seamount, where they rested together in the day, and the open ocean for foraging. His research

---

[11] According to the ISAF, hammerhead shark species have been implicated in 18 unprovoked attacks on people, none of them fatal, placing them quite far down the danger list. The 'Big Three' species involved in most human attacks and fatalities are the great white, tiger, and bull shark.

suggested they were perceiving and orientating using local differences in the earth's magnetic field, and this was controversial.

Klimley recalls presenting his groundbreaking study on hammerhead magnetic orientation at a meeting at the Scripps Institute. It was an interesting experience. 'You know, everybody thinks sharks are just mindless killers, but I went here, and I gave a seminar and I've never been to a meeting so hot. Half the audience were saying that it was impossible that sharks could be sensitive enough, and the other half were saying "He's done good science and he's supporting it."' Klimley pauses, shakes his head. 'People were screaming at each other, screaming at me!' It took Klimley seven attempts to publish this study, because of scepticism from his peers.

Fortunately, he tells me, things are different now. 'The whole perception of sharks has changed – academics don't think they're dumb feeding machines. But when I started publishing there were so many people that didn't believe it.' Klimley shakes his head, and then shrugs. 'And it was difficult to publish because they're the reviewers and they're sceptical about it!' Altered perceptions of sharks in the broad field of animal behaviour mean that today, there are more researchers studying these animals and it's much less controversial for them to publish their findings.

There has also been a change in the types of research questions being asked, particularly in the last couple of decades. 'Before that, we were still very hung up on humans being the gold standard,' Brown says. 'We were always comparing everything to humans, even though half the time it didn't make any sense: natural selection doesn't look at a fish and say, "Oh, we should shape a fish to make it behave like a human", because that makes no sense. For me, that's the whole thing.'

Brown is comfortable saying that sharks are intelligent, citing numerous findings relating to their learning and memory. But far from being evil geniuses intent on terrorising humans, they use their brains for far more innocuous things. Like learning, incredibly precisely, to turn up at the right time to get some fishy treats. This was the finding of a study from Brown's group with juvenile lemon sharks at Bimini, Bahamas. Food was provided at the same time every day for 27 days, and by day 11 the sharks were already showing up on time, if not a little early. Not only that, they kept coming for up to 90 days after the feeding had stopped. Bull sharks take things to another level. When the COVID-19 pandemic halted operations at an ecotourism site in Fiji, the sharks stopped getting their regular snacks. Eighteen months later, when the site was back up and running, it was business as usual for the sharks – they were much quicker to return to it than they had been to originally learn about it.

The same has been found with sharks' relatives, stingrays, in a study of fantastically named females, including: Billie Ray, Desaray, Raylene and Big Momma. As well as finding evidence for a similar social structure to some primates, with one big, dominant female in charge (Raylene), the team also recorded the animals anticipating when fishermen would toss their discarded fish: the rays showed up between about 10.00 a.m. and 2.00 p.m. to take advantage of the free food. Not only this, Brown says, but sharks and rays can learn about weekends too – a completely human thing, but an important cue for when humans are going to be active, because in the recreational fishing community, most activity (and discards) happens on the weekends. 'And the sharks and rays know, this is the time when they show up most reliably: just after lunch on a weekend.'

Tantalising evidence also suggests that, far from being solitary loners, sharks have friends. Sort of. They don't show affection, or mutual grooming, or play together, but studies of several species have found that individuals prefer to hang out with certain others, and these relationships can last for several years. One study of grey reef sharks around the Palmyra Atoll, for example, found that the animals would regularly meet up together in the same groups, with relationships lasting for at least four years (possibly more, but this was when the trackers ran out of battery). Nurse sharks and whitetip reef sharks are known to rest together on the ocean floor during the day, while juvenile lemon sharks actively prefer to spend time with other lemon sharks, compared with no sharks or a different shark species. There's even evidence that great whites, who are perennially cast as solitary ocean wanderers, choose to hang out near other sharks when they might be able to use it to their advantage – at seal colonies, for example, where eavesdropping on who has made a kill may provide an opportunity for some sneaky feeding.

The evidence is there to support the notion that sharks are intelligent and that, like other vertebrates, they possess a cognitive toolkit that they can draw upon to solve problems in their day-to-day lives. They can learn about all sorts of things, including from other sharks, and about artificial sights and sounds in their environment. And they are far from being the antisocial beasts of popular culture.

That they have emotional lives, on the other hand, is far less clear. 'We don't know much about pain and empathy and these sorts of things in sharks,' Brown says, 'but like every other animal, they almost certainly have nociceptors – you have to have them to survive.' Nociceptors are pain receptors, and for a long time sharks were thought to lack them, feeding into the stereotype of the mindless, robotic killer. While it's a lot more complicated than just whether they possess nociceptors or not, and whether they feel pain or not, evidence suggests that sharks do possess nerve endings that allow them to detect harm, but they likely don't function to flag the range of pain elicitors that they do in other animals.

Linked to this, Brown says, and similarly lacking research and public attention to date, is the topic of shark welfare. 'It's just not a thing because they've been the villain for so long. The empathy hasn't been there.' But increasingly people are developing compassion for sharks – such as when they save an animal that has become stranded – a story that nearly always makes the news. This would have been unthinkable in the immediate aftermath of *Jaws*. 'I think that there has been a shift from the seventies, when the shark in *Jaws* was the evil thing out to kill us, and now I think we have much greater empathy and understanding for the role sharks play in marine ecosystems.'

We can only hope that this is true. Sharks have dominated the oceans for 450 million years – but they're now facing their biggest test, and if they're to make it through the current, sixth mass extinction they're going to need all the help they can get.

We know so little about the minds of our big predators. And we're running out of time to discover more. Because while scientific research into the mental lives of crocodilians, sharks and large carnivorous mammals is blossoming, these are still animals that face an extraordinary amount of persecution. Our uncomfortable relationship with these beasts started a long time ago, and we've never really got past it. And that's a big problem, because when we go out with the mission of killing other creatures, we're far more effective at it than they are at killing us.

★★★

It's tempting to romanticise our prehistoric ancestors' relationships with nature, getting misty-eyed about fur-clad neanderthals roaming landscapes teeming with ancient beasts and condemning our modern destruction of the natural world. And while things are certainly phenomenally bad right now, it's worth being aware that humans have always been at it, and not just *H. sapiens*. Research has found that the size of the animals hunted by hominins has been decreasing for as long as 1.5 million years, when *H. erectus* walked the earth. Before 125,000 years ago, during the late Pleistocene,[12] the mean body size of mammals in Africa was already about 50 per cent smaller than in Eurasia or the Americas, suggesting that the long history of hominin–mammal interactions on this continent had already decimated the largest mammals. And when our ancestors migrated out of sub-Saharan Africa, the carnage spread. By 60,000 years ago, several hominin species were widespread across Africa and Eurasia; further expansion to Australia happened about 50,000 years ago, and to the Americas just 15,000 years ago. Each of these places had their own, huge animals: there were mammoths, giant ground sloths, woolly rhinoceroses, and sabre-toothed tigers, as well as a 4m ostrich-like bird called *Pachystruthio dmanisensis*, campervan-sized armadillo-like beasts called glyptodonts, and *Megalania lisca*, the largest lizard ever known. But once humans rolled into town, these beasts were slaughtered – in some cases completely disappearing in just a few hundred years. If future extinctions continue to disproportionately target the largest animals, some scientists have predicted that in a few hundred years, the largest mammal in existence could be the domesticated cow.

The period between 52,000 and 9,000 years ago has been termed the Quaternary megafauna extinction, and during this period more than 178 species of the world's largest mammals (those weighing 44 kg or more) were wiped out. Australia and the Americas were worst hit – Australia lost 88 per cent of its native megafauna, while North America lost 83 per cent. Mammals in Africa and Eurasia fared better during this period, likely because they had co-evolved with

---

[12] The geological epoch known as the Pleistocene, or Ice Age, spanned a period from 2.6 million years ago until 11,700 years ago, up to the point when the agricultural revolution forever changed the face of the planet. The late Pleistocene was the fourth division of this epoch.

hominins over several million years. The beasts of Australia and North America, in contrast, had no idea what to make of this new primate predator, making them woefully ill-adapted to survive.

The killing wasn't specific to predators. Our ancestors preyed on the big herbivores, and they were innovative. They learned to kill entire herds of bison by driving them off cliffs. But sabre-toothed tigers and giant bears were a dangerous source of competition, and once early hunters had mastered the manufacture of complex tools, they became ruthlessly efficient, deadly assassins. They had learned that it wasn't enough to simply survive an attack: killing your attacker before they try again is better, while killing them before they've even had a chance to attack was best of all.

We've been extremely good at it, too. So good that a 2018 study found that 80 per cent of large land-based carnivores are experiencing population declines, and 64 per cent are threatened with extinction.[13] And while species decline is happening across the board, these figures aren't a general consequence of what's happening to all animals – 'only' 32 per cent of mammals as a whole are in decline, compared with 48 per cent of carnivorous mammals.

Almost half of the 38 wild cat species are threatened. Lions, for example, previously ranged across North Africa, south-west Asia, Europe and India, but around 90 per cent of that historic range has been lost. The 22,000–25,000 adult and subadult lions left in Africa are largely confined to protected reserves and national parks. Outside sub-Saharan Africa, a tiny, fragmented population of 670 individuals clings on in the Gir Forest of India, an area smaller than Greater London. It's worse for tigers, which now occupy only seven per cent of their historical range (which

---

[13] All species assessed by the IUCN Red List as Vulnerable, Endangered, and Critically Endangered.

previously extended from Turkey over to the Indonesian islands of Java and Bali and up to Russia's far north-east). With a best estimate of just 3,140 mature tigers in the wild, these beasts have been classed as Endangered since 1986.

Six of eight bear species are threatened, including the sun bear and polar bear. And several of the large wild dogs face precarious futures: recent estimates of mature animals suggest that there are now fewer than 1,500 African wild dogs; around 2,000 dhole (Asiatic wild dogs); 197 Ethiopian wolves and just 20 to 30 red wolves. Grey wolves, on the other hand, are now classed as Least Concern, thanks to decades of concerted conservation effort and reintroductions.

The fates of land animals are inextricably tied to human population growth and our drive for continued development, expansion and consumption of the natural world. The more space we take, the less there is for other animals, and that's a particular recipe for conflict when those other animals are big, dangerous and need a lot of space. We'll return, briefly, to some of the heroic efforts being made to understand and mitigate human-wildlife conflict, but suffice it to say that it's complicated, nuanced, and there are no easy solutions.

In the oceans, we aren't competing with marine animals for the same living space. But our impacts are far from marginal. Overfishing, bycatch, deep sea mining, pollution, global sea temperature rises, all of these are destroying populations of marine wildlife. Sharks and rays are doing particularly badly, with around 100 million of these animals killed every year. The reported global market of shark meat has increased nearly two-fold, from $157 million in the early 2000s to $283 million in 2016. In fact, shark and ray meat is now valued at 1.7 times that of the global fin trade, although tens of millions of sharks are still being killed for fins, despite political and public opinion shifting on the acceptability of this practice.

Jaws hasn't helped. The fear that it generated quickly turned to persecution, as the film's director, Steven Spielberg revealed on BBC Radio 4's *Desert Island Discs* in December

2022. 'I truly, and to this day, regret the decimation of the shark population because of the book and the film,' Spielberg told the show's host, referring to a 'feeding frenzy' in the film's aftermath, in which thousands of sport fisherman hunted for shark trophies off the east coast of the US. According to shark researchers at the University of Florida, numbers of large sharks in these waters halved in the years following the film's release, although the finger of blame can't be entirely pointed at trophy hunters.

Today, all these factors contribute to the sobering statistic that more than 30 per cent of shark and ray species are threatened with extinction. They are the second most threatened group of vertebrates after amphibians. And it's really, bewilderingly, hard to comprehend why it is deemed acceptable to continue decimating the populations of a group of animals with such an obviously precarious future.

As a group, crocodiles are faring a little better, although the combination of unsustainable hunting for their valuable skins, persecution, and accelerating habitat destruction has pushed several species to the brink. The IUCN has assessed the status of 23 of the 26 recognised species, and fewer than half are classed as free from conservation concern. More worryingly, seven species are Critically Endangered – one step away from being declared extinct in the wild.

For those of us living in towns and cities, or in countries where there are no large predators remaining, these can feel like distant issues. Like Charlie said, what does it really matter if we lose these animals – it's not going to impact our lives. The trouble is that's not really true. By waging war on nature's fiercest, we unintentionally set off numerous trains of dominos, and the effects are being felt far and wide.

★★★

It seems obvious today, given everything that has been learned about ecology and the interconnectedness of life, that if you remove a species or group of similar species from the environment, there will be consequences. They might be a prey species, which forms the bulk of another's diet. Or they might be ecosystem engineers, such as beavers. Or they might be apex predators, who keep populations of smaller creatures, including smaller predators, in check.

Not all species in an ecosystem have equal roles, and those with disproportionately large impacts are known as 'keystone species'. This term was introduced by ecologist Robert Paine in the 1960s, based on his research of starfish and molluscs in the rocky tidal pools of Washington State. Starfish eat marine molluscs, including mussels, so Paine wondered whether the diversity of molluscs would increase if he removed the starfish. He found the opposite: diversity crashed. Without the starfish predating the molluscs, numbers of acorn barnacles and California mussels soared, crowding out all other competitors. Both feed on seaweed, and since there were far more of them now, they ravaged it, causing local extinction of other invertebrate species that fed on the algae. His conclusion was that removing the starfish removed an important brake on the shellfish; in his control tidal pools, Paine saw much higher diversity.

In this, Paine was testing observations made by earlier naturalists, including Charles Darwin and Aldo Leopold. Leopold, in his *Sand County Almanac* (1949), had written about the impacts of a 'wolfless' America letting deer browse vegetation unimpeded. He wrote, 'I have seen every edible bush and seedling browsed, first to anemic desuetude, and then to death ... I now suspect that as a deer herd lives in mortal fear of its wolves, so does a mountain live in mortal fear of its deer.'

Paine coined the term 'trophic cascade' in 1980, to describe these relationships, and in the decades since, many more keystone species and trophic cascades have been studied. In Shark Bay, Australia, for example, tiger sharks patrol temperate seagrass beds and in doing so, keep hungry grazers like dugongs and sea turtles from eating too much of it. Temperate seagrasses are phenomenally important weapons in our fight against global heating, not only trapping carbon dioxide but also stabilising ocean floor sediments, which are themselves extremely important stores of this greenhouse gas. By preventing seagrass beds from being overgrazed, tiger sharks keep the whole community healthy.

Perhaps the best-known trophic cascade concerns the return of grey wolves to Yellowstone National Park. As a result of the wolves' extermination in the 1920s, the park became saturated with elk, who played ecological havoc with the landscape. Between 1995 and 1997, 41 Canadian grey wolves were reintroduced, and since 2009 the population has remained stable at around 100 individuals. Their presence has undoubtedly played a role in bringing down elk numbers, both directly and by creating a 'landscape of fear', whereby nervier elk eat less and move around more. Popular claims that wolf reintroduction caused a cascade of benefits, including vegetation recovery, the return of beavers, healthier fish stocks, increased bird numbers and more are frequently shared, and while making a wonderful story, need to be taken with a pinch of salt. Populations of other predators, including cougars and bears, have also increased over the same period, so it's impossible to state how much of Yellowstone's recovery was down to the returning wolves. Nonetheless, what ecologists do agree on is the key role of apex predators in an ecosystem – they eat other animals, and they scare them, and that is a critical ecosystem service.

On the shores of British Columbia, creating a landscape of fear may also restore biodiversity. Raccoons like to hang out on the shoreline, where they feast on marine invertebrates such as crabs found in rock pools. When researchers broadcast the calls of dogs (racoon predators) or pinnipeds (harbour seals or Steller sea lions, which don't predate raccoons), the raccoons immediately adjusted their behaviour to the predators, either spending more time being vigilant as opposed to foraging, or leaving the area completely. Over one month, repeated 10-second playbacks of the dog calls, but not the pinniped calls, led to the raccoons spending 66 per cent less time foraging, and the knock-on impacts were huge: 97 per cent more intertidal crabs, 81 per cent more intertidal fish, 59 per cent more polychaete worms and 61 per cent more subtidal red rock crabs. By inspiring fear, top predators induce just enough stress to keep other animals from getting too comfortable in their environment.

If we lose our top predators, we will need to pick up the job of keeping prey species on their toes and under control. Currently, we aren't doing a good enough job. This is apparent from the fact that approximately 40 per cent of all wild land mammal biomass is concentrated in just 10 species, including five species of deer and two of kangaroo. There are an estimated 45 million white-tailed deer alone. Great for hunters, not so great for the rest of the ecosystem – as Leopold observed 75 years ago.

The impacts of apex predators aren't solely ecological – they benefit us all, and in tangible ways. Let's take wolves again. Or rather, the absence of wolves, for the benefits of predators tend to only become apparent after their removal.

Without wolves and other predators to keep deer numbers in check, their populations skyrocket. As well as eating every green shoot in sight, deer are vectors for ticks, some of which transmit disease-causing pathogens in humans. More deer moving around the countryside means a higher risk of encountering ticks on vegetation, and a higher risk of contracting disease, such as Lyme disease. In the UK, the incidence of Lyme disease has been gradually increasing since the first confirmed case in 1986. In 2017, some 2,000–3,000 new cases were reported each year, meaning that while it's by no means common, it is no longer rare. Climate change and landscape changes are key factors involved in the increased distribution of ticks, but anything that promotes the survival of animals upon which ticks feed and reproduce is undoubtedly also going to contribute. In the US, an average of 46,000 cases of tickborne disease were reported to the Centers for Disease Prevention and Control (CDC) between 2019 and 2022, predominantly Lyme disease, but eight other diseases have been reported, mostly associated with the lone star tick, which is spreading over the country.

What's more, as deer numbers increase, so too do road traffic collisions. In the US, an estimated two million collisions involving deer happen every year, with severe consequences: 440 people lose their lives, 59,000 people are injured and it all adds up to more than $10 billion in economic losses. An analysis of wolf reintroductions in the US state of Wisconsin found that, for an average county, the presence of wolves reduced deer-vehicle collisions by 24 per cent, and that the economic benefit of these reduced collisions was 63 times greater to the state than the costs of wolves killing livestock. Importantly, the study also found that most of the wolves' effect was down to them influencing deer behaviour, again through the creation of a landscape of fear, rather than directly reducing deer numbers through predation. As the researchers conclude, 'It suggests wolves control economic damages from overabundant deer in ways that human deer hunters cannot.'

Of course, this is not to say that we should be reintroducing wolves, tigers or wild dogs to every place that they once roamed: our footprint on the planet has expanded so much that this will never be appropriate. That's because the beneficial impacts of predators on the landscape are inseparable from the risks of those beasts to humans and our livestock. We persecuted large predators, sterilised our countryside from their 'savage' presence, because of these dangers. And that has not changed. They're still dangerous, and people who rely on subsistence farming and using forest products in Africa and the Indian subcontinent know this all too well.

AN AWFULNESS OF TEETH AND CLAWS

The intrinsic conflict between what predators can do for us versus what they can do to us is not easily resolved. And yet, as urban centres continue to spread and encroach on wild spaces, we're starting to see how we may coexist. Completely counterintuitively, large carnivores are starting to move into our cities, despite the concrete, noise, artificial light and proximity to us, and they're adapting. The sprawling megacity of Mumbai provides a good example. Mumbai is home to around 31,000 people per km^2, among the highest population density on Earth, and the city continues to grow. It's also the only city in the world to have a national park within its city limits: Sanjay Gandhi National Park (SGNP) covers 103km^2 (about 20 per cent of Mumbai's total geographical area) and is often referred to as the 'lungs of the city'. It's a refuge for wildlife, and supports a dazzling array of species, including, as of the last survey in May 2025, at least 54 leopards, the highest known density in the world.

While SGNP is officially protected, Mumbai's slums are starting to encroach. Around 250,000 people are believed to live within just 500m of the park's borders, making it a perfect recipe for human–wildlife conflict. But the leopards are doing well, because city living provides them with abundant sources of prey – and I don't mean people. Leopards that hold territories in the middle of the park have plenty of the usual wild prey, but those on the park's borders have become specialists on something a bit less typical: feral dogs. Mumbai is home to some 96,000 of them, one of the largest populations of stray dogs in the world, and they roam freely around the city and the park. It's illegal to kill them, and they live off the hundreds of tonnes of uncollected rubbish and carrion that accumulates within the slums (a consequence of the catastrophic collapse in vulture populations in the Indian subcontinent since the 1990s – we'll return to this in a later chapter). Dogs have been feeding Mumbai's leopards for the past 20 years, and for leopards living on the park borders, they make up around

40 per cent of their diet. That has had a considerable, and welcome, impact on dog populations too: leopard predation has reduced density along the edges of the park to about 17 dogs per km^2, compared with around 680 dogs per km^2 in more central slums. And the prey doesn't run out – as dog territories along the park's boundaries are continuously vacated, a constant stream of dogs move out of the city to occupy them.

By predating feral dogs, Mumbai's leopards are providing tangible benefits to local people. That's because feral dogs are considerably more dangerous to them than leopards. Almost 75,000 dog bites were reported in 2021, and almost 80 per cent of them required medical attention. Many feral dogs carry rabies, a devastating viral disease which kills 20,000 people in India each year. Since they can't cull them, people carry rocks and sticks to defend themselves and the local government must direct resources into sterilising the animals. Leopard predation offers an effective alternative. One analysis found that leopards have reduced dog bites ten-fold for people living immediately adjacent to the city, translating into more than 1,000 bites prevented each year. If leopards were no longer present, an estimated 90 more people would die every year in Mumbai from dog attacks.

★★★

Wildlife conflict is often interpreted as the outcome of competition between people and wildlife for resources, but in recent years conservationists are reframing this. Conflict reflects the level of interaction with wildlife that people think is acceptable. And when it comes to this, there's no one-size-fits-all.

One of the big challenges for predator conservation is that success will always be followed by conflict. Saltwater crocodiles provide a good example. During the first half of the twentieth century, the commercial crocodile skin trade virtually exterminated salties across northern Australia. Formal protection for the species was put in place in 1971, with broad public support: with few animals around, they weren't perceived as being problematic. As crocodile numbers have rebounded in places like Australia's Northern Territory, more attacks have occurred and inevitably people have called for population culls.

These kinds of knee-jerk, emotional responses have also been seen for sharks, with officials often implementing hastily drafted, reactionary policies in the aftermath of attacks. Off the coast of New South Wales in Australia, for example, shark nets were first installed in the 1930s, in response to several shark attacks off Sydney's surf beaches. They're extremely controversial, and for a couple of reasons. First, they're lethal to a lot of other marine wildlife, including whales and their calves, dolphins, turtles and dugong. Second, they're not particularly effective – one analysis found that approximately 40 per cent of shark entanglements occurred on the *beachward* side of the nets, meaning that the sharks are quite capable of swimming over and around them.

While authorities have resisted their removal, shark nets are at odds with the attitudes of those who live near the water and use it recreationally. There is now a growing sense of pride among Australians about sharks, and counter-intuitively, surfers who have been involved in or know of attacks at their surfing spots don't hate the animals. The results of public surveys like the Waverley Council Shark Survey (2023), which included 500 respondents in this area of Bondi Beach, have found a resoundingly shark-positive attitude: 71 per cent of these regular ocean users believed that shark attacks were accidental, 70 per cent would not blame the government if they removed the nets and a shark attack occurred, and only 7 per cent supported shark nets being installed after a shark attack. What's more, almost 60 per cent of respondents reported that the phrase 'shark attack' is sensationalised.

For many people around the world, large, powerful predators hold deep significance, and this can both help and hinder conservation. Religious and cultural factors may promote coexistence, but as conservation efforts pay off and numbers of endangered species increase, patience starts to wear thin.

Nepal's tigers provide a good case in point. When Rajan lost his brother to a tiger attack, on the outskirts of Bardiya National Park, tigers were around but their population was in bad shape. WWF's Tx2 programme was instigated in 2010, an effort in partnership with 13 countries to double global tiger numbers by 2022, and Nepal embraced the challenge. 'We didn't double the tiger population,' Rajan tells me. 'We increased it seven times!' Bardiya went from having 18 tigers to 125, which earned them the prestigious Tx2 award and was cause for great celebration for conservationists. Communities on the park borders, on the other hand, saw only the downsides of increased tiger numbers. That's because while Bardiya, at 968km^2, is theoretically large enough to support more tigers than it had, it is not uniformly prime tiger habitat. Valuable tiger real estate is worth fighting for, but while the winners of territorial disputes stay in the jungle, with everything they need, the losers are pushed out, searching for prey and water until they reach a village, where they are enticed by cattle, goats or people.

Rajan's family belong to the Tharu tribe, and they feel a fundamental connection with the forest – not just as a provider of resources, but as a protector too. Tharu religion combines Hinduism with animism and nature worship; it is built around maintaining a harmonious relationship with the entities of the forest, including the tiger. 'We worship all the animals as gods and goddesses,' Rajan says. 'Most of the people, like 99.9 per cent, love nature; they love tigers; they love the wildlife. Unfortunately, sometimes we are having really unwanted confrontations.'

Rural villagers and subsistence farmers who rely on crops, livestock or products from the forests may well feel proud that their country is one of the best places in the world to see tigers. But that sentiment won't help when a relative has been killed, or a prized cow taken. Retaliatory killings are all too common and it is all too easy for us in the western world to condemn this as irresponsible given a species' precarious conservation status. But we're in no moral position to do this unless we have lived experience of sharing our environment with potentially deadly beasts.

'Conserving wildlife that prey on people is one of the world's great challenges,' crocodile conservationist Webb has written. It's not a problem that's going to just go away, although the outlook doesn't have to be gloomy. Narratives concerning large predators and people are so often focused on conflict, it's sometimes hard to see that there are other ways of thinking about these creatures, but conservationists are doing fantastic work and solutions are being found. The key to promoting coexistence is ensuring that the people living alongside the conserved species feel the benefit of their increased numbers. If a dangerous animal is not also an asset to the local people, and if their needs and values are not integral to the initiatives, conservation efforts won't work. Get those things right, though, and great things can be done.

When it comes to crocodiles, they've been ruling the land–water interface for tens of millions of years – they're not going to stop doing so because we've built a garden or golf course in their territory. We need to find other ways to coexist, and in the Northern Territory, one of the solutions is sustainable crocodile farming. In my youth, I would have reacted strongly against the idea that farming animals for their skins could ever be a good thing, but in this case it seems to be providing a valid way to reduce the conflict. Using a ranching model, the farms pay local landowners for a number of wild eggs and/or hatchlings, which they then raise in captivity for meat and skins. International fashion houses including Louis Vuitton, Hermes and Yves Saint Laurent will pay the crocodile farms anything from $300 to $1,000 per skin, depending on its quality – it's therefore in the farm's best interests to look after their animals well. A report commissioned by the Northern Territory government for 2014/15 found that, overall, crocodile farming was valued at $106.7 million and, importantly, the money is flowing back into local communities. That's provided people with an incentive to maintain healthy populations of the animals in the wild, and it's working: population surveys of salties in the Northern Territory have found no impact of egg harvesting on the wild population (which has stabilised at around 100,000 individuals). It can clearly be an emotive issue, but as Stevenson explains, many of the animals being farmed for their skins are animals that wouldn't have survived past hatchling stage in the wild. 'Crocodile farms *per se* are not good or bad things,' he says. 'It can be done brilliantly, or it can be done awfully. But where it's done in a sustainable way it can have direct, positive impacts in the wild population and ecosystem.'

Crocodile farms have cottoned onto another benefit of crocodiles too: the fact that people will pay to see them. For many people, these animals are both terrifying and fascinating, and that makes them a tourist magnet. Farms and ecotourism companies understand this and crocodile tourism has become incredibly important in the Northern Territory's Top End region. Nobody wants to stumble across a crocodile in the bush, but plenty of people want to see them from the safety of a tourist boat or boardwalk. Companies have sprung up offering crocodile safaris across the range, including in Kakadu National Park, where Plumwood had her horrific encounter (and where *Crocodile Dundee* was filmed). Adelaide River Cruises, some 20km east of Humpty Doo, offers 'jumping croc' cruises, enticing people with the possibility of seeing Brutus and Dominator, the river's two dominant males. At over 5m apiece, these are not animals that anybody would want to encounter from anywhere but the safety of a boat.

Shark ecotourism has also taken off, because these are animals worth much more alive than dead – this was the key conclusion of an analysis published in 2013 which estimated that every year, more than 590,000 people paid to watch sharks, generating more than US$314 million. The authors noted that these numbers could more than double in the following 20 years, generating more than $780 million around the world. That's a vast number, but what's truly staggering is the finer-grained data relating to the value of individual sharks. A single living hammerhead shark at Cocos Island National Park was estimated to have a net value of $1.6 million, compared with just $200 if landed by a fisherman. A single reef shark in Palau had a net value of $1.9 million, compared with $108 dead. And the net value of a single Galapagos shark has been estimated at a staggering $5.4 million over its lifetime, compared to $158 if caught. As long as that money also benefits local communities, then preserving shark populations for tourism should be a no-brainer.

Various studies show that even in westernised countries, people who frequently visit nature show reduced fear to wild predators such as wolves, and greater emotional affinity and willingness to converse biodiversity. Having the opportunity to see these animals and watch their natural behaviour is surely helpful in shifting our perceptions of what they're like, but this could also come from documentaries that portray the animals accurately and sensitively. Indeed, Neves says that convincing the public that sharks aren't the evil monsters of popular culture could be done very quickly: 'The minute we can get Disney on board for shark conservation we're done!' It's a tongue-in-cheek comment but absolutely valid – once the content consumed by the public, particularly children, on television and social media shifts away from the *Jaws* prototype, 'then in 20 years' time sharks will be fine.'

Nonetheless, we can't forget that these are wild animals, and predatory ones at that. They can be legitimately dangerous to us, especially at the boundaries of human and animal worlds, and these boundaries will continue to expand and be challenged by both sides. Our top predators deserve a healthy dose of respect and far greater understanding of what they are and what they do, if we are to stand any chance of coexisting. You can't hug lions or stroke crocodiles and expect to walk away in one piece. But our Victorian compatriots got this wrong – rather than being a symbol of uncivilised disorder, large predators are essential to the functioning of life on this planet. And, perhaps more surprising, they are far from the cold-hearted killers that we've long presumed.

CHAPTER 3

Snake in the grass

Mankind have driven the lion, the tiger, and the wolf from their vicinity; but the snake and the viper still defy their power, and frequently punish their daring interference.
Buffon, *Histoire Naturelle*, 1828

'Is that ... a snake?'

It's September 2023, and we're partway through a hike in Pinnacles National Park, California. Trudging up a dry, dusty path, we've just realised that what, at first glance, we took to be a branch on the path is in fact a snake. Quite a big snake, and unhelpfully stretched fully across the path in the sun, right where we needed to walk. Not long before this, a fist-sized black tarantula had wandered down the path towards us, and before that we'd needed to clamber through a cave where we disturbed a couple of bats. Vultures were circling above. Possibly not everybody's idea of a good nature walk but as somebody writing a book about underappreciated animals, I was in my element.

As we got closer, we could see that this snake was a rattlesnake and it was a beautiful creature, its dark diamond patterns morphing into the characteristic stripes of its tail. We admired it for a bit, before tackling the trickier question of how we were going to move it. As Brits, with only one native species of potentially dangerous snake (the adder, which I've only seen once in my life), we're not bursting with knowledge about the best ways to encourage one off a path, but we figured that, as snakes are animals that rely a lot on tactile cues, vibrations might be the way to go. We therefore started stomping our way up the path and, amazingly, it worked like a charm; the snake lazily slithered out of view and into the bushes, giving a defiant rattle as we hurried past. It felt like we'd reached a good negotiation, one that allowed us all to carry on with our business without animosity.

This western diamondback rattlesnake, I am sure, had a good life. Or at least, a better life than the rattlesnakes that have the bad luck of being born around Sweetwater, Texas. Rather than being left alone to get on with snake things, these animals have a good chance of ending up at the Sweetwater rattlesnake roundup, which happens every year in March. Billed as a 'family-friendly' event, it attracts around 30,000 visitors to the town every year, all drawn to the spectacle of seeing hundreds, if not thousands, of western diamondbacks. But they're not just for show – captured snakes are tossed into a holding pit before being decapitated, skinned and cooked up for visitors to eat. There's a Miss Snake Charmer Pageant and young children are encouraged to contribute to a cheery wall of red handprints, using the blood of butchered snakes.

Sweetwater's roundup started in 1958, with the goal of eradicating snakes from the town, as people and animals were being frequently bitten. Western diamondbacks are a potentially dangerous species, so it was reasonable to want to reduce harmful interactions, but things have evolved since then: today, it's a fully commercial venture and the direction of harm has been reversed. The organisers buy all the snakes brought in, with bumper money for hunters that bring in the heaviest haul and the longest individual. Hunters, therefore, don't mess around – they start catching early and target as many likely areas as they can. Particularly prized are the snakes' winter hibernation sites: typically, old tortoise burrows or rocky cavities where groups of up to 100 or 200 individuals curl up together over winter, emerging in spring when the weather has warmed up. Hunters don't wait for the snakes to naturally emerge; instead, they force them out by spraying gasoline into their winter safehouses, a cruel, lazy and indiscriminate way to catch the animals. Those that aren't killed by the fumes try to escape but are instead caught and crammed into plastic bins where, often lacking food or water, they are kept alive until the festival begins – around 90 per cent of the snakes brought to the event are captured some four to six weeks beforehand.

Sweetwater is not the only rattlesnake roundup, but it is by far the largest, and despite condemnation from environmental groups and the public, it shows little sign of change. This town of around 10,000 residents does well from the roundup – to the tune of an estimated $8.4 million every year. But in a rapidly changing world, it's also important to adapt, and various other roundups already have – those in Georgia, for example, have switched to 'no kill' festivals with a strong educational component. Snakes are celebrated not slaughtered.

The western diamondback rattlesnake is one species in a group of around 3,600, and it carries with it the baggage of thousands of years of fear and persecution. Snakes wear many hats in their relationships with us, often paradoxically: they are killers and cures, predators and prey, pets and phobias. Snake venoms cause death and disability in hundreds of thousands of people every year; but these same venoms may also provide the building blocks for life-changing new drugs. We will benefit from the advances being made with their venom, as well as their pest-controlling prowess, but perhaps we can also benefit from the knowledge that snakes have friends, look after their babies, like to cuddle up, and may have a sense of self? It's a far cry from the common stereotype of them as cold-blooded, cold-hearted, evil beasts. Welcome to our long-standing, deep-rooted, and extremely complex relationship with snakes.

★★★

'Just pretend you're a tree.'

This, I must say, is easier said than done. Especially when you've just been handed a snake and even more so when you've never held a snake and are as excited as I am.

I'm at the Centre for Snakebite Research & Interventions (CSRI), at the Liverpool School of Tropical Medicine (LSTM), to find out more about snakes and their venom. Their herpetarium is the only Home Office accredited facility of its kind in the UK, and it contains around 200 snakes from more than 50 species, ably cared for by professional herpetologists Paul Rowley and Edd Crittenden. The CSRI conducts cutting-edge research into the biology of snake venom, using the insights to help guide the development of new antivenoms, and since there's no point trying to develop antivenom against snakes that aren't a threat to life, the snakes here need to be taken seriously.

The little African egg-eating snake that Crittenden has handed me, on the other hand, is completely harmless. She's the CSRI's 'ambassador' and she's surprisingly cute. About the width of my thumb and the length of my arm, she's an attractive olive-green colour and her large eyes are set low in a dinky little head. She's the sort of snake you could give to an excited child just as easily as an excited science writer and, while this species might not impress in the venom stakes, it's far from boring. These little reptiles belong to the genus *Dasypeltis* and they are true specialists; with no fangs, and in fact no visible teeth at all, they can open their jaws wide enough to swallow whole birds' eggs, which can be many times larger than the snake's own head. It's something that needs to be seen to be believed. During the bird breeding season, they gorge themselves but they're picky: Crittenden tells me that they will shun cracked eggs and will starve if none of the right eggs are around. The ambassador is small and lithe, skinny and strong, constantly seeking with her head while holding onto the branches of my arms for support. To this little snake, I was nothing more than a slightly wriggly, probably very strange-smelling, warm tree, but I was enchanted.

Snakes are characterised by their greatly elongated body and tail and absence of limbs, and are thought to have evolved from a lizard ancestor somewhere in the region of 170 million years ago. Working out from the fossil record the precise moment at which a lizard lost its legs and became a snake is impossible, not least because some modern snakes, such as pythons, retain tiny vestigial hind limbs, and there are also legless lizards, which are very much not snakes, such as the UK's slowworm.

Suffice to say, snakes evolved a long time ago, living alongside the dinosaurs for tens of millions of years, predating insects and small lizards. Then, 66 million years ago, a huge lump of rock hit our planet and everything changed. In this, the Cretaceous-Paleogene (or K-Pg) extinction, around three-quarters of all species were wiped out in a flash of evolutionary time. And in their place, the survivors thrived. It's well known that mammals and birds radiated into an extraordinary diversity of new species, evolving to take advantage of ways of life previously dominated by the dinosaurs, pterosaurs and more. But snakes benefitted too. The diversification of these groups offered up a sudden smorgasbord of potential prey, and snakes grasped those new opportunities with both fangs, moving into new environments (such as Asia, where they were previously not present), diversifying their diets and also starting to specialise. It led to the evolution of some massive forms, such as the 13m *Titanoboa*, a swamp-dwelling behemoth of South America that constricted its prey like modern-day anacondas; and the first tree-dwelling snake. Others became progressively smaller and better able to hunt fast, nocturnal little mammals or, like *Dasypeltis*, they turned to bird eggs.

It's probably a good thing that we no longer have snakes as large as *Titanoboa*, or the Indian equivalent, *Vasuki indicus*, which was estimated to be up to 15m long. These would have been terrifying adversaries. On the other hand, at least you'd be able to see them and hide. Today's snakes may be smaller but some of them are no less deadly. That's because when the snakes underwent their own adaptive radiation around 60 million years ago, some of them evolved an alternative way to dispatch prey which no longer relied on physical strength. Swapping muscles for molecules, they went down the path of chemical weaponry, evolving one of the most devastating weapons of all: venom.

Venom is one of life's most impressive evolutionary innovations. It transformed predator–prey relationships from those based on physicality – brute force, speed, agility – down to the molecular level. Big teeth, claws or muscles honestly communicate their threat level to us: a slavering grizzly bear, for example, lays all its cards on the table about your probability of surviving an encounter with it. Not so with venom. A plain brown spider keeps its cards hidden, and yet only one of these creatures wields enough power to dissolve your flesh, and you may not even notice its bite. With venom, evolution enabled creatures that typically don't have size or strength on their side, such as snakes, scorpions, spiders, wasps, snails and more, to become extremely effective and efficient killers. They could remain small and inconspicuous, prioritising speed and agility to get close enough to their prey to jab it, without needing to try and physically subdue it and risk defensive injuries.

Around 220,000 venomous species are known to science, which is about 15 per cent of global animal biodiversity. And while venom evolution is undoubtedly an ancient adaptation, it didn't just happen once. Scientists estimate that venom has independently evolved in at least 19 lineages, which is a staggering level of convergent evolution and shows just how successful it is. Powered flight, in contrast, which is another extremely beneficial adaptation, has 'only' independently evolved four times.

As well as the sheer scale of it in the animal kingdom, venom evolution is marked by the diversity of animal groups that show it and the diversity in their injection methods. There is no single bodily structure that venomous beasts use to administer their toxins: nature co-opted a bewildering array of different parts. Some use modified leg-like appendages (spiders, centipedes and crustaceans) while for others it's modified teeth (snakes); others use modified antennae (beetles), beaks (octopuses), stingers (scorpions), ovipositors (egg-laying tubes; used by bees, wasps and hornets), barbs (fish), hairs (caterpillars), and harpoons (cone snails). Then there are specialised stinging cells called nematocysts (jellyfish and sea anemones), while the platypus uses spurs on its hind legs. Some snakes, scorpions and ants can also spit or spray toxins into the air as a deterrent. Phew.

Let's also not forget that there are also thousands more organisms that are poisonous – meaning that their toxins are administered if they are simply eaten, inhaled or touched. A popular way of explaining the difference is that if an animal bites you and you die then it's venomous, whereas if you bite it and die then it's poisonous. Biting and stinging animals are therefore venomous, while tropical frogs, fungi and plants that produce toxins are poisonous. When you hear somebody talking about poisonous spiders or snakes, they're technically not right. But whether this alters how you feel about these creatures is an altogether different thing.

Despite any instinctive anxieties that the thought of venomous snakes may prompt, it's worth knowing that there isn't a single species that considers humans as prey. Venomous snakes evolved much further back than hominins, meaning that while our ancestors overlapped with them, they didn't coevolve as hunter and hunted. An obvious clue as to why venomous snakes aren't trying to hunt us comes from their size and jaw structure. Snakes swallow prey whole, but all venomous snakes are too small and their jaws don't come close to opening wide enough to swallow a person. Constrictors are another thing altogether – they had gapes large enough to swallow ancient mammals before 100 million years ago, and primates have been on the menu for as long as they've been around. Chimpanzees and other primates regularly encounter dangerous snakes, and ancestral primates, including our earliest hominin relatives, would similarly have lived with the threat of these predators.

Today, some species, like the reticulated python and boa constrictor, are large and capable enough of eating a person. Even so – according to the USGS, only one to two people in the world are killed by constrictor snakes each year, and in the US all such fatalities have been from captive snakes. Even in Florida, where released Burmese pythons are now doing very well for themselves, there have been no deaths. Snakes aren't slithering around stalking people, and they aren't sitting there plotting how and when to attack.

'A lot of the fear comes from either TV or reading about them, where they've been villainised to the max. In general, though, they're not like that in the slightest.' Crittenden says this as he ushers me into a room filled with, in his words, 'some of the deadliest snakes known to man.' These are members of the *Echis* genus, commonly called saw-scaled vipers, and they are responsible for 20,000–30,000 deaths every year. As we approach one of the tanks a small, beautifully patterned snake edges out, tongue flicking. 'He's come to see what's going on,' says Crittenden. 'This isn't aggression, this is purely inquisitive.' The little snake continues to flick its tongue and stare at us. 'You can see, they're very nosy animals – we'll often be working in here and look up, and all their little faces will just be watching.' He pauses before adding, 'If ever there was a pervert animal, it would be a snake.'

This is not something that I was expecting to hear.

Saw-scaled vipers are ambush predators, in contrast to those that stalk their prey, and they rely on camouflage as their first line of defence. That means that when people get close their first response is to sit still and wait it out. If they continue to feel threatened, they communicate their unhappiness by making warning movements, and by curling into a C-shape and rubbing their rough scales together. I can confirm that this makes a rasping noise not unlike somebody sawing wood. But it's quiet, and if I was out working in the fields or forests, I don't think that I would hear it. This is where the danger lies.

As snakes don't consider us prey, they bite in defence, not offence. Often, that's because somebody has accidentally stepped on one or done something else (unintentionally) that makes it feel threatened. In rural, agricultural settings in lower-income countries, many people working in the fields or forest lack adequate protective footwear, or they may encounter snakes in their homes, often overnight, where the animal has come in seeking warmth and not been noticed. The trouble is that even though the venom might not have been designed for us, vertebrate physiology is fundamentally the same across species, so whether the toxin evolved to incapacitate a lizard, bird or mouse is irrelevant – it can work perfectly well against our boringly animal bodies too.

In June 2017, the World Health Organization (WHO) officially relisted snakebite as a highest priority neglected tropical disease.[14] Their most recent (2023) global estimate is that 5.4 million snakebites happen every year, which breaks down to nearly 15,000 people being bitten *every day*. Anywhere from one-third to one-half of those bites contain venom (termed 'envenomations'); the others are 'dry bites', where no venom is discharged. And the consequences can be devastating. Between 81,000 and 138,000 people die every year, and up to 400,000 people suffer from amputations or other permanent disabilities.

As a continent, Asia is far and away the most dangerous place for snakebite, with up to two million people needing treatment for bites each year, but India is the snakebite capital country, with an estimated 58,000 annual deaths. That nosy little saw-scaled viper is one of the worst offenders: together with the spectacled cobra, Russell's viper, and common krait it makes up India's 'big four'; the species historically considered responsible for most deaths.

Snakebite is both a cause and consequence of poverty. It typically impacts people living in deprived, rural communities, where infrastructure is poor and it can be difficult to get medical treatment. And because the women, children and farmers who are most likely to be bitten tend to be the younger members of a community who do economically important work, it keeps people in poverty too. Similarly to malaria, another tropical disease that is both preventable and treatable, the fact that effective antivenoms exist that could prevent death if there was greater availability and access makes this so much more than a 'dangerous animal' problem. In fact, it's grossly neglected in comparison to other diseases.

In westernised countries, snakebite happens far less often and when it does it's rarely fatal. In the US, the CDC estimate that 7,000–8,000 people are bitten every year,

---

[14] It had first been added in 2009 but was removed for unclear reasons.

resulting in around five deaths. That's a fatality rate of about 0.07 per cent. In Australia, 539 people were hospitalised for snakebite in 2021–22 and seven of them died. Here in the UK, the Amphibian and Reptile Conservation Trust reports that adders are so shy and fearful of humans that only 50 to 100 people are bitten every year and only 14 deaths have been caused by adder bites since 1876. The last one was in 1975.

★★★

I'm having a coffee with Cassie Modahl, lecturer at the LSTM, to find out more about the CSRI's research on venoms. She's been working in venom science for about 15 years and specialises in studying the genetic basis of venom production. My take-home message is that venoms are impressively, dizzyingly complicated.

My mind has already been blown by the diversity of animal species that have evolved a venom system, but things get more complex. Modahl tells me that each venom comprises a chemical cocktail of hundreds, if not thousands, of different biologically active components, including proteins, amino acids, enzymes and other substances, which have evolved over time to produce deadly, targeted effects in the system of their intended prey. 'All these snakes have different toxins,' Modahl says. 'And there's variation between different species, between individuals within the same species, and in some species even within an individual's lifespan – from when it's a young hatchling to when it's an adult. So even trying to approach the question of "What toxin is important?" is really challenging.' Juvenile brown snakes, for example, hunt lizards, and the venom that they produce at this age is targeted for this prey. As they get older and bigger, their diet switches to rodents and, incredibly, the chemistry of their venom changes too.

The study of venom components and diversity is known as venomics, and comprises the fields of genomics, transcriptomics and proteomics, which are essentially just the different levels at which venom components can be studied.[15] By using these cutting-edge molecular technologies, the CSRI aims to develop innovative new antivenoms that offer greater efficacy, fewer side effects and greater affordability. I hadn't realised that antivenoms are still manufactured as they were 100 years ago, by injecting horses and sheep with small amounts of venom and harvesting the antibodies that the animals produce. Improving antivenoms and access to them could improve the lives of millions of people around the world.

To achieve these goals, the CSRI scientists need a reliable supply of venoms, hence the herpetarium full of deadly snakes and the expertise of Rowley and Crittenden. Extracting venom is also known as 'milking', in snakes but also spiders, scorpions and other venomous beasts, and it's a term that conjures up all sorts of weird imagery; in fact, it just involves encouraging the snake to bite down on a membrane-covered pot so that the released venom is collected.[16]

I was fortunate to watch two snakes being milked on my visit and was impressed by the speed of the procedure. Once a snake was released from its carry box, Rowley and Crittenden used poles to pin it to the floor. Rowley then

---

[15] Modahl explains the differences beautifully: 'Genomics refers to all the toxin genes that a snake has. So that's like your cookbook of all your recipes, but you're not going to need all the recipes at any one time, you'll just need one. Transcriptomics looks at RNA, which is just a single recipe, so that'd be just a single toxin gene. And then the final product from the cookbook would be the cake, and that's going to be the specific protein that's produced [proteomics].'

[16] Spiders are knocked out with carbon dioxide and then administered a weak electrical shock, which stimulates a small quantity of venom to be released. Scorpions are milked in a similar way, and a team in Morocco developed the first remote-controlled machine to do so, milking up to four scorpions at once!

picked it up behind its head and brought it over to the collection pot, which was clamped in place just a few centimetres from me on the other side of the viewing window. The first snake, a spitting cobra, was gaping as Rowley carried it over, so he just had to place its top jaw onto the membrane to elicit a bite. It's a surprisingly violent movement, the fangs ripping through the membrane and yellowish liquid dribbling to the bottom of the pot. Rowley massaged its cheeks to encourage more venom release, and then the snake was put back into its box. The first snake disgorged a good amount, but the quantity released by the second snake was dismal; nonetheless, both samples were sealed up and freeze-dried for subsequent research.

Rowley has been hospitalised three times as a result of this 'occupational hazard' but, as I learn, there is a hospital directly across the road from the centre, and I imagine they keep it well stocked with antivenoms. Over the course of a 30-year career at the CSRI, I guess that's not too bad a hit rate. Crittenden tells me that he has never been bitten, but has only worked there for six years. He is remarkably sanguine about the idea that this streak may not last.

When done responsibly, as demonstrated by Rowley and Crittenden, milking is harmless to the snake. That means not doing it too often; the animals need a decent break between extractions to replace the cells that line the venom gland wall, so each snake is usually only milked two to three times a year. They should, therefore, all have the venom available but it's not that predictable. 'No two extractions are the same,' Crittenden says. 'Some days they're happy to give us loads, and some days they don't want to.' He tells me about Frank, a 'geriatric' snake in their collection who started giving them less and less venom at each extraction. He eventually needed to be euthanised and Rowley and Crittenden assumed his old age explained his poor venom production. They were surprised to find that his venom glands were full. 'He was dripping venom from his fangs,'

Crittenden says, shaking his head. 'He was actively refusing to give it to us.'

Venoms can be agents of death and unbearable agony. So it seems a little counterintuitive that those same components that cause tissues to die, organs to fail, and nerves to stop firing can also save lives. But that is exactly what is happening, because the same building blocks of venoms that make them so devastating to essential biological processes can be harnessed to provide incredibly potent and targeted therapies for many human pathologies, including infectious diseases and cancer. It's these components of venom that are providing the blueprints for the development of new drugs, with the potential to save millions of lives.

Broadly speaking, venom components fit into one of three different categories, depending on how they affect biological systems. Neurotoxic components, which typify most of the elapid snakes (including cobras, mambas, kraits and taipans), disrupt the nervous system, causing convulsions and paralysis. Naturally, they're being investigated for neurological disorders and are showing potential in the fields of autoimmunity and neurodegenerative diseases. Cytotoxic components, which are found in elapids and the other major venomous snake group, the viperids (including true vipers, pit vipers, and Fea's vipers) kill and damage cells, causing necrosis. These are being harnessed for their potential anticancer effects, with promising data showing that these compounds can kill cancerous cells. Haemotoxic components, which tend to be concentrated in vipers, impact the blood and its clotting, often by rapidly using up all the clotting factors and then leaving the victim at risk of bleeding to death. Before my visit to the CSRI I'd watched a video where some of a saw-scaled viper's venom was dripped into a blood sample in a petri dish – the blood quickly transformed into a wobbly, jelly-like lump. In the body, this isn't what happens; instead, many micro clots are formed which block the blood vessels, raising the risk for stroke or cardiac arrest, while at the same time enzymes in the venom start to dissolve capillary walls, causing internal bleeding.

As of 2020, 11 toxin-based molecules have been approved for medical use, acting on pathways relating to metabolism, pain relief, blood pressure and blood clotting.[17] Venom complexity and diversity undoubtedly means that many more life-saving drugs and disease therapies are waiting to be uncovered, and scientists working in laboratories worldwide are attempting to crack the clues they offer. It's not just snakes – the venoms of scorpions, cone snails, spiders and more are all being investigated, and one exciting line of research comes from the venom of a wasp: a specific antimicrobial component has unexpectedly shown promising anticancer effects against leukemic, bladder and prostate cancer cells.

Medicine is not the only field to benefit from venoms. The latest research is also exploring their use in next-generation insecticides and pesticides, since venoms can offer a much more targeted way of killing unwanted species than current chemical options. What's more, as Modahl tells me, 'We have so much resistance developing from chemical insecticides.' She's working on early-stage research to see whether venom components might be used to tackle vector-borne diseases, such as dengue fever or chikungiya, both of which are transmitted by the mosquitoes *Aedes egypti* and *A. albopictus*. As our climates continue to warm, these mosquitoes are going to be able to survive in more northerly latitudes and that means a lot more of the global population is going to be exposed to potentially deadly infectious diseases. Modahl says that we're already seeing the spread: 'In the next couple of years, I would say, we're almost at a point

---

[17] One drug (ziconotide) is derived from cone snail venom, two are from lizards (exenatide and lixisenatide), two are from leeches (bivalirudin and desirudin), and six come from snakes (captopril, enalapril, tirofiban, eptifibatide, batroxobin, and cobratide).

where we can say that dengue might be endemic in Italy and France.' She's excited about the potential that venom components may offer to control vector populations and, given everything that I'm hearing, I'm excited too.

Of course, we don't have to extract venom to reap the rewards. We could just allow all those animals that use it to get on with their day jobs. Spiders and wasps, for example, are among the least popular of all animals but they are phenomenal pest controllers (more on wasps in Chapter 7), and they offer this outstanding service for free. If we could hold off squashing them and let them get on with what evolution has fine-tuned them to do, we'd save money and reduce the amount of chemicals going into our gardens. It's surely a win-win.

Snakes are also extremely effective at eliminating pests, especially rodents, whose populations would increase exponentially if left unchecked. As we've heard, adult brown snakes are rodent specialists and they are found in agricultural land across much of Australia. In a recent study into their value as pest-controllers, herpetologist Rick Shine of Macquarie University and colleagues calculated that one adult eastern brown snake likely eats more than 50 mice per year, as a conservative estimate ('probably twice that number'), and there could be 100 brown snakes per km^2 in agricultural areas. The snakes therefore remove thousands of mice per km^2 of farmland per year. Unfortunately, farmers typically kill any snakes they see, a practice that Shine calls 'misguided and dangerous', as it also increases the risks of being bitten. Tolerating snakes would save farmers money, be better for the environment and potentially reduce rates of snakebite, but would require a serious culture shift. I contact Shine to ask how farmers and local people reacted to these results. 'Surprisingly positive. We pitched the story in a responsible way, advocating balance – for example, you may well decide to kill a snake that is close to children or pets – and I think that helped.'

Shine's study is just one of many demonstrating the ecological importance of snakes. Of course, put them in the wrong place and they can cause environmental havoc, as the accidental introduction of brown tree snakes onto the island of Guam in the 1940s has shown. Thought to have stowed away on a military flight, this snake found a land of plenty on Guam, with abundant food and no predators to keep its numbers in check. Its population skyrocketed and is likely in the millions today,[18] and as that has happened, the island's wildlife has taken a big hit: at least ten species of birds have been lost from the island, including the endemic Guam kingfisher and Guam rail. Similarly, in southern Florida, where tens of thousands of non-native Burmese pythons have firmly established themselves, native mammals have been all but eradicated.

But in the places where snakes should be, where we've not messed around too badly with the natural order of things, they're carrying out essential work. Will this help us to overcome our negative feelings? To answer that, we first need to understand where these feelings come from.

★★★

According to the results of several large studies into fear and phobias, around a third of the global population report being scared of snakes, and two to three per cent of these meet the psychiatric diagnostic criteria for having a specific snake phobia (ophidiophobia). That might not sound like very much, but consider the absolute numbers and it's tens of millions of people. Ophidiophobia tops the list for all animal phobias, although spider phobia (arachnophobia) comes close.

---

[18] Despite specific legislation and eradication efforts costing millions of dollars, including parachuting in dead mice laced with paracetamol, which is toxic to snakes (and many other animals).

Most of these people will never encounter a snake but, as we've heard, snakes have been a long-standing, persistent threat throughout the evolutionary histories of hominins and indeed all mammals. Because of this long overlapping history, it's widely assumed that we are biologically programmed to fear snakes: those in our past who responded appropriately to them were more likely to survive, and those traces remain in us today. One popular theory, proposed by anthropologist Lynne Isbell, even suggests that the superior vision and large brains of primates, as well as our human capacity for pointing, are adaptations to surviving the predation pressure of snakes because these things helped us to recognise snakes in vegetation and to communicate this with others.

Interactions between snakes and people can still be seen today, in some parts of the world. The Agta tribe of hunter-gatherers in the Philippine rainforest, for example, encounter snakes on a daily basis. A pivotal study by anthropologist Thomas Headland and snake expert Harry Greene found that around a quarter of adult Agta men had survived a predatory attack by a reticulated python, and six people had lost their lives to snake incidents between 1934 and 1973. On the other hand, the Agta also hunted and ate the snakes, and competed with them for wild pigs, deer and monkeys, showing that this was not a one-sided relationship. It was clear to Headland and Greene that, 'complex ecological interactions have long characterised our shared evolutionary history,' consistent with Isbell's theory.

We can get clues about the strength of this relationship from other primate species, many of whom display an intense fear of snakes. In one famous study, lab-reared macaques were played a video of a wild monkey that was showing fear towards a snake, as well as towards some other animals, including a rabbit. Lab monkeys that had never before encountered a snake subsequently showed intense fear towards a toy snake, but not towards a toy rabbit, suggesting that they were in some way already primed to fear the reptile. Rather than being born with a hardwired fear of snakes, we may be born with a predisposition to learn to fear them. This is known as the theory of biological preparedness, and there's evidence that suggests it applies to us too.

Studies have found that we're faster at picking out little images of snakes from an array than little images of flowers or mushrooms, and that we more strongly associate photos of snakes with an electric shock than photos of these other stimuli. Similarly, infants looked longer at a video of a snake when it was paired with a fearful voice than a happy voice, whereas if the video was of elephants, hippos or giraffes, the voice made no difference. These findings seemed to support the idea of some kind of evolved basis to fear snakes, but not everyone was convinced.

'I used to think there was an evolutionary predisposition [to fearing snakes], but the data have shifted my perspective significantly.' This is Vanessa LoBue, professor of psychology at Rutgers University in New Jersey, who has been researching how children develop fears to negative stimuli, including snakes, since 2004. When she started her graduate studies, she believed, like the rest of the field, that fear of snakes had an evolutionary basis. 'That was the dominant perspective and it's still there. An evolutionary perspective is simple, interesting, and easy.' But her findings since then have nudged her in a different direction.

In one experiment with infants aged 18–36 months, LoBue set up a playroom containing four novel toys – a doll, fire truck, airplane and ball – and four live animals – a spider, snake, hamster and fish, each housed in a little plastic cage/bowl that was fastened to the wall. The children could spend as much or as little time as they wanted in the proximity of each toy or animal, and while you might expect that they'd gravitate to the new toys, LoBue found that the children overwhelmingly chose to interact with the live animals. This makes sense, because animals are clearly extremely relevant stimuli. Studies have shown that infants pay more attention to them, identify them more quickly and ask more questions about them compared with non-animals. However, what was really striking for LoBue is that the children were fascinated by all the creatures: they spent as long with their noses pressed to the tanks of the tarantula and snake as they did for the hamster and fish. Far from being scared, as they should if they are born to fear these creatures, the children seemed to be enjoying the experience.

LoBue has found that our detection of snakes involves an interacting set of factors, drawing in our perceptual, cognitive and emotional systems. At a perceptual level, we're much better at picking out curved lines than straight or angular shapes in an array. But it's not quite as simple as that. Firing up the grey matter by calling a curved line a snake leads to even better detection; making someone feel scared on top of that facilitates detection even more. So what's going on – why are we better at picking out snakes if we're not intrinsically fearful of them?

'Snakes and spiders don't move like other animals,' LoBue says, 'They're weird.' Rather than paying attention to them for being dangerous, she thinks it more likely that we pay attention to them for being novel, strange organisms. 'The only thing that might be innate is a dislike of the unfamiliar. We don't like things that slither, or walk on eight legs, so the novelty might cause us to react to them.' It makes sense, and there are other factors at play too – the unblinking stare of a snake can seem threatening, when in reality the animal is just incapable of blinking; and there's an absence of expressions, which it makes it harder to connect with them too.

Children might simply be fascinated by the peculiarity of snakes and spiders. But it doesn't last. Infants who press their noses to the cages of snakes and tarantulas when they're four years old often aren't doing the same when they're eight. In between, something very important happens, which is that they start picking up the emotional responses of people around them, and they begin to fear what was previously fascinating. In this respect, we do inherit our fears towards snakes, spiders and other animals, but not through our genes.

You don't need to look far in popular culture to see these creatures depicted as scary or threatening, and research clearly shows that infants pay attention to this. In LoBue's study of the live animals vs toys, she also recorded what the infants' parents said and did for a portion of the study when they were in the room. She found that parents made more prohibitive statements towards the spider and snake than the hamster and fish, saying things like 'Don't touch', or 'Don't get too close to that'. In another study at the reptile house of a local zoo, parents said more negative things about snakes and spiders than the other animals in the exhibit. 'Parents are not shy about saying bad things about them,' says LoBue. 'And it's negative everywhere – snakes and spiders are always portrayed badly in the media. It goes back a long way, to the Bible, to Medusa.'

The prevalence of snake and spider phobias in westernised societies fits with numerous other studies showing that the incidence of biophobias is high and increasing. That's despite the risks of encountering dangerous snakes and spiders in these societies usually being quite low. But our progressing extinction of experience means that urbanites are far more likely to learn about wildlife from indirect experience, such as online sources, television or podcasts. This opens the door wide to the spread of unreliable information and the propagation of myths or misconceptions. And since fear propagates fear, does this mean that we're stuck in a reinforcement loop that can only keep on increasing? LoBue shakes her head. 'No. We can change the narrative. We can turn "weird" into exciting. We need to start early, and we need to educate parents, but it can be done.'

I agree. And step one in changing the narrative is addressing the myth that venomous snakes are out to get us. Because it couldn't be further from the truth.

★★★

When Shine started his PhD in 1972, it was very much the case that 'the only good snake was a dead snake'. He remembers national park rangers in Australia killing snakes to protect the public, because that was part of their job. Greene writes to me that it was the same in the US – he remembers his study animals being killed by members of the public despite them posing no threat. Things have changed a little, thankfully, in large part due to the work of snake researchers providing evidence that countered the assumptions of snake aggression. Having said that, there's clearly much to be done, as Greene explains. 'Just last year I encountered a western diamond-backed rattlesnake on the dirt road to my ranch, decapitated – utterly senseless as the snake clearly posed no danger to anyone at the time, and that road runs past three properties in a row with "we don't kill snakes" signs on their gates.'

The late herpetologist, Clifford Pope, famously said that 'Snakes are first cowards, then bluffers, and last of all, warriors.' In this, he was describing snakes' natural proclivity to attack: they tend to only bite as a last resort, only if they feel that their life (or that of their offspring) is in danger. I ask Crittenden about this and he agrees. 'Snakes are massive drama queens. They want to scare us away because a lot of the time they're scared. Then, when they feel they can't scare us away, they want to run away. Snakes are inherently cowards.'

Shine's data on eastern brown snakes support this. We've already heard how big a role these long, slender snakes can play in controlling rodent populations. They hunt by day and move quickly, making them the most frequently encountered venomous snake in Australia, and causing one to two deaths every year despite the availability of an effective antivenom. No wonder they're feared and thought to be aggressive. But Shine's data didn't agree. In one study, he and his colleagues tagged 40 snakes and recorded how they behaved when one of the researchers approached. They found that on more than half of the 455 human encounters, the snakes quietly slithered away, while on most of the other half they relied on their camouflage to stay hidden. On only 12 trials did the snakes approach the human, and only 3 of these were classed as aggressive. That's 0.7 per cent of all encounters. Shine tells me that he wasn't surprised by this data, nor were other snake biologists – 'but the general public were very surprised, I think.' Snakes have a reputation and it's hard to shift. Shine has previously commented that these creatures are in need of a good defamation lawyer.

Similarly, in a study of snake and human use of the coastal bays near Noumea, in the Pacific archipelago of New Caledonia, the data showed that thousands of people and sea snakes shared the same stretches of water at some times of the year. Most of the time, the snakes in question were non-venomous turtle-headed sea snakes, but enough venomous species were recorded in the same waters as people for there to be hundreds, if not thousands, of close encounters each year. And yet, no snakebites were recorded in the area during 17 years of study, and observations showed that the snakes were far more likely to move away from people than towards them.

There's one exception to this, off the southern Great Barrier Reef, where scuba divers frequently report being attacked by highly venomous olive sea snakes. Alarmingly for the divers, the snakes sometimes swim directly towards them and coil themselves around a limb. That's a scary thought. But investigation into these incidents by Shine and colleagues concluded that they more likely reflected misdirected courtship, not aggression. Most of the 158 snake–diver interactions, especially those made by female snakes, were investigatory in nature – the snakes were being nosy about the new arrival in their territory. A smaller subset of advances were termed 'excitable' charges and these tended to be made by male snakes and to occur during the breeding season, often after the male had lost contact with a female. When divers fled, they may have inadvertently mimicked the responses of female snakes, encouraging the males to give chase. Shine and his coauthors acknowledged that the idea of mistaken identity between a diver and a snake 'seems ludicrous', nonetheless they found it the most plausible explanation for their data.

When snakes do bite, of course, they're equipped with some of the most effective killing tools on the planet, and they'll use those tools to defend themselves. You'd do the same. Sadly, sea snakes do kill many people every year, most of them fishermen, who either step on the animal in the shallows or get bitten trying to extract them from their nets. In both situations the animal is behaving defensively and the victims suffer from a lack of safety training and protective clothing.

It makes no sense to pick a fight with a huge, dangerous animal just because it walks or swims past you. If snakes were out to get us, the number of bites and fatalities would be orders of magnitude higher. That's not to downplay the vast number that do occur but to say that, like sharks and surfers, we are often in the same vicinity as these animals and they don't want to attack. Sometimes they will approach people, but not out of aggression – it's a smart tactic that prey species sometimes employ to communicate to a potential predator that they've lost the element of surprise. Hares, for example, will stand up on their back legs when they see a fox, signalling to the predator that the game is up, and snakes may be doing the same. Other times, as Crittenden has said, they're just being nosy.

Back at the CSRI, we've walked into a room full of spitting cobras and Crittenden points out one male who is 'hooding': a threat display where the sides of the neck are flared out to make the head look larger. As we stand there, he starts to relax and drop his hood. Flicking his tongue, he follows us intently as we walk around the room, by this point, with no hood at all. What is more alarming is hearing about the animal's other line of defence, which is apparent from some little splodges on the inside of his tank. Crittenden points to one: 'This is dried venom where he has spat at us. Probably we startled him, and his response is "spit first and ask questions later." It's purely defensive.' Crittenden tells me that spitting cobras can spit accurately to about 3m, and they aim for the eyes because that's the shiniest part. This species, perhaps more obviously than any other snake, has an evolutionary history that is intertwined with humans. Greene first proposed a coevolutionary relationship between spitting cobras and humans in 2013, and subsequent research by CSRI researchers, working with Greene and others, has shown that cobras independently evolved spitting three times, each time coinciding with a key event in the evolution of early humans. For example, when hominins evolved bipedalism, they became more of a long-distance threat to snakes (for example by throwing rocks) compared with their quadruped ape relatives, prompting the evolution of a counter strategy from snakes – long-distance defensive spitting.

With 200 snakes, Crittenden says they don't give them names, but of course there are some exceptions. He points out 'the crazy Cameroonian': a forest cobra who apparently has 'small man syndrome'. At just under 2m in length, for a species that can be more than 3m, the crazy Cameroonian was giving it some from behind the glass – and I thought it was pretty threatening. 'It's not,' says Crittenden. 'In his mind he's big and scary, but he's not. If he was really threatened, he'd be much taller, have a much bigger hood; this is him trying to pretend he's tough and we know it's a bluff.'

I'm interested to know how Crittenden can confidently read the animals – as we heard in the last chapter, it's so much harder to get an idea of what's going on in an animal when its facial muscles are locked in place. But expressions aren't the only clue; it's a question of knowing these animals well enough to be tuned into their other cues. Snakes, it seems, are not the easiest. 'There is a lot of body language,' Crittenden tells me, 'but it's still so hard to tell. We've spent a lot of time around the snakes we know, and even then there are times when we're surprised by them.'

Morgan Skinner, who completed his PhD on snake cognition at Wilfred Laurier University in Ontario, Canada, agrees with this: 'They communicate so subtly, it can be really hard to know what's going on in their brains.' A snake enthusiast from an early age, Skinner recalls finding his first garter snakes when he was about six years old: 'I came down from the back forest with a handful of garter snakes, and I was like, "Look Mom, I'm Medusa's barber!"' The fascination has remained, leading Skinner to do a PhD on snake social behaviour and cognition. He says that reading snake behaviour comes down to experience, but it's not something that can be easily explained. 'I know from interacting with them so much and from handling them. But I don't know how to describe to you how to read snakes.'

It sounds like, given enough time and experience with snakes, they may start to reveal another side, and a more complex one at that. That's surprising, because these animals, just like crocodiles and other reptiles, are often perceived as 'living fossils' with primitive 'reptile brains', incapable of flexible behaviour or emotional states. Crittenden shakes his head. 'Snakes are massively understudied in this but they're a lot more intelligent than we give them credit for: they have personalities, they have behaviour traits, they have good days, bad days, mood swings, all sorts.'

He's right. The current consensus among snake researchers is that we've totally underestimated their behaviour. This is something that Gordon Burghardt has been trying to tell the world since his first publication on snakes in 1967, where he wrote that 'society's antipathy' towards snakes likely accounted for their neglect as experimental subjects, but also acknowledged that, 'The biblical story of the Garden of Eden probably didn't help.'

As we already heard, Burghardt has studied crocodilians, turtles, lizards and more, but at heart he's always been a snake guy. 'Growing up, there were garter snakes in our area, and I was always fascinated by them. I had them as pets from early on.' He pauses, grins, and then adds, 'In grade school my nickname was Snakes.' It's an apt name for the person who has, arguably, done more to overturn people's perceptions of these animals than anybody else.

But it almost didn't happen. Burghardt had no idea that it was possible to make a career out of his snake fascination, so he chose to major in his second passion, chemistry, at the University of Chicago. It was only when a new undergraduate major was established in the field of biopsychology that he transferred from chemistry and started studying snakes, but he didn't leave chemistry behind – his combined interests provided the perfect background to investigate snakes' chemical sense.

Snakes' sensory abilities have been honed by natural selection to superbly equip these limbless predators for their way of life. They lack external ears, and their eyes are relatively simple, but where hearing and sight may be dulled, their other senses shine. Snakes make extensive use of physical, chemical, and, in some species, thermal signals in their environments. The tactile sense enables them to detect ground vibrations (as we had experienced with the rattlesnake in Pinnacles), may enable some sea snakes to detect changes in barometric pressure which indicate an approaching storm, and are used by constricting snakes to detect when their prey no longer has a heartbeat. When it comes to chemicals, snakes have a good sense of smell, but more significantly they have an extremely specialised vomeronasal (aka Jacobson's organ), consisting of a pair of sacs opening into the roof of the mouth. When snakes flick their tongues, they're picking up scent particles from their environment, bringing them back into their mouth and transferring them to the vomeronasal organ for processing.[19] This helps them to trail prey, detect predators and pick up scent from potential mates. The thermal sense seems to be restricted to pit vipers, boas and pythons, who possess specialised thermosensitive organs that essentially give them thermal vision, integrating with visual information to result in a kind of heat map of their surroundings.

In a pivotal review summarising the state of play of reptile learning research in 1977, Burghardt noted that snakes were still largely unstudied. He acknowledged that, practically, they were challenging animals to study in captivity because of their generally sedentary habits and proclivity to hide when stressed. It's also very difficult to run tests using food as a motivator, in an animal that tends to eat huge meals with long gaps between. But Burghardt noted another point that had gone against snakes – they were useless at the typical lab tasks being conducted with monkeys, pigeons and rats. He made the wry observation that, 'This is undoubtedly complicated by snakes' lack of limbs to be used in pressing levers or for receiving electric shock.' Snakes just didn't work for this kind of research. Unfortunately, rather than look to develop other, more ecologically relevant, ways to study them, many psychologists of the early to mid-twentieth century had simply written snakes off.

And yet, as with any animal, if you move away from asking questions that are centred around their similarity with

---

[19] So specialised is this process that snakes even have an indentation in their top lip which allows the tongue to flick without them needing to open their mouths.

humans, and instead ask questions that are guided by their unique sensory systems, morphology and the kinds of problems they need to solve in their lives, you find that snakes have many of the same perceptual and cognitive abilities as other animals. Maybe we'll never find that snakes use tools, but maybe that's because tools have zero relevance to the lives of snakes. Breakthroughs come when scientists ask the right kinds of questions of their animals, something that Burghardt and colleagues have achieved by, for example, recognising the importance of chemical information in the lives of snakes. 'And I'm still working on some of those questions,' he says, 'like the chemical mirror.'

Traditionally, animal self-recognition has been investigated with a mirror: an experimental set-up first pioneered by Gordon Gallup close to 60 years ago when he asked whether chimpanzees recognise their reflection. It's an experimental paradigm that has since been rolled out to all sorts of animals, but many ethologists, including Burghardt, have questioned its relevance in animals whose primary sense is not visual. If they don't appear to recognise themselves in a mirror, does that mean that they lack a sense of self or is the mirror simply the wrong way to ask? The chemical mirror offers an alternative, non-visual way to investigate self-recognition, so, building on previous studies with dogs, who also fail a visual mirror task, Burghardt designed a study to ask whether snakes may recognise themselves based on chemical cues, not sight.

In the study, 24 common garter snake siblings were raised from birth on either earthworm or fish diets, and then on separate days they were exposed to each of four different cage liners: one was clean, one was from the individual's own cage, one was from a same-sex sibling reared on the same diet, and one was from a same-sex sibling reared on the other diet. Burghardt and team measured the number of tongue flicks made by each snake to the different cage liners, as well as their general activity levels, and found something interesting. Male, but not female, snakes behaved differently towards their own cage liner compared with that of a sibling that had been eating the same diet. This suggests they were telling apart their 'image' and that of an unfamiliar sibling based on the only available cue, their chemical signature, which implies a rudimentary level of self-recognition. That it was only seen in males may relate to the more intense male-male competition than occurs between females, Burghardt and colleagues noted, but clearly more research is needed.

'Snakes have this really fantastic vomeronasal system where they can differentiate all sorts of different things. So why not be able to differentiate yourself from other snakes like that? It seems so obvious.' This is Skinner, who was inspired to build on Burghardt's study using eastern garter snakes and ball pythons – two species with markedly different natural ecologies and social lives. This time, snakes' tongue flicking and the amount of time they spent nearby were compared for cotton pads carrying either their own odour, their own odour with an added 'mark' (olive oil), olive oil alone, or the original or marked odour of a same-sex unrelated familiar snake.

Skinner found that garter snakes, but not ball pythons, made considerably more tongue flicks towards their olive-tainted odour than to their plain scent, or to the scents in the other groups, suggesting that they could not only recognize their unique chemical signature, but they could also tell that it wasn't quite right. This behaviour may be analogous to a primate manipulating a mark on their face when they see their mirror reflection. It's the strongest evidence to suggest that snakes have a sense of self, but is it really the same as seeing one's reflection and knowing that it is you? 'Just because self-recognition for us is really complicated doesn't mean that it has to be,' says Skinner. 'Nature can build these really complex things that don't have to function in the same way that we do.' It's a good point, and one always worth keeping in mind when it comes to interpreting animal behaviour – just because we do something in a way that reflects complex cognition, doesn't mean that there aren't other ways of achieving the same thing. Just because, in humans, self-recognition is tied up with self-awareness, theory of mind and consciousness, doesn't mean that all animals that recognise their own image or smell are doing so in the same way.

Nonetheless, if snakes have some form of self-awareness, we'd expect that they might show it in other contexts too. Dogs, for example, as well as responding differently to their own scent and that of other dogs, also pay attention to their body size when navigating their way through physical obstacles, suggesting some level of bodily awareness. And there's some evidence that snakes might too. Copperhead rat snakes get considerably fatter after they've eaten, and in an experiment where individuals were presented with a range of different diameter escape holes after feeding, they were less likely to choose holes that they could no longer fit through. Combining this body-size awareness with the chemical mirror experiments provides an even stronger case for snakes having some sense of self-recognition. The fact that it isn't visual has drawn scepticism from some quarters, but, as Burghardt writes to me: 'Mirror self-recognition is not as much of a cognitive pinnacle as Gallup and others have claimed, I believe, but chemical mirror recognition is certainly a cognitive skill that perhaps many animals have that we downplay because of our anthropocentric focus on vision.'

Another area where snakes have been unfairly written off is social behaviour, and this was a research focus for Skinner, as he explains, 'People don't really think of them as social animals, but almost every animal must interact socially. So, you need some sort of mechanism or some sort of cognition to be able to navigate those interactions, whether it's for mating or for defending your territory from conspecifics [others of the same species].' He studied garter snakes, which show communal hibernation and, every spring in Narcisse, Manitoba, form the biggest aggregation of snakes in the world. Here, tens of thousands of red-sided garter snakes all emerge at once, forming a living carpet of writhing, wriggling, stripy noodles, with dozens of males vying to mate with each female. (Shine once needed to weigh and sex 1,000 of these garter snakes in one day. 'It was awful, they really smelled.')

Because of this natural phenomenon, garter snakes offer a fantastic species to ask questions of social cognition. In a study where he placed 10 snakes into a small arena with four shelters and let the snakes move freely, Skinner found firstly that the animals were more likely to shelter with others than on their own, and secondly that the snakes tended to buddy up with the same individuals. Clearly, they can recognise others and even more surprisingly, they seem to have friends. 'The one thing they will do,' he says, 'which is ironic, considering people don't call them social, is they will cuddle. When you put a bunch of snakes in an arena together, they will group up and cuddle together.'

Snakes cuddling? These are not terms that tend to go together but Skinner is comfortable saying it. I'm curious – does he mean that the snakes are seeking out others for some kind of emotional reassurance or are they just seeking heat? It's known that rattlesnakes become more stressed when they are in a bucket alone compared with when they're with another snake, and one of Skinner's studies showed that after one hour of being with another snake of the same sex, female ball pythons had activation in an area of the brain called the nucleus accumbens, which is involved in processing reward. So, there are signs that snakes might get something out of being with others, but what do we know about what they might be experiencing during these interactions? 'Do they have emotions in the traditional sense?' Skinner muses. 'I don't know.' He explains that being in a group likely increases snakes' survival odds, but that's probably not what compels them to do it — instead, it's possible that their brains have evolved reward structures that mean it feels good to be with other snakes, because that's the way of reinforcing what is ultimately beneficial. It's the same for us — the ultimate reasons why humans evolved to be social and have friendships are because it was beneficial to us in our evolutionary past. But when I'm having a glass of wine and catching up with a friend it's because it feels good to spend time with them in the moment.

Skinner's work has also revealed that our assumptions about certain species are completely false. Ball pythons, non-venomous constricting snakes native to central and western Africa, don't hibernate in groups, and don't form large mating balls like the garter snakes. So Skinner conducted a similar test, placing six snakes in an arena with six different shelters that they could choose to hide in. He assumed the ball pythons wouldn't care about hiding together. He found the opposite — the ball pythons were even more social than the garter snakes, which left him scratching his head. 'I was like "What?! That's not what I hypothesised!" But there's so little we know about these secretive animals and how they behave socially that there's so many questions still to be answered.'

To scientifically study any animal's behaviour necessitates careful observation and experience with that animal — that's why ethologists are trained to first create 'ethograms', catalogues of all the behaviours they observe and the scenarios in which they're expressed. It's a great foundational concept, but clearly one that works better for some animals than others. The gestures of a dog, for example, or courtship behaviours of a gull, are very visible to any observer, although experts will pick up on more subtle signals than students. Snakes, though, seem less willing to reveal the secrets of their minds, being far more impenetrable to observation, and undoubtedly that's a reason why they've both been poorly studied and written off for showing any complexity in behaviour. The scientists who are getting insights into snakes seem to be those that have watched the animals all their lives, kept them as pets, and been truly fascinated by them. That's not to say that they all believed the animals to be intelligent. Harry Greene, for example, whose PhD was supervised by Burghardt, tells me that he 'retained into middle years a preconception that snakes were simpletons.' One of the pivotal things that changed his mind was observing the first convincing evidence for snake parental care: he watched mother black-tailed rattlesnakes looking after their babies for about 10 days, defending them from predators, until they shed their first skins and were ready to go it alone. While the behaviour had been suggested before, most scientists had brushed reports aside as coincidence, rather than the intentional care-giving that Greene and colleagues documented. 'These and other experiences convinced me that snakes have complex inner worlds, including intentionalities, memories, tacticality, and so forth.'

The result of all this work is that snakes are getting a place at the table, after decades of dismissal. Burghardt has documented a clear rise in research papers being published on snake cognition. And people are taking note. So how should we think about snake intelligence? 'They might not do what chimps do in the lab, but they're really good at doing snake things,' says Skinner. 'You know, we might never understand snake social behaviour, but we might not ever understand ourselves.'

★★★

Can we overcome our negative attitudes to snakes? There's so much more to them than popular culture implies and, as we've heard, in many cases, we can live alongside them perfectly peacefully. That's not to overlook the facts: these creatures can be dangerous and the loss of human life caused by snakebite is devastatingly high, but we must remember that snakes bite out of defence, not malice. Because of that, importantly, there are things that can be done to reduce the risks. In 2019, the WHO outlined its much-awaited global strategy to halve the numbers of deaths and disabilities due to snakebite by 2030 – as a preventable and treatable disease, this should be achievable.

In rural India, snakes – particularly common kraits – are attracted to homes and settlements because they provide warmth, shelter and food, in the form of rodents that are also attracted by warmth, shelter and food. If a rodent can enter a house, then a snake can too, and they do, tucking themselves away in dark corners to rest and wait for a rat to pass. Kraits may even try to take advantage of people's body heat by snuggling up to them in bed (which is typically on the floor), and then biting them when they inevitably get rolled or trodden on in the night – with neurotoxic venom, kraits' bites can be painless and cause death by paralysis.

Tackling snakebite here means improving practical knowledge of how to live with snakes. The Indian Snakebite Initiative is working to achieve the WHO's target, with a particular focus on outreach into local communities. Practical education can make a real difference: simple changes like eliminating house clutter, using a light at night, and sleeping inside tucked mosquito nets, would undoubtedly save lives. They have also developed an app, SERPENT (Snake Emergency Response Programme & Response Tool), which people can use to log the location of snakes, locate the nearest snake rescuer, and even chat with the rescuer before they arrive via instant messaging. These are the types of tools that are needed – to build a picture of which snakes are where, to inform local governments as to which antivenoms need stocking, and to make it easier for bite victims to get the support they need from trained personnel.

There also needs to be education on recognising bites and understanding the necessity of swift, medical action.

Rural communities often rely on faith healers instead of western medicine, and that, according to the Indian Snakebite Initiative, is 'probably just as dangerous as the venomous snakes themselves because they ensure that a snakebite victim does not reach the hospital on time.' Antivenoms work, but only if they're administered in time, and precious hours are all too easily being lost through misidentification or misplaced belief. In India, it's policy that all government hospitals have antivenom available free of charge, so there should be good access. But the reality is that rural hospitals may not have the stocks, trained personnel, or life-support equipment to manage a snakebite patient, forcing a decision between travelling further to a better hospital, paying for treatment at a private hospital or taking the word of a local faith healer. Faith healers claim to have an excellent success rate, but the odds are stacked in their favour. If the victim survives, the healer takes the credit, even though most bites are from non-venomous snakes or are 'dry' so no venom is injected. If the patient deteriorates and is taken to hospital, it's usually too late and the patient dies there, which reinforces the negative perceptions of hospitals to the victim's friends and family. In a study of 4,159 households in the North Bihar, two-thirds of snakebite victims first went to traditional healers for help, and only 4.6 per cent of victims presented at the local hospital. Similarly, a direct survey of people in West Bengal found that of nearly 5,000 snakebite cases between 2009 and 2010, only 22 per cent went to a hospital.

In parts of the world where dangerous snakes live but few people lose their lives, including Australia and the US, education and awareness are also of crucial importance for coexistence, particularly around the different venomous and non-venomous species in an area, their ecological roles, and their sentience. The latter continues to be controversial, because, as Burghardt writes to me, 'snakes and other nonavian squamate reptiles do not whimper, squeal, or show typical mammalian responses or facial expressions.' As a result, many people reject the notion that snakes experience any kind of emotions. In reality, all we can really reject is the notion that snakes communicate about their emotions in a human way.

For Melissa Amarello, who in 2014 cofounded Advocates for Snake Preservation (ASP), a nonprofit organisation dedicated to changing the way that people view and treat snakes, communicating about snakes' intelligence and sentience is crucial to changing people's minds. Amarello says that when ASP started, she focused her educational materials on snakes' ecological importance, and while this is still part of ASP's communications, she was inspired to change her approach after listening to somebody talking about whales. As she tells me, 'They didn't talk about how whales were important to the environment, or how these ecosystems wouldn't function without whales. They talked about how they live in family groups and have social lives, and I was like, "Why don't we talk about snakes that way?"' ASP switched focus and started communicating about snakes' social lives, particularly parental care. Amarello tells me that it seems to be working: she's seen great changes in public opinion since she was researching snakes as a graduate student. As we heard for sharks, focusing on the things that snakes have in common with us can really help people to connect.

Rattlesnake roundups, on the other hand, seem set to persist, something that Amarello puts down to rattlesnakes being the most demonised snakes in the US ('they're the ones in all the cowboy movies!'), and the fact that a lot of people do not think they're capable of feeling pain. For Harry Greene, these events are 'disgusting spectacles with no justification from ecological, ethical, or human-health perspectives – I surely do wish they would have long ago ended.' I have to agree. A huge amount of patient observation has gone into investigating some of the mysteries of snake life, and while we're far from fully understanding how these reptiles think and feel, more than enough has been done to overturn many of the fallacies around their behaviour. Look past the unblinking eyes and the alien way that they move and recognise that these nosy, nervous creatures would rather cuddle up with their brethren than slither after you; and if you do happen to meet, know that they would much rather hide or flee than bite.

Unlike a grizzly bear or a crocodile, which elicit pure adrenaline-driven fear, snakes can trigger something else in us too. Something about the way that they move and the way that they look makes them both extremely scary and also a bit creepy. Poor old snakes. But it's this latter feeling that we're going to explore next, which is induced even more strongly by another set of creatures. From cockroaches to maggots, lice to toads, it's the yuck emotion: disgust.

CHAPTER 4

To make flesh creep

It is most disgusting to feel soft wingless insects, about an inch long, crawling over ones body; before sucking they are quite thin, but afterwards round & bloated with blood
Charles Darwin, writing in his field
notebook for St. Fe, March 1835

The hit 1982 horror film *Poltergeist* is not short on scenes which are designed to shock, but there's one that really sticks in my mind. It's when paranormal investigator Marty goes to the kitchen for a midnight snack. He grabs a chicken leg from the fridge and puts it in his mouth, then puts a steak on the counter. Frying up somebody's else's steak at midnight is undeniably a bit odd, as is plopping the meat directly on the counter without as much as a cursory wipe. But those aren't the strangest parts of the scene. Because as

Marty turns to get a frying pan, he becomes aware of a strange, wet, noise, and when he turns back the steak is inching its way along the counter. It then stops and erupts into chunks of rotting flesh. Horrified, Marty drops his chicken leg, only to see that the thing he had just been eating was spewing out maggots onto the floor. He staggers to the bathroom and retches into the sink, before being faced with his own, decomposing face in the mirror. Chunks of flesh drop into the sink as he frantically rips his own face apart, until he's nothing more than a gory skull.

It's hard to think how this scene could have been made to be any more disgusting. Rotting meat, maggots, gore and vomit are all things that scientists have identified as key triggers of disgust; if they'd managed to squeeze in a dead body, some poo and perhaps some unidentified slime too then pretty much all the bases would have been covered. It even covers moral disgust, with Marty's brazen theft of a huge hunk of steak. But how did we become so disgusted by so many things? It's a question that sits at the heart of this chapter, and while our focus is on the other creatures that trigger our disgust response, we need to first understand how and why disgust as an emotion came to be so important to humans. We need to take a deep dive into the unpleasant.

'There are several hypotheses about the origin of disgust. I think the most prominent and most simple explanation is that disgust evolved to prevent oral contamination.' This is Pavol Prokop, professor of zoology at Comenius University, Bratislava, who has long been curious about why some people are naturally more disgusted or fearful towards certain animals than others. Prokop's curiosity was heightened, he writes to me, when he started running zoology practical sessions and noticed that some students enjoyed dissecting animals while others found the exercise repulsive.

The oral contamination hypothesis dates to Darwin, who was the first to recognise disgust as an emotion. In his pivotal book, *The Expression of the Emotions in Man and Animals*

(1872), Darwin wrote that: 'Disgust ... refers to something revolting, primarily in relation to the sense of taste, as actually perceived or vividly imagined; and secondarily to anything which causes a similar feeling, through the sense of smell, touch and even of eyesight.' Like fear, disgust is an emotion that discourages us from interacting with something (unlike anger, which encourages approach). That's where the similarity ends. As we've heard, fear primes us for action – the adrenaline that is released heightens attention, sharpens our senses and readies us physically. Disgust seems to do the opposite: sensory perception and attention processes towards disgusting information are suppressed, and we become worse at solving problems. Remarkably, it takes just 96 milliseconds for our brains to tell apart stimuli that trigger fear and disgust, allowing us to quickly and appropriately respond to these two categories of threat.

Darwin's definition of disgust, linked to things that taste, smell, feel or look revolting, is a good starting point, and one that I'm sure we can all identify with. At its heart is distaste, a reflexive response that helped our ancestors to avoid eating toxins, including natural poisons and gone-off food. Over long evolutionary time, animals fine-tuned their taste receptors to set off alarm bells if they tasted something bad – those animals that didn't experience the 'yuck' sensation as they bit into a toxic caterpillar or poisonous mushroom wouldn't have lasted very long. Almost all naturally produced poisons taste bitter, and animals react in characteristic ways – rats will gape, rub and wash their face; birds will shake their heads and wipe their beaks; if it's really bad, we might spit it out – all of these things work to get something that is potentially harmful away from our mouths. Even three-day-old infants show the characteristic lip curl if they are exposed to noxious smells, so fundamental is this response.

Poisons aren't the only things to watch out for in our food. We can also become sick by ingesting bacteria, parasites, fungi and other microorganisms, and these threats are far less obvious. Parasites and pathogens do not advertise themselves in the same way as a plant poison might, and this means that while our distaste response does a fantastic job at protecting us from toxins, it's not good enough to protect us from infections. And it's here that another theory concerning the evolution of disgust comes in, as Prokop explains. 'Another reasonable explanation is that disgust evolved as a broader mechanism to protect ourselves against infectious disease. Indeed, disgust is a part of the behavioural immune system and can work as one of the avoidance mechanisms included in this system.' Still, he adds, 'oral contamination avoidance evolved first.'

When it comes to preventing disease, we tend to think only of our *physiological* immune system, i.e. the different immune cells, antibodies and other components that jump to attention when microorganisms get inside our bodies. Clearly, the functioning of this system is essential for our health – it coordinates the destruction of these invaders and stops us from getting sick. Disgust is a little different. As part of our *behavioural* immune system, it doesn't help with anything that's already got into the body, but by alerting us to cues that reliably predict the presence of pathogens, it helps to keep us safe. The presence of mould on food that I haven't learned to enjoy (like blue cheese)? No, I won't put that in my mouth. Open sores on another person that are oozing pus? No, I won't touch them (unless I work in a healthcare profession – and if I do, I'll take appropriate precautions). Dead fox starting to decompose behind the garden shed? No, I'm not going to pick that up with my bare hands. You get the picture. For some people, even the sight of clusters of holes, such as the seed head of a lotus, can be enough to elicit revulsion, potentially because it resembles skin that might be diseased or infected.

This reveals something else, too – disgust is not an all-or-nothing trait. While all people will experience distaste towards certain bitter foods or unpleasant smells, the presence or strength of our disgust responses differs between individuals and populations. Foods or behaviours that repulse one group may not be considered disgusting in another, either due to cultural differences or individual circumstances. People who are deprived of food, for example, rate images of mouldy food items as less disgusting than satiated humans. And many people, like nurses, refuse collectors, plumbers and more, are able to get used to sights, smells or sensations that others would find disgusting. Disgust is therefore a trade-off, dependent on the context at the time.

One thing that is certain is that this emotion has developed into bizarre proportions in humans. Compared with other animals, we're positively prudish in the fact that we won't eat food that has touched faeces, lick the snot from our babies' faces, nor groom our friends by eating the parasites that we find in their body hair. We are extremely unlikely to pick out and eat chunks of food from vomit, just as we are extremely unlikely to eat the rotting corpses of stillborn babies. We also feel disgusted by numerous things that are no longer associated with the risk of sickness or infection; instead, we experience moral revulsion towards actions or ideas that are deemed societally unacceptable, including incest, child abuse or ethnic persecution.

That said, we're not the only animals to experience disgust. That's the belief of scientists including Cécile Sarabian, research fellow at the Institute for Advanced Study in Toulouse, France, who has observed tantalising evidence for this emotion in other creatures.

Sarabian's interest in disgust began in 2013, when she was working as a research assistant on the Japanese island of Koshima, where macaques have been studied since the 1940s. One day, she watched a female monkey accidentally tread in fresh poo on the beach. 'And then she crossed the entire beach on three legs and started meticulously rubbing her back foot on a dead tree trunk, repetitively smelling it, and I thought, "wow, that is quite a strong response!"' Sarabian had previously noticed that the monkeys never ate food that was touching poo, and she was intrigued. Monkeys are often stereotyped as animals that go around flinging faeces, but these animals seemed to dislike touching it. Were they showing disgust? This was not something that had been studied – disgust was assumed to be a human emotion, after all, so Sarabian started doing the research and she's built her academic career around this topic. It might seem like a bizarre research niche, but the work has wider implications for understanding how humans came to be so disgusted by so many things in our environments.

In one study, inspired by what she saw on Koshima's beach, she ran a choice test with individual macaques, presenting a grain of wheat on either a real monkey poo, a fake monkey poo, or a control plastic block. Monkeys were less likely to take it from either the real or fake poo than the plastic block, but it wasn't clear cut – more than a third of the monkeys still ate the wheat from the top of the real poo. When Sarabian swapped the wheat grains for a piece of peanut (a treasured treat), the monkeys' manners went out of the window. Every peanut was eaten, even if it was sitting on top of a steaming turd. In follow-up research, Sarabian has proven that this behaviour translates to health – individuals that more strongly avoided the faeces-contaminated food had lower levels of parasitic infection. The least 'hygienic' monkeys had at least seven times more parasite eggs in their faeces than the most hygienic ones.

Her ongoing work explores the key question of whether humans are the only animal to experience disgust towards other creatures, motivated by observations from camera trap footage of wild chimpanzees in eastern Democratic Republic of Congo 'using caves and chasing bats away'. She writes to me that the caves are also home to rats and small carnivorous mammals, making them 'perfect hotspots for pathogen transmission'.

To explore whether the apes are disgusted by bats and rats, Sarabian and team are running a series of tests with chimpanzees and people, asking how individuals respond to images of the animals while they are doing problem-solving tasks (such as matching up images or picking the correct image from a set). She is also going to track where humans and chimpanzees look during tests: do they look away when they see images of bats and rats (as they do for carcasses), and do any specific parts of the rats and bats (for example wings or tail) capture their attention? The work is ongoing, but if the evidence does suggest that disgust is the reason chimpanzees chase rats and bats from their caves then that would be remarkable, and would shed new light on the origins of the emotion. Nonetheless, even if this was the case, chimpanzees would still not come close to being as grossed out about as many other creatures as we are.

A good place to start to identify these creatures is a research study that was published in 2021 with the title, 'The Ultimate List of the Most Frightening and Disgusting Animals'. The team behind the research, based in Prague, compiled their list from the ratings of adult volunteers who ranked sets of animals according to how strongly each one elicited fear or disgust.

Top of the pile for disgust were tapeworms, followed by ticks, roundworms, lice and leeches. Nine of the top ten most disgusting animals were invertebrates,[20] and the results fit with previous work over the last few decades, which has consistently identified the most disgusting animals to be endoparasites (like intestinal worms), ectoparasites (like ticks, fleas and lice), insects and their larvae (such as cockroaches and maggots), other 'creepy' invertebrates (like spiders, slugs or centipedes), and certain small vertebrates (like rats, bats,

---

[20] The single vertebrate was the poor mole lizard, a delightful creature which looks like a huge, pink worm with a little face and dinky hands.

frogs and toads). But what is it that offends us so much about these animals and not others?

If we think about disgust as an emotion that alerts us to things that might make us sick, then it makes sense that animals triggering it most strongly will be the smaller, often parasitic, animals that pose a risk to health. I would agree that little parasitic worms, leeches and ticks are the creatures I most definitely want to avoid. My behavioural immune system gets a metaphorical pat on the back. But what about the other animals? Why do people find frogs, insects or snails disgusting? I ask Prokop, if he was tasked with creating the most universally disgusting fictional animal he could, what would be its key features? His response of 'large, slimy, dark-coloured and slow, something like a big slug,' is consistent with these studies, as is his afterthought that he thinks many people would say a 'big spider'.

For many of these animals, their creepiness is caused by their strange (to us) body plan and the way they move. This harks back to LoBue's conclusion that we find snakes and spiders 'weird'. Two legs good, four legs good; no legs or any other number of legs, on other hand, freaks us out. Spiders, for example, seem to be unique in eliciting high levels of fear *and* disgust: significantly more than any other invertebrate creepy-crawly. A lot of this comes down to their weird, unfamiliar appearance (as researcher Jakub Polák calls it, 'their quirky "too-many-legs" body plan') and the way they move: eight legs is too many; eight eyes is also too many; that silent and stealthy way of moving, until they're startled and start racing around erratically, is creepy; as is the fact that they tend to hide in dark corners or unused areas of our homes.

Disgust can also come down to certain physical features which might be associated with signs of infection, largely concerning the skin. Ironically, given our status as the 'naked ape', i.e. the species that evolved to lose its fur, and the amount of effort that so many of us put into keeping our bodies hair free (our heads are another story, because we don't make much sense), we're not keen on bare skin in other creatures. The bare heads of vultures creep us out, as does the baggy, pink skin of the naked mole rat, and the bare pink tail of a rat. According to Chris Klebl, psychologist at the University of Melbourne, for something like a naked mole rat, their skin looks quite similar to our own, but there's something about it that is also not like normal human skin, and that sets off alarm signals. As he tells me: 'It's very much related to what we see from our perspective as a sign of disease.' Personally, I feel the same towards sphynx cats – I don't know why we have selectively bred them, and I can't understand why anybody would choose a naked cat over one with delightful soft fur. Having said that, at least the sphynx is dry. Slugs, being legless and slimy, were never going to score highly for popular opinion, and while frogs and toads benefit from an appropriate number of legs, their naked, moist or warty skin is a clear trigger of disgust.

Sometimes it's the exceptions that stand out. Because when I saw a photo of *Trichobatrachus robustus*, the hairy frog, I couldn't help but shudder. Also known as the horror frog and the wolverine frog, it's a central African species that has two peculiar traits. First, as suggested by its name, it's 'hairy'. It's not hair, of course, that would be completely bonkers in an amphibian, and it's not across all individuals, or even all the time. But during the breeding season, male frogs develop fine hair-like skin growths called 'dermal papillae' along their flanks and thighs. Each projection contains a blood vessel, and it's thought that these help males to stay underwater to guard their eggs. The wolverine part comes from the fact that when this frog is threatened, it intentionally breaks off the ends of the bones in its toes and forces them through the skin as bony 'claws'. Nature does remarkable things, and the hairy frog is one of them – the more I learned about it the more impressed – and less freaked out – I became.

To sum this all up, animals seem to acquire their status as disgusting creatures in one of three ways. Emeritus professor Graham Davey has proposed the following:

1) being directly associated with the spread of disease (for example rats and cockroaches);
2) having features that resemble primary disgust-evoking stimuli such as mucus or faeces (for example animals that are perceived as slimy, such as worms, snakes, toads and slugs);
3) contingent association with dirt, disease or contagion (for example vultures), or acting as signals for infection or diseased food (for example maggots).

I want to take a closer look at some members of these three groups, because many animals have been tarred with the disgust brush that don't deserve it. And we'll start with what must be one of the most reviled of all.

★★★

In 2015, Tokuyama Zoo in Yamaguchi, western Japan, ran a special summer event. The aim was to raise the public profile of one, rather unpopular, insect. As part of the event, there were live specimens from around the world, races, petting experiences and other fun activities, as well as a special themed mascot. 'They have such a negative image', a zoo spokesperson commented at the time, one can only imagine with an air of apology, given that the insects in question were cockroaches. But Cockroach Fest had an admirable aim — raising the profile of one of the most hated creatures on the planet.

For most of us, these stereotypically greasy, fat, brown beasts are typically first encountered scuttling across a kitchen floor or crawling out of a drain, the little spines on their legs making a 'scritching' sound as they dart to safety. They're unexpectedly fast, and even if you catch one and squash it (which is not entirely straightforward thanks to some super-strength body armour) it'll leave you with another treat – the stench of dirty urinal, thanks to their bodily storage of uric acid.

Or at least this is what I've been led to believe about cockroaches by their depictions in stories and from accounts written by people who have actually encountered them. Most of these come from the US, where these insects feature strongly in popular culture. Horror stories abound, such as the infamous infestation of a home in Schenectady, upstate New York, in 1979, which was described as 'ankle deep in cockroaches'. Some people say there were one million German cockroaches, others say three million – however many there were, they burrowed into the walls, ceilings, floorboards, furniture and every other thing that they could. The house had to be demolished.

Here in the UK, cockroaches feature far less prominently in most people's minds. I hadn't even realised that there were any cockroaches living in the British Isles, having never seen one or heard anything about them. In fact, we have three native species, which live quiet lives in woodland, heath and dunes and are helpful decomposers. But we also have a handful of uninvited cockroach guests, the most bothersome of which are the German and Oriental cockroach species. I'm either very lucky or oblivious to have not encountered these, because a quick internet search pulls up lots of news stories about cockroach infestations around the country, one from a few months ago at a motorway service station just five miles away.

With no direct experience, my views on cockroaches are undoubtedly influenced by Western cultural references, in which they are near-universally detested. While it's true that cockroaches haven't been the subject of as many films as predatory beasts, they have had some limelight – usually either as mutant killers or, more commonly, to paint a scene of poverty or dereliction. They're used to elicit fear and disgust, and those kinds of feelings are contagious.

Why do we despise cockroaches so much? They trigger revulsion in a way that few other insects do, and that's likely down to their association with filth and disease. In a now-classic set of experiments conducted in the 1980s, eminent psychologist and disgust researcher Paul Rozin illustrated our strong reactions to these insects. Participants watched as an experimenter poured out two glasses of fruit juice, and then dunked a plastic candle holder into one of the glasses and a dried, sterilised cockroach into the other. Participants were then asked to choose which glass they would like to drink from and, despite being assured that there was absolutely no risk from the cockroach, overwhelmingly chose the other option. I suspect that most of us would do the same. Even if the cockroach isn't a contaminant, there's something a bit 'icky' about knowing it was there — why risk it? Rozin explained it from the perspective of 'sympathetic magic', invoking something called the law of contagion, or 'once in contact, always in contact'.

When a cockroach is in your house, touching your things, the same principle is at play. These insects will eat just about anything, and they don't understand the difference between food and filth. To a cockroach, the nutrients in poo are just as valuable as the nutrients in bread, or beer, or dried skin, toenails, soap, paper, etc. How are they supposed to know the difference? These are nature's ultimate waste disposal agents, indiscriminately munching up anything they can find, and if they would only do this out of sight, in the leaf litter and mulch of the woods, that would be fine. But no, they bring it into our space, and this is the issue — when a creature with zero sensitivity to disgust scuttles happily between a carcass, a poo and our cupboards, and when that creature is as resistant to deterrents and breeds as rapidly as the cockroach, that's when we have a major problem on our hands.

While it's an exaggerated depiction that cockroaches are synonymous with disgusting things, we are right in not wanting these animals living in our homes, as Beulah Garner, senior curator of the Blattodea (cockroaches and their close relatives, termites[21]) at the Natural History Museum (NHM) in London, explains: 'Certain species within certain families, including the German cockroach, communicate by leaving pheromones or a faecal trail. And so, depending on what species or what family it is, it's those faecal trails that are being deposited in our kitchens or bathrooms that potentially are causing a health risk.'

Faecal trails. The ultimate ick. I looked into it and indeed, all pest cockroach species are attracted by faeces. According to entomologist and cockroach expert Coby Schal, professor at North Carolina State University, 'fecal smears contain aggregation pheromones that serve as beacons to attract cockroaches to aggregation sites.' Individuals use their two antennae to compare the concentration of pheromones or faecal matter in their environment, using that information to guide their movements. When scientists messed with their navigation system by crossing their antennae and glueing them in place, the animals consistently turned in the wrong direction when navigating a pheromone maze.

On top of this, swabs of the little beasts have shown them to carry an astonishing array of pathogens – including bacteria causing salmonella and tuberculosis, viruses, fungi, parasitic worms and protozoa. And yet, incredibly, there is no hard evidence that cockroaches cause disease. 'Yes, this is indeed surprising,' says Schal. He explains that the potential is there, given how many pathogens have been isolated, but that nobody has documented clear evidence of transmission. However, he notes, 'Documenting transmission is very challenging.' Researchers have found evidence of salmonella

---

[21] Termites were historically grouped in a separate order called the Isoptera, but recent genetic analyses indicate that they evolved from an ancestral wood-feeding cockroach – making termites a lineage of eusocial (i.e. living in a colony with only some individuals breeding) cockroaches.

transmission in the lab, so it seems quite likely that the absence of evidence in the 'wild' does not absolve cockroaches of spreading disease. What there is strong evidence for is that they transmit allergens, and there's a clear link between this and the development of asthma. However you look at it, you don't want cockroaches infesting your house. Schal agrees: 'In my view there are no redeeming features to cockroaches that evolved an association with humans in the "built environment".'

No redeeming features. Ouch. And yet. Tokuyama Zoo was onto something.

In his foreword to the 2016 book, *Cockroaches: Ecology, Behavior, and Natural History*, by William Bell, Louis Roth, and Christine Nalepa, eminent entomologist Edward O. Wilson opened with a plea: 'Let the lowly cockroach crawl up, or, better, fly up, to its rightful place in human esteem!' There are around 5,000 species of cockroach in the world, and entomologists estimate that there could be another 5,000 undiscovered. Yet humanity's hatred of the group results from the 'bad' behaviour of about 10 problematic species, including the German, American, Australian and Oriental cockroaches. That's a tiny fraction of the whole, making them an unreliable set of ambassadors. Just as with sharks, our mental template for a cockroach has been constructed from the species that we like least; in this case, the ones that live among us, invade our space, and may transmit disease. And while I'm not suggesting that you fling your doors wide to let these creatures in ('faecal smears', shudder), I do agree that cockroaches as a whole deserve a bit more recognition for being a wonderfully diverse and interesting group. As Wilson wrote, the pest cockroaches are only 'the least pleasant tip of a great blattarian biodiversity'. I appreciate that this is a tall order and can already visualise some headshaking but hear me out.

Cockroaches have been around for some 125 to 140 million years, although 'roach-like' animals were in existence as long ago as 300 million years. Ancestral roaches would therefore have been scurrying around in the undergrowth, probably feeding on the excrement and dandruff of dinosaurs and other prehistoric beasts, as well as the sorts of things that they still do now. But unlike the dinosaurs, they are survivors. They survived 66 million years ago, and I'd hazard a guess that they'll continue to survive long after we've gone; that is, unless the entire planet is nuked into oblivion. That's right, the old adage that cockroaches could survive nuclear war is nothing but a myth: they're tough, but not *that* tough. What they do have is incredible tolerance when it comes to coping with temperature and humidity extremes, as well as a lack of food and water.

Their relationship with us goes back a long way, too. American entomologists Roth and Edwin Willis proposed that some species lived in our ancestors' cave dwellings in the Palaeolithic era, surviving on our food and waste products. From those origins, they would have spread with us into every kind of human structure. But before you feel too creeped out about our little blattarian stalkers, note that they're not interested in us. As Roth and Willis wrote: 'Man is only incidental to these associations. Only the shelter and food that man unwittingly provides for these unwelcome guests attract cockroaches to him; man's physical presence is unnecessary.' This is true not just of cockroaches, but of many of the animals that we call pests (more in Chapter 7) – we've created perfect environments for them, so why are we surprised if they choose to live in them?

Garner agrees. 'They're doing what they would do, but they've been taken out of their so-called natural environment and ended up in an environment where there's a lot of crumbs. Why wouldn't they take advantage of that?' She says this as she leads me to a counter on which she has lined up a series of diverse specimens from the museum's collection of around 3,200 cockroach species. 'Cockroaches are nature's caretakers,' she says, explaining that all species are detritivores, meaning that they play an important role in breaking down waste – they're less obvious than the big scavengers like vultures or hyenas but no less important. One study estimated that cockroaches constitute approximately 24 per cent of total arthropod (the group comprising insects, spiders and other invertebrates) biomass in tropical tree canopies worldwide, representing a vital part of our ecosystem. Some species specialise in wood, including the termites, while others munch away on general detritus found on the forest floor. And 30 of them are synanthropic, meaning that they exploit the waste created by humans.

We start with a case containing the smallest cockroaches in the world. At first glance, these tiny brown grains could be anything, and Garner says they're often confused with beetles – measuring less than 3mm in length, these miniature beasts spend their lives pretending to be ants or termites, exploiting the resources available in these colonies.

Moving to the other extreme, I'm keen to see the biggest cockroaches, and Garner doesn't disappoint. *Megaloblatta longipennis* holds the title of largest cockroach species in the world, and I can confirm it is a huge insect. Native to Colombia, Ecuador and Peru, it measures up to 97mm in length, and its long, ochre and brown wings can span 200mm. While long, *M. longipennis* is quite slim, unlike the next specimen, *Macropanesthia rhinoceros*, which is the heaviest cockroach. This burrowing behemoth can measure up to 85mm in length and weigh in at 30g or more. Built more like a tank than *M. longipennis*, and lacking wings, it's the only species of roach to build permanent burrows underground, which can be a metre below the surface.

In general, cockroaches have smooth, flattened bodies, and that's down to their crevice-inhabiting lifestyle. There are variations on this, of course. In the Neotropics, some cockroaches have evolved more pancake-like bodies, which allow them to flatten themselves to whatever surface they're on and prevent ants getting to their vulnerable underbellies. Others, like desert-dwelling species, have evolved to be hairy. Some have the same colouration as bees and wasps, while the domino cockroach is black with bright white spots, closely resembling a monochrome ladybird.

'They need a marketing campaign,' says Garner. 'They need for the information that I'm talking about now to be more common knowledge, I feel, because the things that they do in the world are so important, and they're just beautiful.' She says this as she points out an absolute stunner, *Polyzosteria viridissima*, which is metallic green and bronze. Surely, if all cockroaches looked like this, people would find them less disgusting? 'Absolutely,' says Garner. 'They've got more of the cute factor.'

Cute cockroaches! I never thought I'd hear it. But it goes to show that the concept most of us have of these animals needs a bit of expanding. Especially because those species that live amongst us are no longer typical of the rest of the group. Schal tells me that the German cockroach now lives its life so intimately associated with humans that there are no known 'wild' populations. That means that we know little about their truly natural behaviour and, importantly, Schal adds, 'the German cockroach is far from a typical cockroach in several regards.'

Molecular analyses show that the German cockroach evolved from its 'sister species' the Asian cockroach around 2,100 years ago, probably by adapting to human settlements in India or Myanmar. Then they spread, and it's all thanks to us. First, they went west to the Middle East, coinciding with various Islamic dynasties in the region of 1,200 years ago. Then, there was another movement, eastwards, around 390 years ago, coinciding with the European colonial period. Ironically, given the name, Europe wasn't central to the early domestication and spread of the German cockroach. However, European advances in long-distance transportation and temperature-controlled housing were likely important for the more recent global spread, increasing chances of successful dispersal to and establishment in new regions.

The global genetic structure of German cockroaches is therefore interesting not just from the perspective of mapping how this species came to colonise the world, but because it also tells a story that aligns with geopolitical boundaries and global commerce.

They're also anatomical and physiological marvels, as you'd expect for a creature that can squeeze through the narrowest of gaps and scuttle up walls and ceilings, and studies of American cockroaches have revealed some of their physical feats. By flattening out their pliable exoskeleton, they can squeeze through gaps less than a quarter of their height (3mm) in just one second. They can run 50 body lengths per second (210 miles per hour for a human) and even when flattened to half their height they can still run at 20 body lengths per second. They can also withstand compressive forces of 900 times their body weight with no apparent ill effects. And when it comes to their ability to move over rough ground, they are exceptional. In one study, discoid cockroaches were fitted with tiny exploding cannons glued to their backs. As the animals were running, researchers would trigger a 10-millisecond horizontal blast from the cannons, which would be enough to knock most creatures off balance. Not the cockroaches – the study reported that the insects regained their footing in a single step, never breaking their stride.

Cockroach physical superpowers haven't gone unnoticed by researchers in diverse fields. Among them are roboticists interested in developing new solutions to improve search-and-rescue efforts. Could the physical prowess of cockroaches be used to help rescuers to navigate through rubble in the aftermath of an earthquake or tornado? The answer seems to be yes, and it's fascinating.

One team in California is working on developing a palm-sized, soft-legged robot (catchily titled CRAM, or 'compressible robot with articulated mechanisms') with the same cockroach physicality and shape-changing abilities.

Another team, in Singapore, is exploring the alternative option of cyborg cockroaches, because using real, live creatures is considerably cheaper than building robots and eliminates the serious challenge of battery life. The Madagascar hissing cockroach offers the perfect biological component for these 'cyborg bugs'. Each animal, which measures an average of 6cm, is anaesthetised and fitted with a little backpack comprising a microchip, electrodes, sensors and an infrared camera. Once the cockroach regains consciousness, the microchip emits electrical signals, effectively plugging into the animal's neuromuscular system and allowing the team to take control of its movement. The result combines the cockroach's locomotor abilities with the controllability of a robot, which is an extremely attractive proposition for deploying into search-and-rescue situations. Within the chip is a human detection algorithm, and initial results are promising: the cyborgs can distinguish between human and non-humans with 87 per cent accuracy. Cyborg cockroaches might be coming soon to a disaster area near you!

Other aspects of cockroaches that make them so despised are also proving to be beneficial to us. One of those is their voracious, 'eat-anything' approach to food which, combined with their tolerance of overcrowding and aridity, has led some scientists to investigate whether they could help with humanity's waste problem. It has led to a new avenue for waste processing called blatticomposting, in which the animals are set loose to gorge themselves on organic waste, with the added bonus that what comes out at the other end makes for extremely good enriched compost.

They are also being explored for what's inside them. Cockroaches have been a component of Chinese traditional medicine for centuries, and the world's largest cockroach breeding facility in Xichang has been tasked with breeding six billion of the insects per year to meet demand for a potion said to relieve stomach pain and other gastric problems. Allegedly, when jazz musician Louis Armstrong was a child, his mother fed him a broth made from boiled cockroaches whenever he was ill. Then there's evidence suggesting that cockroaches produce their own antibiotics: a species of bacteria isolated from the gut of the American cockroach showed activity against *Klebsiella pneumoniae*, a major pathogen of hospital-acquired infections, which is showing broad resistance to available antibiotics.

I had no idea how beneficial cockroaches could be to us, particularly that they may one day help to save lives. But I'm not satisfied with just working out how to best exploit them for humanity's benefit. I want to know how we can like cockroaches too – surely there must be something about them that is endearing?

'Endearing?' writes Schal, and I wonder whether he thinks I'm mad. I'm relieved that he elaborates. 'The nuptial gifts that cockroaches share during courtship reminds one of Valentine's gifts (the chemistry is similar to the chemistry of chocolate!) and the maternal care of some species and parental care in some is pretty sophisticated. I think many of these behaviors are pretty endearing!' Indeed, it is the case that in some cockroach species the female looks after her babies, making a nest or carrying them around. Garner tells me that immature roaches don't possess the necessary gut microbiomes to digest their typical diet of wood, making them reliant on parental feeding until they reach adulthood. 'So they behave in the same ways birds do, in the sense that the adults regurgitate the food for the young.' That's incredible, but there's more. 'In return, the young groom the adults – it's pretty cute!' Garner thinks for a moment and then continues. 'In a sense, that's an argument for understanding them as clean animals, because they engage in grooming within a community. And that ensures the health of the population as well.'

Cute again, as well as caring and clean. This is not what I was expecting! But the truth is that the more that scientists study the diversity of cockroach species, the more we are learning about their behaviour. It's not an easy task; these are well camouflaged, nocturnal little animals, meaning that virtually nothing is known about many species. Even for those that are more visible, such as the hissing cockroaches, which are commonly kept in homes as pets, in laboratories for experiments, and in museums for educational purposes, parental feeding behaviour was only recently observed.

So, how should we think about cockroaches? 'I admire the evolvability of the German cockroach,' writes Schal, but overall, when it comes to the pest species, that's the best he can say, and I agree. The rest of the cockroach group, though, are fantastically important and interesting insects, that perform a great service to us far beneath the radar. We should appreciate how much these animals do to keep environments healthy, but it may still be a losing battle. Those inbuilt cues that alert us to the presence of potentially harmful stimuli are part of the cockroach body plan, and it's hard to adjust our programming. As Christine Nalepa has written, even the impressive traits of the insect, such as the ability to survive extreme temperatures and higher radiation levels than people, likely reinforce the 'monstrous' stereotypes in people's minds. The fact is that, just as with sharks, the negative beliefs that we hold about cockroaches are rooted strongly, and it is difficult to reconcile those beliefs with conflicting information about positive, even human-like traits. It's tough, trying to override inbuilt emotions with biological facts. It can be done though, when there's enough at stake. And nothing illustrates this better than the curious case of animal slime.

★★★

Few things evoke such revulsion as slime, or other oozy substances produced by living creatures, such as mucus, snot or exudate. The exception to this is tears, which are classed very differently and much more positively than other excretions. But slime is not a substance that we tend to intentionally manufacture, especially for things that we might intentionally consume ('side of slimy peas with your fish, sir?'). It sounds unpleasant, irrespective of which word you choose. Slime is something that happens to unfortunate gameshow contestants, or provides telltale signs of bacterial growth or unwanted nocturnal visitors over your tender succulent plants. Mucus or other secretions might reveal illness or infection – avoiding these sticky liquids therefore makes a lot of sense in terms of staying healthy, right?

Yes and no. Your body produces at least one litre of mucus every day and it is essential for various functions, including as a barrier against germs, and for lubrication of our eyelids and gut. We need our own mucus, and while we might not like the idea of contacting anybody or anything else's, scientists are discovering that the slime and secretions of an array of other animals have superpowers too.

The most impressive oozers are hagfish, a group of jawless and almost eyeless fish that has changed little over the past 300 million years. When it comes to disgusting animals, hagfish would surely occupy a top spot if only people were more aware of them. As it is, they live quietly in the oceans, feasting on dead carcasses that drift to the seabed, using whisker-like projections around their mouths to navigate and detect food. Being scaleless and squishy tubes of flesh, they are also very appealing snacks for bigger fish, like sharks. Or at least, they seem appealing until the shark tries to take a bite, because when a hagfish is under attack it can direct a jet of slime straight into the mouth and gills of the potential predator, causing it to choke and release its grip. Hagfish slime is the stuff of scientific legend. Unlike other animal slimes, it contains not only slippery mucus ('mucin'), but also ultrafine protein fibres termed 'slime threads', which provide strength and cohesion. These fibres are tightly coiled within slime cells until they are released, at which point they rapidly unravel and tangle together with the mucin to trap water, forming a huge quantity of soft, elastic slime. It's unlike anything ever made by man. Sounds gross? Yes, undoubtedly, but remember that one man's disgust is another's delicacy: five million pounds of hagfish are eaten every year in South Korea, showing that disgust is very much in the eye of the beholder.

Closer to home, slugs and snails are your key oozers. We had a bumper crop of them in summer 2024, thanks to a mild and wet spring, which was a disaster for my sedum plants and for gardeners across the UK. You'll notice that if you pick up a slug or a snail, it will ooze slime as a defensive reaction. This is likely the main reason why people don't like them. But, while most people are familiar with the fact that snails are considered a delicious and nutritious foodstuff in France and various other countries, did you know that snail ooze forms the basis for an almost billion-dollar skincare industry? Perhaps you even use it – various products with the active ingredient of mucin are available, and it has been used in skincare, again in South Korea, for decades. Mucin-based lotions are touted as moisturising, full of antioxidants, and capable of stimulating new collagen, and while they're promoted as being exclusively produced by snails, slug mucin would work just as well – but may need a greater marketing budget.

Then there are all the wonderful things found in the slimy secretions of amphibian skin. Some frogs ooze a sticky mucus that essentially becomes glue. This, like hagfish slime, makes life very difficult for an attacking predator. The Mozambique rain frog uses the glue for another reason too – males literally stick themselves to females during the mating season. Other frog and toad secretions contain toxins, antimicrobial substances, or psychoactive compounds, like those contained within the Sonoran Desert toad's defensive skin secretions, which include a strong psychedelic called the 'God molecule'.

It's not just the obvious slimers that are producing potentially beneficial compounds. There's another mini beast that even more strongly elicits the disgust response, and I want to tell you its story, because it's remarkable. It's the maggot, a creature that hangs out in infected wounds, rotting meat and corpses, usually as a writhing, seething mass of little flesh-eating bodies, just as depicted in *Poltergeist*. And, spoiler alert, it's a mini medical marvel.

Maggots are fly larvae, and when it comes to carrion flies, their lifecycle is intimately tied to dead bodies. These flies are so highly attuned to specific chemical signals caused by decomposition that they can arrive within minutes of death.[22] It's not just about food. Fresh corpses make wonderful nurseries, providing moisture, sustenance and protection to a developing brood, so female flies make the most of this by laying their eggs in any body cavities they can find (nose, ears, anus – they're not squeamish). A single carcass can be colonized by thousands of eggs from different flies, which all hatch into hungry maggots. Research has found that a single blowfly larvae will consume close to 2g of meat during its development, meaning that all those maggots can easily strip bare a dead animal.

That sounds unpleasant, but maggots are also 'helpful and marvellous!', according to Yamni Nigam, professor of biomedical science at Swansea University. Nigam is head of the maggot lab at Swansea, founder of the Love A Maggot campaign, and an all-round maggot champion. She's on a mission to change people's perceptions of these unloved creepy crawlies, and all because of their oozy secretions.

Using maggots to clean wounds has been practised for centuries, even millennia, including by Indigenous people in the Mayan civilisation, aboriginal tribes in Australia, and the

---

[22] So good are their carrion-finding abilities that these flies are now being explored by conservation biologists as potential indicators of biodiversity, the rationale being that DNA isolated from their stomach contents can reveal what species are living in an area, information which might be otherwise practically impossible to collect in remote or difficult to access areas.

Myanmar Hill People. The technique re-emerged to treat infected wounds on the battlefields, where Napoleon's military doctor observed that the little grubs only ate infected, not healthy, tissue. Maggot, or larval, therapy started gaining popularity in the clinical setting in the 1930s but before it could properly take off, antibiotics were discovered. These compounds, particularly penicillin, provided a much more convenient solution to bacterial wound infections; maggots seemed primitive by comparison. Since then, however, humanity's carefree over-use of antibiotics has led to a new and far more deadly problem – the emergence of antibiotic-resistant pathogens with the potential to kill millions. Coupled with the rise in infected wounds and ulcers associated with diabetes, attention turned back to the tried-and-tested natural method of wound cleaning. 'And of course, they discovered that it worked,' Nigam says. 'It worked really, really well.'

Nigam set up her maggot research group in 2000 and started looking into how the little beasts did such a good job. We're talking about one specific kind of maggot here: larvae of the common green bottle fly (*Lucilia sericata*). Nigam is quick to point out that not all fly larvae are the same – some, such as the human botfly or screwworm can invade healthy flesh, which is called myiasis, and that can cause pain, lesions, bleeding and infections. But these will never be an option for medical treatment. Green bottle larvae, though, are literally only able to eat dead tissue – they will die if left on the healthy stuff because they are physiologically incapable of ingesting it. And that makes them perfect little contractors for the job of wound care. It seems like a contradiction for a creature that is so intimately associated with death and disease. But when it comes to cleaning out an infected wound, there's no better agent.

Although maggots are voracious consumers of infected flesh, they are toothless little beasts, meaning that they're not actually nibbling away at it. Rather, like adult flies, they obtain sustenance through something called extracorporeal digestion.

Nigam explains that they produce salivary and bodily secretions, which contain powerful protein-digesting enzymes. These function like chemical scissors, turning the dead tissue into a sort of soup, which the maggots can then drink up. This cleaning (called 'debridement') is the first step in wound healing and it's essential: a wound will never heal unless it has been cleared of dead tissue and infection. Maggots can clean and debride a wound in just four days, whereas traditional wound healing may take many months and still run the risk of requiring amputation.

An abundance of published studies show that maggots work extremely well: they have undoubtedly saved numerous toes, feet and legs from amputation, as well as prevented surgical procedures and helped with healing where surgery was not an option. It's not just down to their ability to debride the wound. 'We discovered lots of lovely, brilliant molecules that the maggot secretes in the wound,' Nigam tells me. In particular, the little creatures secrete a novel antibiotic called seraticin, which Nigam and her team have found kills many dangerous pathogens, including *Clostridium difficile*, *E. coli*, and 12 different strains of methicillin-resistant *Staphylococcus aureus* (MRSA). Another research team in Germany recently identified 47 different antimicrobial peptides from maggot secretions; these are now being synthesised in the lab for evaluation as novel anti-infectives in wound dressings and bandages.

This makes perfect sense. These are organisms that have been exquisitely honed by natural selection to do just one thing at this stage of their lives: eat dead tissue. And since they're sharing their meal with a range of potentially deadly bacteria, fungi, and other pathogens, evolution placed a strong selection pressure on them to evolve some potent protective mechanisms. The diverse molecules that maggots secrete are their defence against whatever else they might come across in such a dangerous environment.

The trouble is, despite all this positively glowing evidence, maggots are still under-used in medical practice. Why? Because patients and staff find them disgusting. In one study from the Tver region of Russia, nearly 60 per cent of 576 enrolled patients reported that images of maggots were *more repulsive* than images of gangrenous wounds. From a medical perspective, this is extremely troubling, because it translates into a reluctance to use what is a proven, effective, therapy. This was the finding of a study by Nigam and collaborators, which involved surveying people across the UK, US, Canada, South Africa, Australia and New Zealand. Despite 90 per cent of the 412 respondents having heard of maggot therapy, only 36 per cent said that they would accept it as their first choice for a (hypothetical) painful wound. There was greater acceptance as the severity of the wound increased, but around eight per cent of patients were still either against or unsure of maggot therapy, even when the alternative was having a limb amputated.

That's bad enough, but the negative attitudes are present among healthcare providers too: almost one-third of non-wound specialist nurses in the UK said they found maggots disgusting and the idea of maggot therapy made their skin crawl. Wound specialist nurses were much more positive about it, but there's clearly work to be done to overturn people's negative perceptions. And Nigam's onto it. She set up Love A Maggot in 2016, a public-engagement campaign which was launched with a fantastic close-up photo of a single maggot balanced on her nose. Since then, she and her team have been on a mission to overturn the stigma surrounding maggots. They've set up maggot races at schools and science fairs, and taken the little beasts to a staggering number of golf club, yacht club and Women's Institute meetings. They even got maggot therapy into an episode of the British medical TV drama, *Casualty*, and reported significant increases in public acceptance as a result.

As we've already heard for snakes and spiders, our negative emotional responses don't seem to be baked into our genes. Somewhere between the ages of four and eight years we learn from others that snakes are scary, spiders are creepy and bugs are bad. And it's the same for maggots. 'I've put a maggot on a three-year-old,' says Nigam, 'and they're absolutely enthralled with it, they love it, because it's like a little caterpillar. But when you put a maggot on a nine- or ten-year-old kid they're like, "Eww, get that off me".'

What is it about maggots that makes us learn to dislike them so much? Some of it comes down to a lack of knowledge about fly biology. Given that the animals are literally dissolving your flesh, and that other species of fly larvae will not restrict themselves to infected tissue, it's reasonable to be wary of these little animals on a vulnerable part of your body. Education from trustworthy medical professionals can help to reassure people that medical maggot treatment is both safe and effective. But without the knowledge of how superb a role maggots can play in wound healing, people will always gravitate to the emotional salience of the 'yuck factor'. The fact is that for many people, the mere thought of these animals makes their skin crawl – they are creatures of death and disease, so why would anybody want them squirming and spitting right into their wounds and their bloodstream? From the perspective of the disease-avoidance hypothesis, it seems obvious; but from a medical standpoint, the opposite is true. As the global population ages and rates of diabetes skyrocket, wound care is going to become increasingly important, and if we can use the science to balance any knee-jerk shudders of disgust, far fewer people will suffer from chronic infections and amputations.

Maggots aren't maggots forever. Once they've had enough to eat, they start to pupate and eventually metamorphose into their final fly bodies. Do we, at this point, cut them some slack and start to appreciate them? Of course not. Flies, and indeed most insects, are reviled at all stages of life.

★★★

At Japan's Chiba University and the University of Tokyo, researchers Yuya Fukano and Masashi Soga have been looking into the reasons why people find insects so disgusting. City-dwellers tend to have more strongly negative views towards insects than those in rural settings, leading Fukano and Soga to propose their 'urbanisation-disgust hypothesis'. They suggest that stronger disgust towards insects and other arthropods in modern societies results from several species adapting to live alongside us, becoming more abundant in urban environments, and therefore being more likely to 'trespass' inside our homes. In essence, our negative feelings came down to an invasion of personal space and the perception that indoor environments are most vulnerable to infection. When Fukano and Soga presented images of different insects to participants, ratings of disgust were higher when the animals were presented on an indoor background as opposed to outside, and this was particularly the case for cockroaches and ants.

In fairness, there is some truth to this. We live in a world full of intruders, and only a very small proportion of them are criminals. It's always been the case: for as long as our early ancestors have lived in fixed dwellings, other organisms have shared those dwellings too. I'm not talking about microorganisms, in which we and our homes are covered; I'm talking about proper little animals, which won't make you feel any better. The truth is that arthropods have lived and evolved alongside us for all our history. We've already heard about cockroaches, but bed bugs (then called bat bugs) and kissing bugs are also thought to have been cave dwellers alongside prehistoric people, and with the dawn of agriculture, opportunities for arthropods exploded.

They still live alongside us. Our homes are not the sterile environments that many of us might believe.

In my own house, I'd say that we have occasional flies, ladybirds and spiders, but that's all I'm aware of. In fact, of all the creatures that could be in our house, apart from our cat Hattie, I think I'm least bothered by spiders, except in autumn, when male giant house spiders roam the rooms looking for love. Even then, I only evict them from our bedroom and only because the thought of one scuttling over my face in the night is a step too far. I did once wake up to find an assortment of spider legs and other little brown pieces scattered under me on the sheet, indicating some unintended nocturnal incident, and that still makes me shudder; but overall, I think our house is reasonably pest-free.

I may have been a little naïve.

When entomologists were let loose inside 50 houses around Raleigh, North Carolina, they collected more than 10,000 specimens of arthropod, comprising at least 579 different species. Their aim was to document diversity, by recording the number of different species, rather than the total number of individual critters in each house, and they found that each home contained, on average, at least 61 different arthropod families and 93 different species. These were conservative estimates, so the reality is almost certainly higher. The larger the house, the more families were collected. Cobweb spiders, carpet beetles, gall midge flies and ants were present in every house, while most houses (80 per cent or more) also contained book lice, dark-winged fungus gnats, cellar spiders, weevils, mosquitoes, scuttle flies, leafhoppers and non-biting midges. Dust mites were found in three-quarters of all homes.

As tempting as it might be to believe that this is just a 'Raleigh, North Carolina' thing, it's not. It's a 'being human' thing, and it's enough to make you want to cancel your weekend plans and do a thorough disinfect of your house; or possibly burn it down, depending on your perspective.[23] But there's reassurance from the data too, because among all the thousands of little creatures found, only a small proportion were classified as pests. German and American cockroaches, for example, were found in only six per cent of houses, while subterranean termites were in 28 per cent, fleas in 10 per cent and not a single bed bug was found. Smoky brown cockroaches were more common, but the authors note that this species does not generally achieve pest-level populations due to its need for high humidity and moisture. As the authors summed up, 'It appears that the vast majority of arthropods that live among us cause no direct harm.' This should offer some comfort, and the take-home message should be that it's impossible to bug-proof your home and that's OK. I suspect that for some people this might not be the take-home message though. I suspect that, despite these animals having no direct impact on us or our possessions, the mere thought that there are any arthropods in the home will be enough to make some people's skin crawl.

It won't help to know that as well as easily entering our homes, many bugs are active at night, which happens to be an approximately eight-hour window in which we're practically motionless in the same spot, and that means they are liable to wind up close to us. Or under us, in the case of my spider. Or, most alarmingly but very rarely, sometimes even in us. In 2017, a woman living in Chennai, India, was admitted to hospital and found to have a cockroach living in her sinuses – thought to have crawled up her nose while she was sleeping. Numerous other unlucky people have experienced cockroaches going into their ears; indeed,

---

[23] On at least three separate occasions in the US, people have burned their houses down after using a flamethrower to kill a spider.

one study found that over a two-year period at a hospital in Cape Town, 24 arthropods were extracted from people's ears. Ten of them were German cockroaches, eight were flies and three were beetles; there was also one tick, one assassin bug and one 'badly damaged adult clothes moth'.

Fukano and Soga elaborated on this in a later paper, where they explored reasons for insect fear (entomophobia). They noted that, while the terms entomophobia and arachnophobia literally mean a fear of these organisms, negative feelings towards insects and arachnids mostly stem from disgust, not fear. The exceptions are species that are capable of physical harm to us, including scorpions, venomous spiders and wasps. They outlined how easily disgust towards insects in cities can grow and lead to a self-reinforcing feedback loop: 'Annoying insects are easily eliminated from people's living environments, knowledge of these insects is lost, and thus, more insect species are perceived as disgusting.'

The dial on our behavioural immune system, in other words, has been cranked up because of urbanisation, and this is a problem because it was already a blunt instrument. Our brains have been honed for efficiency, and that means we cannot possibly accurately identify and make judgements about every animal we encounter. Instead, cognitive tricks called heuristics help us to respond as appropriately as possible by picking up on commonalities and general object features. Imprecise systems are subject to errors, and when it comes to identifying things that could be one of two types, we can either wrongly identify something as harmful when it's safe, called a false positive, or we can wrongly identify something as safe when it's harmful, called a false negative. When it comes to disease avoidance, it's clearly better to err on the side of false positives and false alarms, wrongly avoiding things that tick some of the boxes indicating risk, than not avoid a creature that is genuinely harmful. This is known as the 'smoke detector principle' and, evolutionarily speaking, it is undoubtedly a good thing. It may be the case that only 30 cockroach species are known to enter dwellings, but if you see a cockroach scuttling over your decking in the direction of your house, you're probably not going to take the time to get out a field guide and identify it. What's the downside?

As Fukano and Soga point out, while awareness of different species can help to hone the error management system and reduce the expression of disgust, a lack of knowledge can lead to people feeling disgusted by anything that resembles an elicitor, and this can spread. What's more, we excel at learning from others, which is highly advantageous when it comes to learning about genuine threats, including what to avoid to reduce the risks of exposure to parasites, disease or danger. We start picking up on these things from an early age, but even as adults our tendency for emotional contagion is strong, and in modern society, bombarded as we are by social media, that leads to the rapid spread of fears and dislikes towards certain animals, even when they aren't grounded in facts. The more knowledge and understanding that we lose by interacting less with nature, the easier it is to plug the gaps with other people's fears.

It's a devastatingly simple positive feedback loop, involving a synergy of all these characteristics. Let's say that a woman who dislikes moths moves to a city for work. There, with less nature interaction, her conception of scary flying insects may widen from moths to include other kinds of insects too. She may become less keen on going into nature, because of anxieties about encountering insects. This will accelerate her loss of insect knowledge, possibly leading to more generalisation of fear towards other insects, which she may encounter because of urbanisation. Her children may see her negative emotional responses to insects and learn that they are scary, picking up on the same avoidance of natural environments and reinforcing the response of killing insects as reasonable.

You can see how this sequence of events could happen. In many ways, it's understandable, given that certain insects do carry serious pathogens. But there are two, extremely important, points to consider here. One, there *is* a downside to indiscriminately killing insects, and it's a big one too. The downside is that increasing entomophobia is accelerating a global insect apocalypse, and that is a serious cause for concern. More on that later. The other is that while our behavioural immune system is busy alerting us to non-harmful moths, cockchafers, or daddy-long-legs, it's ignoring the tiny, whiny, annoying elephant in the room. It's not flagging the false negative that is mosquitoes, the deadliest non-human animal of all.

★★★

By some estimates, mosquitoes have been responsible for almost half the deaths of humans ever. If true, and it's disputed, that would be 52 billion lives claimed from a total of 108 billion. Even if that is hyperbole, it's undisputable that mosquitoes are responsible for more deaths each year than any other animal, and more deaths than there are human homicides.

They do this by carrying deadly diseases, most famously malaria, but also dengue fever, Zika virus, yellow fever, chikungunya and more. And the numbers are astronomical: 263 million people are infected with malaria every year, 390 million people are infected with dengue fever, and tens of millions more contract Zika, chikunguya and West Nile virus. Around 40 per cent of the global population is considered at-risk for dengue infection, which causes an estimated 25,000 deaths each year, while in 2023, malaria claimed the lives of close to 600,000 people. This is actually an improvement on historical figures: when the WHO started publishing global death estimates in 2000, malaria caused more than 895,000 deaths. Nonetheless, for a preventable and treatable disease, that's far too many lives lost, especially when three-quarters of them are children younger than five years old.

Malaria is not a new disease – humanity's history with it stretches back tens of thousands of years, and so entwined have our pasts been that malaria has left its mark on us in several ways. It may have contributed to the fall of the Roman Empire, for one. It's also why we have gin and tonic.[24] And it has left its trace in our blood, in the form of sickle cell anaemia, an inherited blood disorder in which the production of abnormal haemoglobin leads to red blood cells becoming deformed. Sickle cell disorder causes pain, anaemia and infections, and usually cuts the sufferer's life short. But it also defends against malaria, because the abnormally shaped red blood cells hamper the parasite's reproduction. Evolution favours the route with the best odds of passing on one's genes, and having sickle cell disorder was a better bet than falling sick and possibly dying with malaria. Today, in regions where malaria is endemic, there's a far higher prevalence of sickle cell disorders.

Let's get one thing straight from the off – mosquitoes don't cause malaria. These little insects are not directly responsible for making people sick. What is responsible is a single-celled protozoan parasite belonging to the genus *Plasmodium* – in Africa, where most cases and deaths of malaria occur, the species is *Plasmodium falciparum*, which specifically infects humans (some other species infect other primates, birds and even reptiles). If *P. falciparum* was only transmitted between humans via direct contact of blood or

---

[24] Tonic water contains quinine, a compound that comes from the bark of the cinchona tree. Quinine is an effective malaria treatment, and was a mainstay of medicine until the 1920s, when it was replaced by more effective synthetic antimalarials, such as chloroquine. But in the nineteenth century, British soldiers in India were given quinine, in the form of a rudimentary kind of tonic water, as a malaria preventative. These soldiers also had a daily gin ration, and so it's not a great stretch of the imagination to see how the two got combined.

other secretions, then malaria would not be such a big problem. As it is, *Plasmodium* parasites rely on an insect stage to complete their ridiculously complicated lifecycle, and this is what makes the disease so transmissible. That insect vector takes the form of about 70 species of *Anopheles* mosquito, which are essentially the parasites' public transport, sucking them up from the blood of one individual and squirting them back into the blood of another as they feed. As Jonathan Balcombe wrote in his 2021 book, *Super Fly*, this turns mosquitoes into 'flying contaminated needles, extending an ill person's infectious range for miles.'

And yet, mosquitoes aren't disgusting, which is baffling, given everything that we've heard about the link between disgust and parasite avoidance. What's going on?

'I think that it's hard for the brain to relate the disease that it experiences to mosquitoes, because it's just not intuitive to us that the disease is being caused by the bites of these mosquitoes.' This is entomologist and mosquito expert Lawrence Reeves, of the University of Florida. He tells me that it was only in the 1900s that the disease-vector role of mosquitoes was discovered, and there's likely a disconnect because mosquitoes are the vectors rather than the organism that makes us sick. It's not quite the same as being chewed on by a leopard, or falling sick after eating a death cap mushroom, where there's a clear and immediate link between the preceding event and any ill effects.

Having said that, Reeves then asks if I've seen the 'mouldy' mosquitoes, and shows me a photo on his screen. Belonging to the genus *Mucidus*, which means mouldy in Latin, this insect does indeed look as if it has been infected by some kind of fungus, with patches of white 'fluffy' scales. Now, if all mosquitoes looked like this, that would probably be enough to trigger the disgust response, but it would still have nothing to do with its status as a disease vector.

That's all well and good, I imagine you're thinking, but even if mosquitoes aren't the organism that directly causes sickness, they're still the reason that billions of people are at risk of serious sickness and death from deadly infectious diseases. And even when they aren't spreading deadly diseases, when one punctures you with its proboscis (aka 'face needle') and starts sucking out blood and spitting in saliva, you'll likely get an unwanted souvenir. I know about this because I'm one of the unlucky ones that seems to give off the perfect combination of carbon dioxide, heat and smell that mozzies find irresistible. And every bite puffs up into an itchy, red, sometimes blistering lump that drives me mad for days. It's not from the proboscis stabbing into our skin, as this has the precision of a hypodermic needle and a much finer gauge, so we rarely even feel it; instead, it's their spit that our bodies dislike. It contains a cocktail of chemicals that do useful things for the mozzie, in the form of messing up our blood's normal clotting process – this keeps the blood flowing for longer and allows the mosquito to drink her fill. Our immune system detects these foreign chemicals in our blood and mounts a response and it's this, and particularly the release of histamine (which is also released during allergic reactions), which causes the skin around the bite to flare up.

By several polls, mosquitoes rank as the most despised group of animals on the planet; one that elicits hatred and a desire for total eradication rather than fear or disgust. And total eradication is surely a fair aim for a creature that causes so much death and suffering?

Not so fast, say the world's entomologists. Mosquitoes have been around for 217 million years and there are 3,700 known species. That's a vast amount of fine-tuned diversity that you're talking about throwing out and, even less conveniently, *they're not all bad*. In fact, mosquitoes are mostly innocuous plant feeders – fuelled for almost all their daily comings and goings by nectar. Males never feed on blood, and females only do so for a few days of their lives, when they are ready to reproduce, for the sole reason that blood contains specific proteins that are essential for egg development. Looking at it like this, those bitey nuisances are simply little animals doing what they must to become mothers. Each species is also highly specialised towards the animal that it targets, based on smell – a few feed on human blood, while others are specialised to feed on rats, birds, manatees, alligators, fish and even earthworms. Reeves says that one species is so specialised it only bites the nostrils of a specific type of frog.

To date, scientific research has, understandably, focused on what Reeves calls the 'bad apples'. These are the species that cause us problems, and they comprise less than 10 per cent of all species: in fact, only 2.5 per cent of mosquito species are known vectors for human pathogens, while seven per cent are likely vectors. The bad apples are concentrated in three groups of genera: *Anopheles* (transmitting the malaria parasites), *Aedes* (transmitting the pathogens for dengue fever, Zika, yellow fever, and chikungunya), and *Culex* (transmitting the pathogens for encephalitis, West Nile virus, filariasis and elephantiasis). We don't yet know enough about all the other mosquito species, but what entomologists are discovering about some of them should be enough to nudge us away from wanting total eradication.

Take *Toxorhynchites rutilus*, for example: commonly termed the elephant mosquito, it's the largest species in the US, but completely harmless. In contrast to the typical way of life outlined above, females of this species don't require blood to reproduce – they've instead evolved to use nectar. This is the case for all other species of *Toxorhynchites*, as well as those of the *Malaya* genus, and a few outliers whose relatives are more typical blood-feeders. Reeves tells me that this may tie in with another feature of their biology, and it's a human-positive one. Because as well as not being dangerous bloodsuckers, all *Toxorhynchites* larvae are voracious predators of other mosquito larvae, particularly those of the disease-spreading *Aedes* genus. Like most mosquitoes, the eggs of both groups are laid in water, and they hatch into larvae that mature in the same watery world. It can take elephant mosquito larvae several weeks to six months to mature and in this time one of these giants can consume up to 5,000 *Aedes* larvae. Reeves says that they may save resources gained from predating other larvae for later egg development, meaning that blood-feeding is unnecessary. So beneficial are these mosquitoes that they are actually being *introduced* to places outside their native range to control other species. 'Unfortunately, they're not quite the magic bullet,' Reeves says, explaining that populations never get big enough to fully control the disease spreaders; nonetheless, they can be helpful in reducing *Aedes* numbers, suggesting that this is one mosquito species we may want to keep around. Reeves nods. 'Yes, we can think of *Toxorhynchites* across the board as beneficial.'

Mosquitoes are also pollinators. Unequivocally so. In the high-resolution photographs made by his team to document mosquito diversity, Reeves says they sometimes see individuals dotted with pollen grains, and while mosquitoes lack the specialised pollen sacs or furry bellies of bees, enough pollen can stick to their bodies, including the eyes, that it makes a difference. With such large numbers of these insects, might it therefore be that mosquitoes could be important pollinators? 'We don't know a lot,' Reeves says, 'but based on the bits that we do know, I would say that is very likely.'

More surprisingly, some mosquitoes are incredibly beautiful. Please take a moment to look up the genus *Sabathes* ('the blue morphos of the mosquito world,' according to Reeves), who combine sparkling iridescence in turquoise, indigo and teal, with fantastically funky legwarmers (called 'paddles'). Think 1970s aerobics but made of feathery scales and used for elaborate courtship displays. You can imagine *Sabathes* whirring around the forests of central and South America looking absolutely fabulous, waving her paddles in the tropical sunlight. Were you to be there she would have no qualms about taking a bite, so it's best to admire from afar.

As mentioned, it's only the females that have a taste for blood; the males are entirely innocent and spend their short lives quietly buzzing between flowers, supping nectar and minding their own business. But we shouldn't even get rid of the females either, because these little insects may hold the clues to major medical advances. When a creature has been on the planet for as long as mosquitoes have, you know that they've hit upon an extraordinarily successful way of life, and by studying the secrets to their success we can benefit too.

One of those secrets is in the saliva, because those chemicals that our bodies react to so strongly have extremely potent and selective anti-clotting properties. We've known the value of naturally-derived anticoagulants for millennia – the archetypal molecule is hirudin, which comes from the medicinal leech, itself an extremely disgusting creature thanks to its legless body plan, sliminess and habit of sucking blood. Leeches have been used medicinally for bloodletting since ancient Egyptian times, and hirudin was first extracted in the 1950s, spearheading the development of more potent variants. The anticoagulants bivalirudin and desirudin are based on hirudin and extensively used today to prevent blood clots, and ongoing research is investigating the molecules produced by ticks and mosquitoes to keep blood flowing.

Rather than kill all mosquitoes, let's get to know them better. We only know a fraction of what this group has to offer right now, and as scientists like Reeves and others are discovering, there's more to mozzies than meets the eye. We also shouldn't ignore the fact that they are insects, and insects are in big trouble worldwide.

Setting out to intentionally eradicate the whole group before we know the extent of their ecosystem roles just doesn't seem smart.

★★★

In case you hadn't noticed, we're in the midst of a global insect apocalypse. For too long has scientific evidence about the serious and persistent impacts of insect decline been overlooked or blatantly ignored; governments urgently need to wake up and pay attention, because insect populations are in free fall around the world. In the back of my head, I can hear Charlie asking, 'Why should I care?' and this time it's much easier to answer. The reason he should care, in the words of leading entomologist Dave Goulson, when interviewed for the *New York Times*, is that: 'If we lose the insects, then everything is going to collapse.' Now, scientists usually shy away from making definitive statements, preferring the softer options of 'may' or 'is likely to'. But Goulson pulled no punches here. Nor did an article authored by 25 biologists in 2020 entitled, 'Scientists' warning to humanity on insect extinctions.' The fact is that without insects, there will be widespread ecosystem collapse, and that's not something that we'll be able to ignore. For as much as we might like to think that we've severed our ties with nature, we are wholly reliant on insects for our survival, end of story. And it will be the end of our story if we don't do something about it.

Insects are the most diverse group of organisms on the planet, with just over one million species known to science, but an estimated 5.5 million species in total. Of the known species, there are around 400,000 beetles, around 150,000 each of flies, butterflies and moths, and bees, wasps and ants, among others. In contrast, the total number of known vertebrate species (that's *all* fish, amphibians, reptiles, birds and mammals combined) is about 70,000. One statistic that blew my mind is that, with about 6,000 species, there are about the same number of species of ladybirds as all the mammals combined.

That's an awful lot of insects, and they perform an awful lot of important roles in our natural spaces. Most obviously, they pollinate more than 75 per cent of all our crops, which is valued at up to $577 billion per year, and is also essential for humanity's continued existence. Pollination isn't just done by honeybees, though they're the most familiar. Wild bees, including bumblebees, mining bees and solitary cavity-nesters, as well as hoverflies, butterflies, moths, wasps, beetles and flies, including those little mosquitoes, are all important parts of nature's rich pollinator web. They're also pest controllers and decomposers, as we've already touched on, and they provide food for a huge diversity of other animals, meaning that if their populations collapse, entire food webs will fail.

Study after study is showing the same alarming results – there are fewer insects in the world. A 'splatometer' analysis of insects hitting car number plates in the UK showed 50 per cent fewer splats in 2019 than 2004, while similar analysis of car windscreens in rural Denmark found an 80 per cent decline in insect splats from 1997 to 2017. A German study found a decline of 75 per cent in 27 years. In the rainforests of Puerto Rico, analysis showed that arthropod biomass decreased over a 36-year period by 98 per cent for ground-foraging species and 76 per cent for canopy-dwellers. We're losing insects and we're losing them fast. More than 40 per cent of all species are threatened with extinction.

Addressing the global decline in insect populations will necessitate coordinated actions at a national or regional level, most obviously by protecting habitats and imposing regulations on the use of broad-brush insect-killing chemicals. I'm not going to go into the murky waters of what historical evidence was swept under the carpet by governments and industry officials past, other than to say that the present crisis hasn't come out of the blue.

And yet, astonishingly, given the proportion of animal life made up by insects, they are the recipients of only 10 per cent of conservation funding. A big part of that comes down to a lack of awareness and knowledge about the group – by the public, policymakers and even scientists. It's impossible to have accurate data on long-term population change for so many species, meaning that many of them are going extinct before they've even been flagged as at risk. As of July 2025, the IUCN Red List, for example, only includes 13,442 records of insect species out of the one million species described, meaning that only around one per cent of the group has been assessed for their extinction risk. It's so much harder to conduct these studies on miniature, highly mobile, nocturnal or subterranean insects than it is for larger vertebrates, and it requires a much greater research effort – both in manpower and money. And even once flagged as being at risk, conservation is a harder sell for organisms that are not large, cute or charismatic, as we'll see in Chapter 6, but particularly so when the animals in question creep us out.

Getting over our disgust towards nature is possible, but it takes experience and an adjustment to our thought processes. Direct experience is crucial – study after study shows that exposure to the things that creep us out can reduce our negative feelings. For example, students felt less fear and disgust towards woodlice after doing hands-on work with them. Tenants living in cockroach-infested houses expressed more rational views towards the insects compared with those without a cockroach infestation. A survey of people living in Kabul, Afghanistan, found that those who raised animals or grew plants reported lower feelings of disgust towards wasps and ants, and also lower motivations to kill them. Frequent gardeners are more likely to express biophilia and perceive invertebrates as beneficial. Disgust can even be reduced towards bedbugs – students who were exposed to live animals were significantly less disgusted by them than students who only saw pictures. 'Nonetheless', Pavol Prokop tells me, 'Gaining acceptance for these organisms is undoubtedly much more challenging than for wolves.'

He's right. We're never going to find it easy to love the bloodsuckers, slime-producers or squirmy wrigglers of the world. But perhaps we can be a little more aware of the value that they provide, or could provide, if we adjusted our preconceptions. Cockroaches and mosquitoes live in tropical forests and other ecosystems that in many cases are highly threatened, yet the stigma they carry with them makes it unlikely that they'd ever muster much in the way of conservation concern. The same goes for many species of bat and toad, and countless species of fly, worm and snail. Historically, this has also been true of a group of creatures that, through their proximity to death and disease, have traditionally been thought of by the public as disgusting. But, as we'll see, these are some of the most important beasts on the planet for the work they do in clearing up the environment. Let's take a closer look at scavengers.

CHAPTER 5

Keep calm and carrion

*This disgusting bird ... its bald scarlet head formed
to wallow in putridity*
Charles Darwin, observing a turkey vulture off
the deck of the *Beagle,* January 1835

The smell hit us first. That cloying, pungent odour that is hard to place except that you know it means death. Most people would agree that it is a truly disgusting smell. Now imagine that magnified one-hundred-fold. And then imagine seeing a river full of bodies – mounds of dead wildebeest, their lifeless limbs protruding at sickeningly jaunty angles from bodies swollen with water. It's fair to say, when we hopped out of the safari vehicle, that we were completely unprepared for this. I was at the Mara River in the aftermath of the great migration, and I was consumed by a heady mix of awe and nausea.

Every year, around 1.3 million wildebeest, plus 175,000 zebra, gazelle and other large hooved mammals, embark on the great migration, one of the most iconic wildlife spectacles in the world. This epic, 1,200-mile journey takes the form of a colossal loop, the animals moving from Tanzania's Serengeti National Park up into Kenya's Masai Mara National Park for the dry season, and then sweeping back down to the Serengeti for the rainy season, where they give birth. It is a breathtaking, chaotic impossibility of movement on a mind-boggling scale, appropriately labelled as one of the Seven Wonders of the Natural World. I've never seen it in person, but I've watched enough nature documentaries to be blown away by the seemingly unending caravan of animals, each one willed on to cross rivers and deserts, driven by primal urges for greener pastures and fresh water.

To complete the loop, the animals must cross the Mara River, and the image of these wildebeest stampeding across crocodile-infested waters, trampling each other in their panic to reach the other side, is probably a familiar one. What the documentaries typically don't show in much detail is what comes next. The crossing claims the lives of several thousand wildebeest each year, which is just 0.5 per cent of the total herd size, but in absolute terms it's a scene of carnage.

And yet, while death stretched in every direction, the river was by no means dead. Everything is connected and as one creature falls, so a community of others get a leg up in their quest for survival. White-backed, Rüppell's and hooded vultures were perched on rocks or on the bodies, some with their heads already hidden inside a carcass. Nile crocodiles were motionless in the water, likely digesting the flesh they had already stripped from below for this, their one big feeding event of the year. And then there were the marabou storks. Oh my. In a scene more reminiscent of a gory horror film, one of these storks, which are also known as the 'undertaker birds' (for their hunched stance, long skinny legs, and neatly folded big black wings), stood still and silent on top of a wildebeest, holding about a metre of taut rope in its enormous, dagger-like beak. Or that's what it looked like. With a collective, disgusted groan, we realised that the rope was coming from inside the carcass, and it was not rope at all but the end of the wildebeest's intestines. The image of that bird perched there, its scrotum-like throat pouch huge and pendulous, tugging out guts, has been seared into my memory.

We all know about the circle of life. But historically, little attention was paid to the stage of the circle that involved the breakdown of carrion, being termed an 'academic backwater' until recently. As we heard in the last chapter, contact with death is a prime elicitor of disgust, and some, such as raptor expert Keith Bildstein, have suggested that the lack of research interest in carcass degradation 'has much to do with humanity's long-standing aversion to the dead.'

In fact, it's an incredibly important component of all ecosystems, because as carcasses break down, they release organic material back into the environment, enriching it with nutrients that support new life. This organic material is termed biomass, when we use it as fuel. That word has a second, ecologically based definition, which is the collective mass of all organisms that are living at any given moment – that's all the plants, animals and fungi, plus bacteria, viruses, parasites, algae and all other microorganisms making up the kingdoms of life. Biomass is usually measured as the amount of carbon available in a particular organism, and the total biomass of planet Earth has been estimated at 550 gigatonnes (gT) of carbon. This is distributed unequally between the kingdoms, with plants accounting for the vast majority (450gT), followed by bacteria (70gT) and fungi (12gT). Animals only account for 2gT of carbon. Which doesn't sound like a lot, until you remember that 'giga' means one billion of that unit of measurement, and one billion is one thousand million. So 2gT is two thousand million tonnes, or more than 400 million African elephants. Given that most animal life on this planet comprises lightweight insects, not heavyweight elephants, that is a lot. Then let your mind be blown by the idea of multiplying that 225 times to cover the mass of plants. That's 90 billion African elephants. These are incomprehensibly large numbers, and they translate into an enormous amount of organic matter being cycled between the living and the dead. We tend to think only about the miracle of life but for this to work, death is just as important.

Carcasses don't break down of their own accord – this stage of life's cycle relies on other organisms, specialists that help to speed up the process of decomposition and return nutrients to the environment. The gruesome scene at the Mara River provided us with a snapshot of this process, for from the moment that a wildebeest drowned, a complex chain of interactions was set off, involving a diverse community of living organisms: scavengers. These are the life forms, like the obvious crocodiles, vultures and marabou storks, as well as unseen fish, carrion beetles, fly larvae and more, who mechanically and chemically break down bones and soft tissues until the nutrients within are released to the environment. And they're vital. No organism, plant or animal, can create all the elements that it needs for life. That means that constant recycling of nutrients is an essential process for healthy ecosystems. And while organic matter breaks down eventually, it needs a helping hand to keep the elements moving through the system smoothly. Like enzymes in our bodies, working to speed up chemical reactions, scavengers speed up decomposition, keeping the building blocks of life freely moving and available.

It has been estimated that wildebeest mass drownings contribute more than 1,000 tonnes of organic material to the Mara River each year. The carcasses persist for around 28 days before they're no longer visible, and during this time they release massive quantities of dissolved nutrients – the equivalent of ten blue whale carcasses entering the river each year.

And yet, despite the crucial recycling of nutrients that was going on before our very eyes, we couldn't help but feel collectively sickened by the guts and gore. Scavengers present as a formidable bunch, and have mixed reputations across cultures. From vultures, whose stomach acid is on a par with battery acid, to hyenas, whose jaw strength can literally crush bones, and of course the carrion fly maggots we heard about in the last chapter, these are not beasts that the public tend to love. Their intimate association with death and disease makes them 'creepy', 'ugly', or 'revolting'. What's less appreciated is that nature's clean-up crew perform one of the most vital roles on the planet: without them, we'd live in a world of putridity and pestilence. They may not be the most graceful of creatures, nor the most delicate of eaters, but what scavengers do is critical to the continuation of life. And they're in desperate need of a PR overhaul.

★★★

It's one of those crisp, bright spring mornings, where the countryside is bursting into vibrant shades of the freshest green and the sun's rays are starting to emit a radiant warmth. I'm driving up a narrow country lane, praying that nobody is driving the other way and keeping mental track of suitable passing spots. Off to my left are phenomenal views across the valley. It's a perfect start for an eagerly anticipated trip – I'm off to meet some vultures.

I'm not in Africa, Asia, the Americas or the Middle East. None of the usual places that you might expect to see these birds. In fact, rural Wales might rank as one of the least likely places to see vultures. And yet, some 30 years ago, if you lived in these Carmarthenshire hills, you'd have gotten used to the sight of the birds soaring overhead. After vulture enthusiast Manfred Horstmann moved his private collection here in the early 1980s, griffon vultures were free flown around the Welsh valleys, often visiting the local pubs where signs would ask patrons not to feed them.

I've come here because I want to get a sense of what these birds are like. Because, Mara River aside, my experience of vultures is limited to seeing other African species hunched in trees or squabbling over a carcass, or turkey and black vultures soaring above the California hills. And those stereotypical images of the birds provide little insight into their true natures. I needed to get close to a vulture, and for that I needed both a captive collection and some willing vulture experts. I needed to go to Wales.

The Horstmann Vulture Conservation Trust was founded in 2020 to continue the work of the late Horstmann and his partner, Brett Sloman. It's the UK's only charity dedicated to the captive breeding and release of vultures. Adam Bloch, the Trust's chief executive, and Holly Cale, curator and head of research and aviculture, are waiting for me as I pull up, and the tour begins straight away. It's one of the most bizarre and enjoyable research trips I've ever done. Bizarre, because the Trust's site is some 44 hectares of manicured gardens and parkland, with giant rhododendron bushes and ornamental bridges spanning streams, the sort of estate that you'd more likely associate with a country house than a vulture charity. And yet, dotted around the lawns are giant aviaries filled with vultures, including some of the largest-known captive populations of hooded vultures and Egyptian vultures in the world.

The Trust's work is pure vulture conservation. It's not open to the public, meaning that while they miss a potential income stream, they can be laser-focused on their mission: building sustainable, genetically diverse and consistently breeding collections of vultures, with the ultimate aim of supporting wild populations. They have 61 birds from eight different species, but have a particular focus on hooded vultures, Egyptian vultures, bearded vultures and Andean condors.

The first three belong to the family Accipitridae, a group that includes the more familiar birds of prey (including eagles, kites and hawks) as well as 16 species of vulture. These are found across Africa, Asia and Europe and are commonly called Old World vultures. The group is further divided into two distinct subfamilies: Gypaetinae (palm-nut, Egyptian and bearded vultures) and Aegypiinae (including the griffon vultures and all other Asian and African species). Andean condors, on the other hand, belong to the family Cathartidae,[25] the New World vultures, a group of seven vulture and condor species found in the Americas and Caribbean. While the two families appear very similar anatomically, physiologically and behaviourally, they independently evolved to be full-time scavengers, providing a striking example of convergent evolution.

Of the Trust's four focal species, hooded vultures have the most precarious future: they are listed as Critically Endangered on the IUCN's Red List, which is one step from being extinct in the wild. Egyptian vultures are listed as Endangered, while bearded vultures and Andean condors are Near Threatened. That's a reasonable representation of the group's conservation status as a whole – only seven of the world's twenty-three vulture species are free from conservation concern, while nine, or 40 per cent of the whole group, are Critically Endangered.

We'll come back to the many threats facing vultures worldwide, but first, we need to get to know the birds, and that starts with their appearance. Think of a vulture and you'll probably imagine a large, black-feathered, bald-faced bird, perhaps hunched in a tree and silhouetted against a moody sky. And while this does sum up many species, may I direct

---

[25] The genus name *Cathartes* was named after the Greek *kathartes*, meaning a cleanser or purifier, and subsequently adapted to become the family name, Cathartidae.

you to the wonderfully jazzy king vulture, a South American species that fully rebelled against the drab uniform. The only black on this bird is its tail and wing tips; it has white body feathers, a grey scarf, a bare head and neck resplendent in shades of orange, purple, green and yellow, and it's all topped off with a fleshy orange wattle called a 'caruncle' bulging from the top of its beak. The king vulture makes a compelling case that vultures do not need to be sombre.

Even the more monochrome birds have a lot more going on, appearance-wise, than we might initially think. Hooded vultures ('hoodies'), for example, may at first glimpse look like boring, bare-faced, brown birds, but take a closer look. Soft, cream little feathers stretch up the back and sides of their neck, and extend over their heads almost to their eyes, like a little judge's wig. Up close, they have pretty blue eyelids and their faces and necks flush pink when they're excited, as they are when Holly and I go in with a bucket of food. They share an aviary with Cape griffon vultures, whose 2m wingspan makes them one of Africa's largest species. These magnificent birds are cloaked in cool tones of dove grey, white and tawny brown, and their featherless faces are a striking steely blue; combined with their commanding stare and huge, curved beak they have a real air of authority. They certainly have the upper hand over the hoodies, chasing them away from the food at every opportunity. Watching these birds squabbling over food you get a sense of the interactions taking place on the African savannah, and in the wild the intermediate-sized white-backed vulture would also be in the ruckus.

Different vultures have evolved to fill different niches, although all are what's known as 'obligate' scavengers, meaning that eating carrion is not a choice but a necessity. That's in contrast to part-time, or 'facultative' scavengers, like hyenas, crocodiles, crows or any other opportunist that will eat fresh carrion but does not rely on it. Vultures are the only obligate scavengers that live on land, and within that niche each species has its role at a carcass. Holly points to Linton, one of the juvenile hoodies who is hovering nearby, unsure about coming closer to snatch a snack. 'The hoodies have a proportionally thinner, more slender beak than the Cape griffons because they're typically stripping the smaller, sinewy bits – they get what's left once the big boys have been in and scoffed as much juicy stuff as they can.'

We move on to the really big boys. Or girls, actually, as they're all females. Pookie, Paisley and Real (pronounced ray-AL) are the Trust's imprinted Andean condors (meaning they were raised by humans), and Adam's favourites. These behemoths weigh up to 15kg and have wingspans of up to 3.5m, among the largest of any living bird. Real is a glossy black-and-white adult, with a collar of thick, soft, fur-like white feathers and a bald, pinkish grey head. Pookie and Paisley are younger, and their plumage is more brownish grey. All of them are curious, playful, fascinating birds, who also happen to sport a serious piece of weaponry on the front of their faces. If they were male, they'd also have a fetching wattle at their throat and a large caruncle on their forehead, used to charm the females.

That powerful beak is used to rip open the thick hides of animals like guanaco, a relative of the llama that will have historically formed a major component of their diet. Smaller vultures are unable to tear through the guanaco's tough skin, so the condors play an important role – like a battering ram, they can break inside and that allows the smaller players access too. It comes down to their size and strength, but also to unique adaptations, like a bizarre, ridged yellow tongue that helps them to pull food into their mouths. Adam tells me that no other vultures have the prehensile quality to the tongue and that it helps them to eat things fast, but that sometimes 'they pull the food in so quickly that it starts coming out of their nose.' Like their Old World brethren, they are demonstrably quick at stripping bare a carcass, as Charles Darwin observed while exploring South America as part of the voyage of the *Beagle*. In April 1834, he recorded the following in his diary:

> The Captains servant shot two Guanaco: Before the men could arrive to carry them to the boats the Condors & some small carrion Vultures had picked even the bones of one clean & white, & this in about four hours. — The Guanaco probably weighed 170 or 180 pounds. — When the men arrived, only two Condors were there & some small Vultures within the ribs were picking the bones.

They also use that beak for exploring things, and they are extremely inquisitive. Textured objects are particularly interesting for them, especially those crinkly, rattly, sparkly toys for infants. This exploratory tendency isn't limited to hand-reared birds either. In May 2021, a group of 15–20 of their Critically Endangered smaller relatives, California condors, descended on a house in Tehachapi, at the southern tip of the Sierra Nevada mountain range. Congregating on the deck and roof, they explored (and therefore destroyed) pretty much everything they could: potted plants, a screen door, a spa cover, ornaments, furniture, even the fence. Oh, and they pooped all over the deck too. They basically had a condor party on this woman's deck and then left her with the bill. According to the Fish and Wildlife Service, who responded to tweets about it at the time, the house was in 'historical condor habitat where natural food sources occur … unfortunately they sometimes perceive houses and decks as suitable perch locations.' They recommended 'hazing' the birds with non-harmful things like spraying water, but the condors were unbothered and stayed for more than a week.

Real would only tolerate Adam's presence in her aviary, but later that day I got to see the full extent of her wings when my loitering outside prompted an extremely impressive display: stretching her wings out wide, she slowly turned on the spot and started chugging like a train. I've never seen anything like it. Adam later told me that it's a courtship display that imprints use as a way of getting attention, 'sort of like children learning to swear when they don't know the meaning.' He thought for a moment and then elaborated: 'In their case, the meaning is, "I want attention. This gets me attention, so I do it."' Whatever the reason, Real's wingspan blew me away – her primary feathers were the length of my arm. Indeed, wild Andean condors are hunted for these feathers, which are used in traditional South American ceremonies and are considered to have spiritual significance. And they also hold the key to why vultures are so successful at scavenging.

Vulture wings are fantastically adapted for soaring and gliding flight, and this helps the birds to locate food in two ways. First, giant wings allow the birds to ride thermals high enough to scan the landscape for carrion or other vultures, which may indicate the presence of carrion. Sometimes they can get really high, like the Rüppell's griffon vulture who, in 1973, collided with a commercial aircraft at 37,000 feet over the Ivory Coast. Second, because soaring is so efficient, the birds can glide for long distances at little energetic cost. Himalayan griffon vultures, for example, fly around 85km each day, and rack up an annual cumulative flight distance of approximately 30,000km.

For Real and other Andean condors, who have evolved to soar over the high Andes and adjacent coastal regions, their main issue is that they're almost too large to get off the ground.[26] They spend more than 75 per cent of their total

---

[26] Male kori bustards are the only living birds that can fly at heavier weights, with big males reaching 18kg or more. Yet all of these pale in comparison to the ancient vultures, the teratorns (aka 'monster birds'), that roamed the skies between 25 million and 12,000 years ago. The largest of them was the predatory behemoth *Argentavis magnificans*, the heaviest-ever flying bird, with an estimated weight of 72kg and a wingspan of 7m. *A. magnificans* could not have flapped its way into the air. Instead, it must have used slopes and headwinds to launch itself, much like a modern hang glider.

flapping time achieving this, but once they're airborne and have found a thermal, all they need to do is glide. In one study, a young condor soared on thermals for five hours without flapping, gliding for more than 100 miles with virtually no effort. For a creature that doesn't know when it will find its next meal, this is an extremely useful skill.

When it comes to sensory tools, vultures have exceptional visual acuity, especially in the large Old World species that soar at the highest altitudes: the measured acuity of the Indian vulture, Egyptian vulture and griffon vulture approach that of the standout bird, the wedge-tailed eagle. New World vultures of the genus *Cathartes* have much lower values, and that fits with their ecology. They forage a bit closer to the ground, and make use of another powerful tool to locate food: their outstanding sense of smell.

The olfactory bulb of the turkey vulture is the biggest of any bird studied. This part of the brain manages our sense of smell – it is responsible for interpreting signals from olfactory receptors in the nose and relaying that information to other brain regions. The turkey vulture uses this fantastic sense to detect chemicals, such as ethyl mercaptan, that are released from decomposing carcasses. Indeed, it was this chemical that outright proved the superiority of turkey vultures' olfaction, thanks to clever work by American ornithologist Kenneth Stager in the 1960s. Along with carefully controlled experiments, Stager learned that oil company engineers used turkey vultures to locate gas leaks. They had spotted groups of the birds congregating at spots along a 42-mile leaky pipeline and realised that the birds weren't detecting the gas itself (which is odourless), but the organosulphur compound, ethyl mercaptan, that is added to the gas for human detection.

The other set of adaptations that equip vultures so well for the obligate scavenging lifestyle is their physiological armour. That's essential, because the moment that an animal dies, enzymes begin digesting cells and the flesh starts to decay. It's because of these enzymes that your dry-aged steak is better than a freshly cut piece – by starting to break down proteins in the meat, amino acids are released, together with chemicals from the oxidation of fatty acids. All of this makes for a more flavourful and tender piece of meat. And outside the controlled, refrigerated conditions in beef production, it's not just enzymes that get to work. No longer kept in check by the immune system, the invisible microorganisms that comprise the animal's microbiome start to multiply. These are the decomposers, the other group of essential organisms that break down organic material and recycle the building blocks of life, and they've evolved their own strategies for monopolising carrion. To deter competitors, microbes engage in chemical warfare, producing unpleasant and potentially dangerous toxins, including botulism, anthrax, and tetanus. All of these could easily kill us. We mitigate the risks by keeping food cold enough that the microorganisms cannot grow, or by preserving meat in particular substances that also prevent pathogenic growth. But out in the African savannah or Utah desert, things happen a lot faster.

Add to this the fact that many animals die from disease, and you can see how scavengers are at high risk for infection. But vultures shrug off such concerns. Their constitutions are so tough that they show no ill effects of consuming even the rottenest of meat, and while they much prefer fresh carcasses, those that are a little riper can also be a bit easier to get into. And on that topic, the way that vultures typically get inside carcasses isn't the most hygienic either, because to avoid tackling the tough hide that is typical of large mammals, they readily take advantage of natural orifices, particularly the anus. For the vultures, it's 'in for a penny, in for a pound' – carrion is carrion, and they can handle it all.

Clearly, vultures don't have our well-developed sense of disgust. They don't need to, and in any case, life as an easily disgusted obligate scavenger would be extremely confusing. These are animals whose gizzard walls can handle fragments of bone, and whose stomach acid is corrosive enough to eliminate almost all toxins. This reaches extremes in the bearded vulture (which you may know as the 'lammergeier', thanks to its historic, unfounded, reputation for predating lambs), whose diet is typically 85–90 per cent bones. It's the bearded vulture that was said to have killed the ancient Greek playwright Aeschylus, when it mistook his bald head for a rock and dropped a tortoise on it. Whether or not that's true, these birds do drop large bones onto rocks to break them into more manageable pieces. And with such incredibly powerful stomach acid, these birds can monopolise a source of food that few others would consider.

Vulture physiology sits at the heart of their importance to ecosystem health. They're essentially a super-fine environmental filter, trapping and eliminating almost all pathogens. And they're extremely good at what they do. In the Serengeti, vultures are estimated to consume more meat than all mammalian carnivores combined. So effective and efficient are they that a group of vultures (aptly termed a 'wake') can reduce an adult cow carcass to bare bones in 40 minutes, and I mean bare bones. Nothing is left to rot and contaminate the surroundings and, as we heard, the vulture's gut is an environmental dead-end for most pathogens. Their bare faces reduce the risk of feathers being clogged by rotting flesh, and once they've finished stomping around in the gore, New World vultures often do something called urohidrosis – they poo on their own legs and feet. That doesn't sound like it should be contributing to good hygiene, but with a high concentration of uric acid, the poo helps to kill any lingering pathogens. Unlike the cockroach, vultures at least go to the trouble of cleaning their feet.

★★★

Our early ancestors will have recognised vultures' carcass-detecting potential from the moment that they started incorporating meat into their diet, sometime around three million years ago. A substantial portion of these early humans' dietary meat would have been gained through scavenging, and this may have enabled them to migrate out of Africa and into southern Europe, some 1.4 million years ago. It may have also promoted the evolution of enhanced cooperation and communication, since stealing carcasses from the giant hyenas and sabre-toothed cats that dominated Eurasian landscapes would have necessitated working together. Since these early people lived alongside vultures and meat-eating mammals, their relationship would have been competitive – all wanted the lion's share of any fallen prey. But there were benefits to living alongside these beasts, too. For watchful observers, the presence and behaviour of vultures was also an information source, their presence revealing the likely location of food.

Today, land-based scavengers such as hyenas and lions will often use vulture activity to locate carrion, but even with this eavesdropping they'll never get there first, so the birds normally get their pick of the spoils. Once study found that vultures in the Serengeti stripped bare 84 per cent of carcasses that researchers had put out before the mammals arrived. This is why there are no land-based obligate scavengers – they'll never rival the balance vultures have struck between speed and energy efficiency.

Just a few thousand years ago, scavengers became part of human cultures, taken to represent spiritual and religious values and, in turn, worshipped. The Egyptian vulture (aka 'Pharaoh's chicken'), for example, is prominent in ancient mythology. Nekhbet, the Egyptian goddess, was portrayed as a vulture or a woman with a vulture's head, often with outstretched wings. She was worshipped as the guardian of Upper Egypt, her vulture form symbolising her protective nature and her ability to soar above, surveying the land. Around the same time in the Americas, Andean condors started to appear in Andean art, where they were associated with the sun and portrayed as rulers of the sky. For the Incas, condors represented the Jananpacha, the upper world, and the birds were considered divine messengers. They are still spiritually important in South America, symbolising strength, power, nobility and freedom, and have been immortalised as national symbols of Bolivia, Chile, Colombia and Ecuador. They're also used in Peru's Yawar Fiesta (blood festival) to celebrate the liberation of the Incas from Spanish rule. The condors represent the Incas, and the bull the conquistadors, which sounds like it should be good for the birds, but the reality is that the bird's feet are sewn to the bull's back and the two animals are then goaded into fighting each other. The audience wants the condor to win, and if anything happens to the bird it is taken as a bad omen. But Adam tells me that about 25 per cent of the condors die either during the fight or later from injury. 'And in the old days, there's probably one or two of these festivals, and now there's dozens of them and they're catching lots of birds for each one.' He pauses, and then adds, 'But I don't know any other bird that you can tie to a bull, fight the bull, and have any survive. They are that tough.'

Sadly, the traits that make vultures so fantastically adapted for carrion removal, and which have been celebrated in some cultures, are leading to their downfall. As we heard in Chapter 2, in their quest to find food, apex predators are increasingly coming into conflict with farmers and local people, who retaliate against livestock attacks by leaving out poisoned baits. Since vultures are much quicker at finding carcasses than large carnivores, they are feeling the effects of the retribution. They're deliberately targeted, too. Even though condors are revered in the Andean countries, their speed at finding stillborn calves or livestock that died of other causes means they are often blamed as the killer, and farmers hit back in the same way. The effects can be devastating. In 2018, for example, a single sheep carcass laced with the pesticide carbofuran killed 34 Andean condors in

Argentina. Carbofuran is a neurotoxic chemical, interfering with nerves' ability to communicate – poisoning leads to convulsions, system failure and an excruciating death.

Pesticide poisoning is the leading threat for Andean condors today, and while the IUCN currently 'only' classes them as Vulnerable to extinction, conservationists are putting measures in place now. These birds fall into the class of animals that take a 'quality not quantity' approach to their offspring. They don't reach sexual maturity until they're about five or six years old (although first chicks have been reported in parents as old as 11 years), and when they do breed, they only lay a single egg every two to three years. Both parents feed and look after the chick for about six months until it fledges, and then both continue to feed it for several months after that. All of this means that the species is extremely vulnerable to mass mortality events – 34 poisoned birds don't get replaced quickly, and when that's scaled up to reflect the true extent of deliberate poisoning events across South America, together with the other threats of habitat loss, indirect poisoning from lead shot, and collisions with power lines, you can see why conservationists are worried. Establishing a stable breeding programme now is important, before it's too late.

Of the other New World vultures, five of the seven species are listed as Least Concern by the IUCN, while the California condor is Critically Endangered. Things are far worse on the African continent, where populations have been declining since the 1970s. Today, seven out of eleven African vulture species are threatened with extinction, and some species have seen their populations decline by up to 97 per cent in the last 50 years. Here, too, poisoning is the major threat: an analysis published in 2016 showed that 61 per cent of nearly 8,000 vulture deaths recorded across Africa were attributed to it, while 29 per cent were attributed to trade for belief-based use.

As with the condors, poisoning is both a direct and indirect threat. In Kenya, for example, most vulture poisonings are indirect, stemming from the frustrations of farmers and pastoralists who are losing animals to lions, leopards and hyenas. Although there are compensation schemes for those who lose livestock, bureaucracy and delays mean that poisoning is often the easier option. Poisoned carcasses are also being left out intentionally to kill vultures, because the birds are unwittingly acting as snitches on criminal gangs. When poachers kill an elephant, it takes them time to remove the tusks (which are actually massive teeth, deeply rooted in the skull). It could take more than an hour to do this, and since vultures can locate an elephant carcass within 30 minutes of its death, groups of the birds can act as a useful alert for anti-poaching units, providing a brief window in which they may be able to locate and apprehend the criminals. That's great for conservationists but not for criminal gangs, and they've turned to poison to eliminate the birds, hoping to reduce their numbers for future poaching events. Since vultures are attracted to the presence of other vultures, a single carcass can kill tens or even hundreds of birds, and depressingly there are numerous examples. In South Africa's Kruger National Park in 2024, 86 vultures were killed by a buffalo carcass laced with the insecticide aldicarb; in Zimbabwe in 2012, a single poached elephant carcass was found surrounded by the bodies of 191 poisoned vultures; and just outside Botswana's Chobe National Park in 2019, three poisoned elephant carcasses were found surrounded by 537 dead vultures – most of them Critically Endangered white-backed vultures. Many more examples exist.

While vultures' phenomenal food-finding abilities are deemed a nuisance by poachers, in other parts of Africa those very same qualities are celebrated. But that has created a whole other problem: the harvesting of body parts for belief-based use. As Adam explains, 'People think that vultures can see into the future. So, the thought is that if you smoke the brain of a vulture, you'll be able to foretell the future too.'

This belief in vulture foresight has created a lucrative trade in vulture parts for traditional medicine (for curing everything from bad eyesight to infertility, leprosy and cancer) and charm-oriented mystical beliefs (for example to bring good luck, political success or protection against witchcraft and evil spirits). Many birds are decapitated and the heads sold at markets, although numerous other body parts are used, particularly in Nigeria and other West African countries.

'The belief in the mystical powers of vulture and other wild flora and fauna is as old as time in Nigeria and other parts of the world.' This is Stella Egbe, senior conservation manager with the Nigerian Conservation Foundation (NCF), writing to me from Lagos. She explains that the trade in vultures and vulture parts is an economic pursuit that spans generations and is traditionally passed down from parents to the children. It's certainly a good income stream for people who may have few alternatives. In Nigeria, the price for a whole vulture in 2002 was around $1 to $1.50. In 2020, a carcass was fetching $92 – close to a 100-fold increase. In Ghana, whole vulture carcasses may reach $140 and vulture eggs may be sold for up to $127. It's a lucrative business all round, as local communities will pay large amounts for traditional treatments – in some cases more than they would for western medicine.

Demand for vulture parts has led to horrifically large mass mortality events, including the world's largest vulture poisoning to date, in which more than 2,000 hoodies were poisoned in Guinea-Bissau in 2020. As the historically most abundant species, hoodies have been the most frequently targeted: in one survey of medicine traders in Nigeria, 90 per cent of all vulture parts came from this species. But as numbers of previously common hoodies, white-backed vultures and others crash, other species will start to feel the heat. The enigmatic little palm nut vulture may be one of them, as Holly explains while we're feeding Neville, one of the Trust's residents. 'I think they're going to be overlooked.

Right now they're Least Concern but what's happening in Nigeria is that as it becomes harder to find the other vulture species, you're getting more palm nut vultures at the markets. There has been a very shocking shift. I suspect we'll spend a bit of time not really noticing because they're not being monitored, and then suddenly the world's going to go, "Oh shit, they're endangered too."' Neville glares at us with his yellow eyes; it feels almost accusatory.

The state of vultures in Nigeria is 'dire', Egbe says. But the NCF is on it, and a key goal is reducing the trade in vulture parts. They have partnered with the conservation charity BirdLife International, on an initiative to engage local faith-based healers and encourage the replacement of vulture parts with plant-based alternatives. 'Since 2019, the NCF/BirdLife has engaged more than 100 traditional medicine practitioners across the country,' Egbe writes. She explains that demand for traditional medicine is highest in the south-west and northern parts of country, so engagement efforts have been focused there, with a particular aim to engage the leadership of the state or regional traditional medicine organisations. Meetings are run by conservation officers, involving these local leaders sharing their experience as practitioners of using plant-based alternatives. She sends me the booklet that is used and distributed, which was produced by the NCF in 2022 in collaboration with practitioners of traditional medicine and herbal medicine. It sets out the case for protecting vultures and distills the knowledge gained over preceding years of workshops and discussions with the traditional medicine community. The summary of medicines for which vultures or vulture parts have traditionally been important is an eye-opener, covering everything from 'get rich quick' medicine to medicines for clairvoyant powers, job promotion, improved business success, insurance against spiritual attacks, memory stimulants, protection against madness, cure of epilepsy, headaches, rheumatism, bed wetting and diabetes. The authors note that the vulture head was traditionally the most culturally important body part for treating human ailments and to support business success, the feathers were in demand for several traditional medicines, while the intestines were used to treat many kinds of infectious disease. Numerous alternative medicines are presented, including the updated, vulture-free recipes and a description of the process. In other words, and importantly, the initiative is not about disparaging or shutting down traditional healing; rather, they hope to nudge practitioners towards plant-based alternatives that, the authors note, perform similar functions to vulture parts.

It's a drop in the ocean right now, but the hope is that as the educational information cascades, use of plant-based solutions will start to replace the use of vulture parts. BirdLife International reported in 2022 that fewer than 50 percent of the traditional healers in Nigeria were using vulture parts, down from more than 95 per cent in 2019. Egbe writes that there are other factors at play in West Africa's vulture decline, including habitat loss and electrocution from powerlines; nonetheless, she says she is 'optimistic about the work we are doing', noting that there are still sites with viable populations that are potential sources of vulture stock for habitats currently under restoration. Most importantly, she adds, 'awareness is increasing, and people are more aware of the importance of vultures in the wider ecosystem.'

Back at the Horstmann Trust, I'm watching Holly feeding and weighing two hoodie chicks and I can't help but feel a pang of sadness. These bug-eyed little babies, at the time of my visit in May 2024, represented 40 per cent of the captive hoodie chicks in the world.[27] They're so precious, and the amount of effort that's going into making sure they grow up strong and healthy is phenomenal. Ultimately, the aim of the

---

[27] Sadly, after my visit I heard from Holly that one of the chicks had died from an infection.

Trust's work is to release birds back into the wild but, as Adam says, right now that's not an option – there is no point in sending these birds into the world until the world has changed. It would be sending them to their early deaths.

The situation in Africa is shocking, but it has not yet reached the severity of what happened in Asia in the mid-1990s. It is, however, much more complex and multifactorial. The Asian vulture crisis was driven by one simple thing – a cheap veterinary drug called diclofenac.

★★★

In the 1980s, tens of millions of vultures could be found across India (40 million white-rumped and slender-billed vultures alone). But during the 1990s, vulture numbers went into free fall and by 2000 the situation was so bad that the IUCN reclassified the white-rumped, slender-billed and Indian vultures as Critically Endangered. By 2007, numbers of slender-billed and Indian vultures had crashed by at least 97 per cent, and the white-rumped vulture by 99.99 per cent. It was the fastest decline of any bird species in recorded history and the largest since the extinction of the passenger pigeon.

Vibhu Prakash, principal scientist with the Bombay Natural History Society, was the first to document the vulture decline, through his survey of nests in Rajasthan's Keoladeo National Park. In 1988, there were 353 nesting pairs in the park; by 1996 this number had halved and by 2000 there wasn't a single vulture remaining. Prakash and others were baffled. Food shortage couldn't account for it: India is home to an estimated 500 million livestock, and plenty of carcasses could be seen across the birds' ranges. Disease seemed more likely: the birds were being spotted sitting in trees with drooping necks for days and weeks before they collapsed and died.

Post-mortems of dead birds found no evidence for pesticides, herbicides or heavy metals, but many of the birds did have gout, a build-up of uric acid that manifested as a white paste coating their internal organs. They seemed to be dying from kidney failure, but it wasn't until 2004 when researchers identified the cause – a non-steroidal anti-inflammatory drug (NSAID) called diclofenac, marketed as a human pain killer since 1973, had entered India's veterinary market in 1994. No longer under patent, diclofenac was cheap, easily administered, and a lifeline for rural communities to relieve pain and sickness in their livestock. Cattle are revered as sacred animals in Hinduism, meaning that the slaughter of old or sick animals is prohibited in many regions. A cheap veterinary drug that kept those cattle moving and working was therefore extremely valuable. People had no idea that by protecting their cattle they were killing vultures too.

Given the toughness of vulture constitutions and the fact that they can happily eat meat infused with anthrax and other deadly toxins, it's surprising that the chink in the vultures' armour was a common NSAID; ironically, one that became a standard treatment for gout-associated pain and inflammation in humans. Diclofenac is, essentially, a more potent form of ibuprofen, and harmless to us at therapeutic levels. But for vultures, it's a deadly poison, causing the kidneys to stop removing uric acid from the blood, which leads to rapid gout and death. For some reason, which is still not fully understood, vultures are so sensitive to diclofenac that the lethal dose is about one-tenth of the therapeutic dose for mammals by weight. Mathematical modelling estimated that a diclofenac concentration of just 0.8 per cent in a carcass would be enough to kill a vulture, and analyses by Prakash and team found that average concentrations were more like 11 per cent.

India, Nepal and Pakistan announced a ban on diclofenac in 2006, and Bangladesh followed suit in 2010. Since the ban, the decline in vulture populations continues in India, albeit not at the catastrophic levels of the early 2000s, and we're far from seeing any signs of recovery. Populations are a fraction of what they once were: 0.002 per cent of the 1992 level for white-rumped vulture, and 0.02 per cent of the 1992 level for Indian vulture and slender-billed vulture combined. There's better news in Nepal, where populations of white-rumped and slender-billed vultures have risen sharply since 2013. It's likely that this reflects national differences in the availability of diclofenac and other harmful NSAIDs. While diclofenac is banned in India, undercover surveys of pharmacies found that in certain states its illegal use remains high, and in others, diclofenac was simply replaced by other, similarly harmful, NSAIDs: nimesulide, ketoprofen and aceclofenac. The latter two were banned in 2023, but while some states are getting tough on the problem, there's clearly more to be done to safeguard the future of India's vultures. In Nepal, in contrast, diclofenac and other harmful NSAIDs have virtually disappeared from pharmacies, replaced by vulture-safe meloxicam, and this, combined with a greater effort to establish vulture-safe zones and vulture 'restaurants', has helped the birds to recover.

Diclofenac isn't an exclusively Asian problem. It's marketed in five European countries and was actually *approved* for administration in two different veterinary drugs in Spain in 2013, a decade after its role in the Asian vulture crisis came to light. Given that Spain is home to 90 per cent of Europe's four vulture species, including the globally Endangered Egyptian vulture, it's difficult to understand how these drugs came to be approved, and many conservationists, members of the public and politicians expressed strong concerns to the European Commission following the decision. As Stefan Oppel, conservation scientist at the Swiss Ornithological Institute, who led a successful project to arrest the decline of Egyptian vultures, which he describes as 'a somewhat privileged species in that very few (if any) people actually hate them', writes to me: 'Diclofenac is a known toxic substance for vultures, and permitting its veterinary use in areas where wild vultures live and can potentially consume livestock remains ... is a huge and unnecessary risk.'

The European Medicines Agency (EMA) has confirmed that risks are not unfounded, concluding a report into the medicine's approval with the clear statement: 'Diclofenac use in animals poses a risk to European vultures.' However, it proposed that the drug should be regulated, not banned. Since 2013, sales of diclofenac in the EU have tripled and one analysis found that its annual use in Spanish livestock continues to increase. And, while there's a prevalent attitude that European systems for managing livestock should be effective at preventing diclofenac from entering the vulture food chain, it has not been fully contained within livestock, and dead vultures with gout and traces of NSAIDs in their system have been discovered. Oppel notes that so far there's no suggestion of a repeat of the south Asian crisis. 'But that is no reason to be complacent about the issue and permit the use of a toxic drug in my opinion.'

Egyptian vultures are declining in almost every part of their range, which stretches from southern Europe through the Middle East to India, and south to Tanzania in Africa. The decline is greatest in India, unsurprisingly, as populations haven't recovered, and in Africa may be more than 90 per cent in some parts. Europe should be a stronghold, with a decline of 'only' 10 per cent over three generations, but in Spain, which with around 1,300 pairs may support as much as 40 per cent of the European breeding population, the number of territories declined by at least 25 per cent between 1987 and 2000. Authorising the use of a drug that is known to kill these birds, when vulture-safe alternatives exist, doesn't send a great message about the perceived value of these birds.

The thing about protecting vultures is that it's not just a 'nice to have'. These are animals that natural selection has fine-tuned to be scavenging superstars: no other animal comes close to doing what they do as well as they do it. When we lose the vultures, we lose a vital player in the functioning of the environment. And the outcomes are being felt.

★★★

The dawn of farming 12,000 years ago signalled a new, mutualistic role for vultures – as hygienic waste disposal agents for livestock carcasses and, also starting during this time, human carcasses too. As such, vultures likely helped to reduce the spread of disease to both humans and animals; a service that they have continued to provide to this day.

In India, people historically relied on vultures to deal with livestock carcasses, dumping them at 'animal landfills' on the outskirts of towns and cities. In the pre-diclofenac days, vultures made easy work of these landfills, consuming an estimated 12 million tonnes of carrion every year. Without vultures, that's 12 million tonnes of rotting meat and waste that's no longer being efficiently processed, and that has consequences.

According to economic analysis by Eyal Frank and Anant Sudarshan, at the Universities of Chicago and Warwick respectively, those consequences include more than half a million additional human deaths between 2000 and 2005. They found that, in areas where many of the birds would have been found in the pre-diclofenac years, around 104,000 additional human deaths were reported each year, translating into an overall mortality cost of $69 billion per year. The prime reason for the increased mortality, according to Frank and Sudarshan, was a 'negative shock to sanitation'. Losing vultures means that other, less specialised, scavengers feed on the carrion, such as feral dogs. That leads to an uptick in rabies cases, and also (since dogs are much worse at completely cleaning up) a lot of left-over rotting meat, full of pathogens that easily spread into drinking water. In urban areas, where animal carcasses were dumped on the outskirts, dissolved oxygen levels in the water dropped by seven per cent and faecal bacteria more than doubled. The pair concluded that their results 'suggest high returns to conserving keystone species such as vultures' yet acknowledged that these birds evoke quite different emotions to the more charismatic poster animals of wildlife conservation. Nonetheless, they cautioned, 'subjective existence values alone may not be the best way to formulate conservation policy.'

Without a good natural replacement for vultures, we must look to our own solutions, the most straightforward of which is carcass incineration. But that has costs too. In India alone, with its 300 million cattle, the annual operating costs of a nationwide network of incinerators would be around $768 million, a massive expense for a country that had never anticipated such a need. And because it's such an unprecedented change, there's no guarantee that farmers would even use the incinerators – vultures have always come to them and done the job for free, so asking people to transport their carcasses to the nearest municipal processing facility poses a significant behavioural barrier.

The costs aren't just financial. Transporting carcasses and incinerating or otherwise processing them has environmental impacts, and these are also substantial, as became clear during the European BSE/CJD outbreak. To combat the disease, first detected in 2001, rapid sanitary legislations were passed, including the European Commission mandating that carcasses of domestic animals had to be collected from farms and transported to authorised plants for processing, rather than being left to natural scavengers. In Spain, this meant less food for the vultures, which member states were legally obliged to protect, and an increase in CO_2 emissions of 77,344 tonnes per year, just from carcass collection and transport to processing plants. Data weren't available to accurately model the emissions caused by incinerating the carcasses, but they would also be considerable. Oh, and farmers had to pay for the service too, in the form of $50 million in annual payments to insurance companies. The authors of this study concluded that replacing the vultures' services in this way had created 'unnecessary environmental and economic costs, which can be saved if we simply let nature do its job.'

Finally, the loss of vultures has resulted in considerable cultural problems, especially for the Parsi community in Mumbai. Parsi religion teaches that water and earth are sacred and must not be contaminated with dead bodies: instead, corpses are left on 'Towers of Silence', for natural disposal. These sky burials rely on the action of the sun and vultures, and date back to the birth of Zoroastrianism in the sixth century BC. Without vultures, kites and crows are scavenging on the bodies but, as with dogs, they don't do a good-enough job, leaving the towers covered in decomposing remains and pathogen hotspots. There's talk of setting up vulture breeding pens for the Parsis to use to continue this ritual, but so far that has not come to fruition. There's also talk about integrating solar-powered technology to help speed up the process, something that many of the elders would not support.

These are all good reasons to step up our support for vultures. There's another reason too, and it's far less known. It's the knowledge that there's much more going on in the minds of these birds than we could ever imagine.

★★★

Back at the Horstmann Trust, I'm at the Egyptian vulture ('EV') aviary for feeding time. These unmistakable birds are predominantly white, with contrasting black flight feathers, a bare, yellow face, a hooded collar of spiky white feathers and a curved, slender yellow beak. And when I say, 'predominantly white', they probably started out that way but very few of the 11 birds housed in this aviary are pure white – most of them have a pinkish, brown tinge to their feathers which make them look a bit grubby. Indeed, Adam affectionately (I think) refers to the EVs as 'filthy little monsters', and we'll come back to this shortly.

I comment that things feel a bit more relaxed here, and Adam nods. 'It's a very different kind of energy level. They're not all charging around, being massively pushy with each other.' He's right. Even though Holly has just thrown a bucketful of dead chicks around the aviary, it's much more peaceful than it was with the hoodies and Cape griffons. 'I think of them as "the zombies"', she says, smiling, 'because of the way they move around.' It's true that the birds are slowly drifting about, gradually getting a little closer, which does have something of a miniature zombie apocalypse about it. And watching their cautious but deliberate footsteps, I can't help but be reminded of corvids (birds in the crow family). The way that they move is uncannily similar, and I'm not the only one to have made this comparison.

'For me, the Egyptian vultures really looked like crows in the way they behave,' says Mathjis van Overveld, of the Doñana Biological Station in Spain. 'And crows are considered as very intelligent animals. So, I was impressed but I thought, how is it possible that nobody has looked at vultures in detail?' He quickly realised that most people dismissed vultures as dirty birds that spent all day hanging around carcasses. But having spent many hours in a hide watching the behaviour of Canarian Egyptian vultures, van Overveld could see so much more complexity. 'They gather around carcasses but it's not just about food – they preen each other and have these special dominance displays. There was a lot of stuff going on and this is how I came to think that these are really interesting birds.'

Around a carcass, Egyptian vultures are silent – in stark contrast to, say, a group of ravens who would be croaking and cronking and all sorts. They don't interact vocally, says van Overveld, although he notes that the male bird 'screams very loudly' during sex, so they're clearly capable. Without sharing information through sound, the birds instead rely on sight and touch. On Fuerteventura, the Egyptian vultures are provisioned with pig heads, which only one bird can feed from at a time, allowing van Overveld and team to record how the birds interact with each other around this resource. They've identified some consistent dominance hierarchies: female birds always outrank males, and dominance increases with age and territorial status. A territorial female aged more than 10 years is pretty much the boss, and any lower-ranked individuals that try to muscle in on her food are dealt with by a small kick or peck. But overall, the dominance relations are well respected, and there are low levels of aggression around carcasses, just as I saw at the Trust. Not only that, but the birds frequently preen each other, which is common in many birds within their mated pairs, but which these birds seem to do willy-nilly: adults preen young birds, members of different pairs preen each other, females frequently preen other females, and males have even been spotted preening other males. It doesn't seem to be reciprocal, where one bird preens the other and the other bird returns the favour; instead, one bird just starts preening another until the recipient decides it has had enough and gives it a peck.

One of the other signals used by Egyptian vultures relates back to my initial perception of these birds looking a bit grubby. They often are, van Overveld says, but the birds at the Trust are nothing like the birds that he's observed on Fuerteventura, whose white feathers are frequently striking shades of strawberry blonde. It's not because they are bumbling around in the dirt more, or not washing properly. They're intentionally 'mud bathing', which in the wild takes the form of splashing around in iron-rich muddy pools and smearing themselves with it, staining their neck feathers varying shades of orange, red and brown. It was already known that bearded vultures, close relatives of Egyptian vultures, use mud to stain their feathers, but while the media have likened this to the birds applying make-up, the reasons remain elusive. It intrigued van Overveld enough to set up a study of the behaviour in Egyptian vultures. As he says, 'The question is why? Why would a completely white bird develop a behaviour to make itself completely red?'

He dug two pools at the feeding station on Fuerteventura and filled them with water, also dumping a few spadefuls of reddish mud into one of the pools. In one day, 18 different Egyptian vultures were seen rubbing themselves in the muddy pool, painting their feathers various shades of red. In contrast, only one bird bathed in the clean water. However, from more than 600 total mud-bathing events, the only conclusion that van Overveld has drawn is that mud bathing is very common. The reasons why they do it remain a mystery. One hypothesis suggests that the mud has hygiene benefits, protecting against pathogens, but if that was the case, all birds would be expected to do it to some degree, whereas many birds did not show the behaviour at all. Another hypothesis suggests that the muddy feathers act to signal something to other individuals, such as dominance; however, the data didn't line up with what the team had already documented as consistent dominance hierarchies. Another option is that the mud is being applied for some sort of courtship display, but again the data are not yet there to support it. Could it be that the birds just enjoy splashing around in mud? 'This is also possible,' says van Overveld. 'There is so far no clear evidence why they do it.'

In 2022, van Overveld and colleagues published a paper calling for more attention to be paid to vulture cognition. As they outlined, these birds have relatively large brains, a slow pace of life (with long lifespans, a low number of eggs, long chick development times and an extended juvenile period), and, as obligate scavengers, they face a unique set of problems. In his book, *Vultures of the World* (2022), raptor expert Keith Bildstein wrote that, 'social behavior serves as a key innovation in the development of obligate scavenging,' and this is key for van Overveld. 'Everybody knows that searching for scarce food is difficult. This is definitely important for vultures. So, I can see how it would be really beneficial to be intelligent because it's how to find this food.' By paying attention to other birds, vultures can locate patchily distributed carcasses. From that foundation, enhanced abilities in the field of social cognition may have developed, such as individual recognition, awareness of dominance hierarchies, scrounging tactics and cooperation.

It makes sense, so how did the call to action go down with the rest of the scientific community? 'Well, it got a lot of attention from the media!' van Overveld shrugs. 'But I think many people were quite sceptical. Even scientists like to see vultures as dumb animals that just hang around carcasses and fight for the biggest pieces.' He says that it's been difficult to get papers published and to secure funds to continue the work. '[The reviewers] say things like, "Why would a vulture be able to recognise others – why would that be beneficial?" And I can name 10 or 15 reasons why this could be the case.'

Vultures aren't just impressing researchers with their social smarts. Egyptian vultures are one of the few birds that regularly use tools, a behaviour that makes them unique within the group. Unlike other well-known tool-using birds, like New Caledonian crows or woodpecker finches, they're not using twigs to prise out grubs from cracks and crevices. Instead, their tool-using prowess is shown when they are faced with a large, thick-shelled ostrich egg and no way to get inside. Their solution is to find a good-sized rock, which they hurl at the egg to smash a hole. The behaviour was first described scientifically in the 1960s,[28] and while it's frequently cited in scientific literature, it has received very little research attention. One study found that

---

[28] Although subsequently, accounts of the behaviour have been found in texts from the nineteenth century.

hand-reared birds developed the behaviour without any demonstration, suggesting that it is at least partly innate. Another has shown that the birds' responses to ostrich eggs are highly individual-specific, implying that there is flexibility in the way in which it is expressed. Other observations suggest that Egyptian vultures simply have an urge to throw things, as they will also throw small eggs against rocks to crack them, and in one observation one bird was seen throwing a stone at a carcass. It may be that thwarted egg-throwing led them to redirect their throwing urges at other objects, but not enough research has been done to conclude anything with confidence.

I mention this to Holly while we're at the EV aviary, asking whether they ever provision them with ostrich eggs. To her credit, she only slightly raises one eyebrow, before explaining that that would not be advisable in a breeding program context. 'The last thing I want is them to get in the habit of smashing eggs,' she says patiently, 'because they may well smash their own, or each other's.' In hindsight, I probably should have anticipated this.

One scientist who agreed with van Overveld about the potential for studying vultures is Jorg Massen, at Utrecht University. Massen had initiated a collaboration with Rotterdam Zoo for undergraduates to conduct short-term projects, and needed to identify a suitable bird species to work with. He told the zoo that he had three criteria: the species needed to be quite large, so that it could take big rings for easy identification; it needed to not move around too quickly; and it needed to be a social species because that's the focus of his group's research. 'And the zoo said, "Well, we have this group of 20 Rüppell's vultures ..."' Massen started reading up on vultures and quickly became interested. 'I noticed that they are relatively understudied. They are social. And they have relatively big brains.'

Massen's PhD student, Eva van Dijk, has been running the vulture work, and while the project is still in its early stages, a couple of things are already obvious from her observations. 'If you just walk by an aviary and see them sitting still, you'd think they're very inactive. But if you study them more closely, you notice that they are quite quirky. They have these interactions, they are very vocal with each other; they do clumsy things, destroy things in the aviary. They're very fun to look at.' Van Dijk is interested in the social complexity and social cognition of vultures, and as she says: 'Corvids and parrots are very interesting, but you can't figure out how intelligence has evolved if you're only looking at those two groups.' She's a year into her PhD and has lots of questions based on watching the birds' natural interactions. It's a question of 'watch this space' – I have a feeling that she's going to find some fascinating things. 'Anything I can do that sheds more of a positive light on them would make me very happy,' she tells me. 'If you can figure out that they indeed have a more complex society, it can inform zoos in how they structure their social groups, and also hopefully get the word out to the public about just how important these birds are.'

The turkey vulture, that super-sniffer of the Americas that Darwin referred to as 'disgusting', has also been the subject of intelligence testing. So far, only one study has been conducted, the string-pulling task, in which a piece of meat is tied to the end of a length of string and suspended from a perch. To get the treat, the animal must pull up the string, securing it as it goes to stop it falling back down. Immediate success on the task suggests that the animal has some form of causal understanding about the connection between the string and the treat, whereas birds that lack this would be expected to simply fly at the treat, focusing on that rather than the top of the string.

The experiment was conducted with individual turkey vultures from different wildlife centres in British Columbia, Canada, with the excellent names Judge Dredd, Jury, Phoenix, Igor, Vladimir and Frank. Judge Dredd and Frank both solved the task on their first trial and within five minutes, which is impressively rapid problem-solving. Phoenix failed on his first nine trials but then closely watched Judge Dredd and subsequently solved it. All three birds continued to solve the task and more quickly, demonstrating they were learning about the problem. In contrast, the other three birds never solved it, with Igor and Vladimir too fearful of the string to really interact with it. When this task has been set to ravens, keas or other birds, the technique for securing the string as it's pulled up is to step on it. Turkey vultures' large, flat feet are not designed for grasping, so they employed a novel technique, teasing the string through their beak with their tongue, and storing it in their crop until the food was within reach. This is exactly how they would deal with pulling intestines and other viscera from a carcass, so this certainly seems to be a task that is ecologically relevant for vultures. Remembering the marabou stork at the Mara River, perhaps this species should be tested too.

Other species may not have been the subject of scientific study, but observations of their behaviour are offering some tantalising clues into vulture minds. Black vultures, in particular, are exceptional at finding food, and in some pretty innovative ways. As well as the usual carrion feeding, these vultures preen mammals for ticks, feed on sea lion placentas by cutting through the umbilical cord, and have mastered the art of urban scrounging, with records of them even entering houses to steal food. Having learned how to rip open garbage bags at dumps and in bins, the birds are now making a nuisance of themselves on the beaches of Sao Paulo, Brazil, where swimmers leave their clothes and other possessions in bags of similar appearance.

The stories I've heard from Adam also suggest that if Andean condors were studied scientifically, they would likely show evidence for the kinds of creative, complex problem-solving that other species are so lauded for. He tells me that one bird landed on the door handle of the visitor centre shop and opened it on her first opportunity, having previously watched people going in and out. She was apparently a regular thereafter. So what's his view on their intelligence? 'I think a condor is probably up there with a three- or four-year-old child in its problem solving – some aspects will be older and some aspects will be younger.' He thinks for a moment. 'Yeah, I'd say like a three- or four-year-old with a chainsaw.'

★★★

Although our history with vultures goes back a long way, there's so much that we still don't know about them. For thousands of years, we've lived with vultures for mutual benefit – our livestock providing a reliable food source, while they remove the carrion from our settlements. But the balance has tipped too far in current times – we're asking too much of them and for too little in return. We need to do something about this, because if we keep going as we are, driven by excessive production, consumption and wastage, and we keep losing the creatures that help keep our planet habitable, we're going to be in a lot of trouble. How do we turn things around?

'We're fighting several battles,' says Adam. 'We're fighting the perception of vultures because there's the association with death. I've been working with someone on fundraising who has been doing it for a long time. And he said he's never found it so difficult to fundraise for anything as he has for what we're doing.' The vultures, Adam says, can't compete with the pandas, tigers and donkeys championed by the big conservation charities, who have spent years creating marketing campaigns. But, as he says, 'There are now more rhinos than there are some species of vulture. People don't know about it, and when you tell them, it still doesn't mean anything to them: forty to eighty million vultures gone from Asia. But people can't comprehend what that looks like and why they should care.'

That's depressing, but Adam and Holly don't seem too weighed down by the enormity of the task. ('No, you see, you've got to be stupid and optimistic in our game.') Having had a year running the charity and figuring out where the greatest needs are, they have big ambitions, particularly regarding the EVs. '[They] have become probably the most important species we work with at the moment,' Adam says, due to the perilous status of European populations. He notes that EU-funded conservation projects under the LIFE programme in Bulgaria need to release six to nine chicks each year to support the population, but that existing breeding programmes are falling short right now. This is where the Trust can step in. 'This is the second largest captive collection of Egyptian vultures in the world. So everybody wants to know what's going on, what we're doing, and "Can I have some chicks please?" We're trying now to look at building another six aviaries to separate what we hope in here are breeding pairs. Then we can probably provide much of Europe's requirement from here.'

That would be a phenomenal achievement. However, the Trust can and should only be a last resort. Vultures are in big trouble and turning things around means addressing complex issues on the ground, most of which are not specific to the birds. And while it's easy to feel a bit hopeless about this, there is one thing that we can all do, and it does make a difference. Appreciate what vultures do, tell others about it, and fight for their future.

That's easier said than done. Realistically, how do we get people on board with the vultures' cause? 'It's really tough,' says Adam. 'We've been doing it for the last ten years and, to be honest, the easiest way is usually just to let them meet a vulture. But you can't let everybody meet a vulture.' He's got a point – I think that if everybody could spend time with these birds, they would be as invested in saving them as I've become. Because the next morning, as I drive away, navigating the same tiny lanes and admiring the same expansive views, I realise that I've gone from thinking about vultures as a somewhat nebulous group of scavenging birds that do something important, to a full-blown vulture fan. These are thinking, feeling, complex individuals, with personalities, likes and dislikes, and a range of funny quirks. They've evolved to do something that no other animal can, and that no human would want to, and we've never properly valued it. It has only become apparent in the last few years how intertwined vulture health is with our own. And, like the passenger pigeon, which people saw in its giant flocks and assumed could never go extinct, public awareness of the threats to vultures needs to catch up.

I just hope that we can do it in time. And that those hoodie chicks get the chance to one day spread their wings in Africa, where they were born to be. Too much is riding on it.

CHAPTER 6

Easy on the aye-aye

Similarly we cannot find beautiful the amphibia, many sorts of fish, crocodiles, toads, numerous kinds of insect, etc.
G. W. F. Hegel, *Lectures on Aesthetics,* 1835

As part of their 1990 art installation, *Survival of the Cutest (Who Gets on the Ark?)*,[29] artists Mark Dion and William Schefferine crammed a bunch of cuddly toys into a wheelbarrow. Panda, orca, zebra, toucan and elephant were there, as well as various other 'charismatic megafauna'. Along the wheelbarrow was a painted message about the rising extinction rate, together with the names of various

---

[29] Part of their *Wheelbarrows of Progress* series, which comprised five different wheelbarrows, each created to give a different message relating to conservation issues.

species. The message was clear – to be considered worthy of conservation efforts, animals needed to be beautiful, charismatic or cute.

Survival of the Cutest was fun, visually appealing, and took serious aim at the way conservation organisations were raising awareness and funds for animal preservation. As well as being overwhelmingly biased towards large mammal and bird species, the crowded wheelbarrow portrayed a conservation field that cared more about the survival of specific species rather than the bigger picture associated with those species. Why not educate the public on the interrelationships between these species and the rest of their natural environment and advocate for habitat protection instead? The panda was case in point: the animal was chosen by the Worldwide Fund for Nature (WWF) as its logo based on Chi-Chi the giant panda, who arrived in London the year that the organisation was formed (1961). Founding member of the WWF, Sir Peter Scott, drew the first iteration based on sketches by wildlife artist, Gerald Watterson. According to the WWF website, he said at the time, 'We wanted an animal that is beautiful, endangered, and loved by many people in the world for its appealing qualities.' There was a practical consideration for Scott too, however. 'We also wanted an animal that had an impact in black and white to save money on printing costs.' The team felt that 'the big, furry animal with her appealing, black-patched eyes' was perfect as the public face of the organisation.

A few decades later, in 2009, British television presenter Chris Packham controversially called time on the giant panda, saying in an interview with the *Guardian* newspaper that he would 'eat the last one' if it freed up money for conservation projects. Calling the animal an 'evolutionary cul de sac', Packham argued that too much money was being channelled into trying to preserve a species that, in his opinion, had reached the end of its time. Rather than Save the Panda, or Save the Tiger (a species that he also felt received more conservation effort than it was worth), he argued that the focus should instead be on habitat preservation as that would give more bang for your buck.

Packham's comments certainly sparked debate. I remember discussing it with friends, one of whom was fully supportive of Packham's stance, and outspoken in her belief that pandas should be left to go extinct. I, on the other hand, being idealistic and naïve, wasn't onboard with letting such an iconic animal fade from existence. Yes, we must preserve habitats as a priority, but surely we can still save the panda – why can't we do both?

It's a complicated issue, but the short answer is, 'We can't do both, because: "Money".' Packham, it should be acknowledged, knew exactly what he was doing in making these comments. He doesn't, as far as I know, hate pandas and want them all to die – he's a conservationist and his ideal world would be one in which no animal's existence is threatened by humanity. But he also recognises that conservation funding is not limitless. Gut-wrenchingly difficult decisions must be made and they're getting harder all the time, as more and more species become imperilled.

The panda is a single species, but it's an instantly recognisable, extremely charismatic and attractive one. People love it and are rooting for it, particularly in China. In fact, so important is the panda in China that in 1963, the government established the Wolong National Nature Reserve and three others to protect their national animal. Today, Wolong, together with numerous other reserves situated in the Sichuan, Shaanxi and Gansu provinces, forms the Giant Panda National Park: the largest contiguous area of giant panda habitat in the world. The park was officially opened in 2021, and it has a combined area of nearly 10,500 square miles – about three times the size of Yellowstone National Park in the US. It covers 70 per cent of the animals' existing habitat, as well as also providing homes for other rare creatures like the (unrelated) red panda, golden snub-nosed monkey, takin, snow leopard and clouded leopard, along with untold numbers of rare plants and insects. That land wouldn't be protected if not for the panda. In the same *Guardian* interview in 2009, Packham's position was balanced by that of Mark Wright, chief scientist at WWF, who countered that pandas capture the public's attention and so of course conservation organisations capitalise on that. He emphasised that charismatic megafauna can be extremely useful for conservationists, noting that when it comes to raising money it's better to go for something 'further up the food chain', because larger animals need more space, and by protecting a bigger area you will also be protecting lots of smaller animals. Recent research on the economic benefits of panda conservation agrees – giant panda reserves were estimated to contribute between $2.6–6.9 billion per year in ecosystem services in 2010. Protecting the panda and its habitat yields roughly 10–27 times what it costs to maintain the current reserves, and that is a figure that could motivate expansion of the reserves and other investments in natural capital in China.

It's a good argument, so how come it didn't happen for the Yangtze River dolphin (aka baiji), which also lived in China and was declared extinct in 2006? This large aquatic mammal was pretty far up the food chain, and its home was the largest river in Asia, meaning that if it had been protected many other species could also have benefitted. Packham also had opinions on this, commenting that the animal 'looked like a worn-out piece of pink soap with piggy eyes', and that it went extinct because it was 'pig-ugly and swam around in a river where no one saw it'. Can it really be the case that if this animal had seemed beautiful to us, it would not have gone extinct?

Extinction of the baiji set several records. It was the first known global extinction of a large vertebrate for more than 50 years, the first extermination of an entire mammal *family* for about 500 years, and the first species of cetacean (whale, dolphin or porpoise) to have ever been driven to extinction by human activity. The baiji was the only living member of the family Lipotidae, which had branched off from other cetacean lineages some 20 million years ago, and was therefore important for being evolutionarily distinct. The Yangtze River had been its home for millions of years, and the baiji evolved to exploit this ecosystem fantastically. In murky water, sight was never going to be its prime sense, hence its tiny eyes. Instead, the baiji relied on echolocation to get around and hunt, something that became progressively harder as human activity increased on the river. Humanity wiped it out in less than 50 years.

In his book, *Witness to Extinction*, which details the baiji's story, zoologist Sam Turvey castigated the lack of effort to save this animal, writing that the recovery programme that he and others established could have saved it, 'or at least would have had a damn good go at doing so,' if it had been done in time. But, he added, 'Who could really be bothered to put themselves out for the baiji?'

It's hard not to feel sad, angry even, that the baiji slid out of existence and most of the world didn't notice. But the truth is that, as a large mammal, it's getting considerably more attention and lamentation now, having been lost, than most of the animals we've driven off the edge. What about the San Marcos gambusia, a 2.5cm-long fish that was found only in the (once) crystal clear, cool waters of the San Marcos River? Or the flat pigtoe mussel, last recorded in 1984. These were among 21 different species that the US Fish and Wildlife Service delisted from the Endangered Species Act in October 2023, because they were all believed to be extinct. Where was the angst and handwringing for the flat pigtoe, the seven other species of freshwater mussel, or even for the little Mariana fruit bat, that all suffered the same fate?

The blunt, devastatingly simple truth about humankind is that we pay more attention to, care more about and are more willing to try and protect things that we think are attractive. This chapter seems like it should be the superficial one, the one where we laugh and think, 'Well of course I'm not shallow enough to value some animals over others just because of their looks.'

Let me tell you: you are, and you do, even if you're not consciously guided by these thoughts. When it comes to conservation, we may hold up ideals of egalitarian support for every species, but it's just not the case: when it comes to looks, some animals are more equal than others.

★★★

Like many of you, I remember hearing Hans Christian Andersen's classic story, The Ugly Duckling, when I was a child. In it, a swan's egg accidentally gets mixed up in the brood of a mother duck and the chick, upon hatching, was scorned and shunned for being a giant, ugly mess compared with its cute little fluffball siblings. It's a sad tale, and while you know it'll probably end up OK for the ugly duckling, you're probably not expecting that it only comes about because the little bird metamorphoses into something beautiful. It's not quite aligned with current ways of thinking: 'Hey, it's OK kids, as long as you're able to transform your ugly little face into something more attractive you'll be accepted.' But it really speaks to the values that society places over physical appearance. Or at least, that it clearly once did.

For as long as records have existed, people have admired the aesthetic qualities of animals. Maybe prehistoric humans had the same thoughts about the creatures that they represented in cave art – I'm not sure that we can ever truly know. Nonetheless, philosophers in more recent history have long speculated about what makes an animal beautiful or ugly.

For Victorian philosopher John Ruskin, the beauty of living things was linked to their vitality: 'Those forms will be the most beautiful ... which exhibit most of power, and seem capable of most quick and joyous sensation.' Similarly, German philosopher G. W. F. Hegel, in his 1835 *Lectures on Aesthetics*, wrote about the beauty of nature:

> *We make distinctions according to which we call animals beautiful or ugly; for example, the sloth displeases because of its drowsy inactivity; it drags itself painfully along and its whole manner of life displays its incapacity for quick movement and activity. For activity and mobility are precisely what manifest the higher ideality of life ... Similarly we call animals beautiful if they betray an expression of soul which chimes in with human qualities such as courage, strength, cunning, good nature, etc.*

That we judge other animals based on their looks shouldn't be surprising, given that we also do this routinely towards other humans. It's known as the 'what is beautiful is good' stereotype, a term first introduced by psychologist Karen Dion in 1972 to account for the fact that people expect more physically attractive individuals to also be more competent, kinder, and more intelligent than their unattractive counterparts. Since then, thousands of studies have confirmed the presence of this expectation, and the depressing finding that physical attractiveness confers certain societal advantages too, from greater employability to lower prison sentences.

Given how ideals of beauty seem to bombard all aspects of our lives, it would be easy to say that societal expectations are responsible. And they certainly do shape our developing view of the world, conditioning us to appreciate objects, animals and even people that are more attractive over others. But we can't fully blame this on nurture. No, appreciation for beauty starts at a much earlier age. Research has found that infants aged just two to three months, who have no real clue about what's going on in the world around them, prefer to look at women's faces that have been digitally manipulated to be more versus less attractive. One study even found this for newborn infants, who averaged under 3 days of age at the time of testing. It's not just about people either. Infants aged three to four months preferred to look at cat and tiger faces that were rated as attractive vs unattractive by adults.

This means that even from the earliest age, before societal norms have had chance to shape emerging minds, we possess some inbuilt representation of a 'good' face. It's near-universal too, as much as we may like to say that 'beauty is in the eye of the beholder'. That may well be the case on an individual basis but at a population level, facial attractiveness matters.

What underpins our responses to beauty? Theory goes that we're hardwired to appreciate certain natural forms because they conferred survival benefits to our ancestors. This has been suggested for natural patterns such as symmetry and fractals, and those based on the Golden Ratio of the Fibonacci Sequence, because these were thought to be associated with higher-value foods or better-quality mates. In humans, perceptions of beauty are linked to facial symmetry and 'averageness' – studies have shown that when lots and lots of images of different faces are morphed together and 'averaged', the composite face is rated as more attractive than any of the individuals that went into it. Symmetry, it is thought, reflects health and genetic quality, making it a good signal for a potential mate.

Ugliness, in contrast, may be another cue that feeds into our behavioural immune system. That's the suggestion of University of Melbourne psychologist Chris Klebl and colleagues, who have suggested that 'ugliness judgments constitute the aesthetic dimension of the disease-avoidance system.' This is supported by some (disheartening) lines of evidence. For one, people feel disgust towards and are less likely to approach people with leprosy, an infectious disease; but also to people with facial disfigurements, who pose no risk of infection. Bias against individuals with disfigurements is also reflected in popular culture; a notable example being that most of the all-time top American film villains, but none of the all-time top American film heroes, have skin conditions. In the battle between good and evil, it seems that only baddies can have blemishes.

This seems to fit with what we've already heard about the evolution of disgust for pathogen avoidance, but there's another aspect of Klebl's research that I find a lot more surprising: that the way an animal looks strongly influences our perceptions of its 'worth' (i.e. its perceived moral standing). In one of his studies, participants were asked to rate the beauty, intelligence, sentience, harmfulness and moral standing of a large selection of animals based on their photographs. Animals rated as highly beautiful were attributed greater moral standing than their less beautiful counterparts; but more remarkably, moral concern was more strongly influenced by an animal's attractiveness than its perceived harmfulness.

In a second part to the study, Klebl used these initial scores to pair up seven sets of animals, matching the images so that each pair differed only in beauty. A blue morpho butterfly, for example, was paired with a slug, because they scored similarly on their perceived cleverness, sentience and harmfulness, but had wildly different beauty scores. Different participants were then presented with either all seven 'beautiful' or all seven 'ugly' animals and asked to rate each on its beauty and moral standing, using questions such as, 'How morally wrong do you think it would be to harm this animal?' and 'If this animal was endangered, how important would it be to protect it from extinction?' Again, participants attributed greater moral standing to attractive animals: people's moral concern for the blue morpho butterfly was greater than for a slug, and this was based purely on its looks.

Why are beautiful animals afforded more moral concern? Klebl and colleagues have identified one more puzzle piece: perceptions of beauty are related to perceptions of moral purity. In studies using images of people, they've found that unattractive (vs attractive) individuals are judged as more likely to engage in 'purity violations' (such as spitting in the street or eating mouldy food) compared with harm violations (such as shoving someone out of the way or swearing at strangers), which relates back to Dion's stereotype that what is beautiful is good. Good, it seems, overlaps with morally pure. Ugly evokes the opposite of pure, and the opposite of pure is disgusting.

The consequence of all this research is that when it comes to determining animals' fates, we find it much harder to care for those that we perceive to be ugly, because traits that are associated with ugliness are often also associated with disgust and impurity. 'And if you feel like something is disgusting', Klebl says, 'it's very difficult to make you care about that animal.' It seems like ugly creatures are doomed from the get-go — surely all of this is saying that we're never going to think them worthy of concern and protection? 'I don't think there's a simple solution to it,' Klebl says, 'because you cannot just disable people's disgust response.' But, he reminds me, disgust can be overcome. 'I think the only way is to make people aware of it — to say that we dislike an animal because it is ugly to us, not because there's something wrong with it.'

We'll come back to the ways in which people are doing just that, but there's one big, outstanding, question. If unattractive animals elicit disgust and less moral concern, as the evidence seems to show, why do we also gravitate towards certain, ugly, animals? Peggy the pugese (pug crossed with a Chinese crested dog), for example, was crowned Britain's ugliest dog in 2023, yet now has her own social media profile and starred alongside Ryan Reynolds in his 2024 film *Deadpool & Wolverine*. In an interview with the BBC after Peggy's crowning, the competition's founder commented that, 'I never once thought we'd find a dog like her who manages to be both ugly and so, so cute all at the same time.'

Peggy's case suggests there's an alternative to being the prom queen. If it's not possible to win hearts through beauty, be so ugly that you push through the disgust barrier and come out the other side. By doing so, you might find that you've become cute, and that's a whole other subject.

★★★

The word cute derives from 'acute', meaning sharp or quick-witted, and this is the context in which it was first used in eighteenth-century Britain. The modern meaning of the word originated at least a century later in the United States, initially for things that were both clever and charming, before moving further towards aesthetics alone. Modern usage is typically to describe something that is attractive, particularly in a childish, youthful or delicate way, although sentences such as 'Don't get cute with me' betray its etymology.

In humans, as we've heard, beauty is attributed to objects of high adaptive value, signalling sexual attractiveness or moral purity. Cuteness is different. It's not linked to morality or virtue, but to our instinctive, biological urges. It was Konrad Lorenz, one of the pioneers of animal ethology, who first connected cute features with evolutionary theory, writing in the 1940s that certain physical features typical of human babies – including large heads, big eyes, chubby cheeks and stubby limbs – trigger innate feelings of affection and an urge to provide care. By reminding us of our own babies, these *kindchenschema* ('baby schema') activate protective instincts, and increased caregiving tends to increase infant survival rates. In other words, we're biologically programmed to gaze at babies with a goofy grin.

Since then, numerous studies have explored Lorenz's theory, fitting some of the biological and psychological pieces together. One, a pivotal study published in 2008 by neuroscientist Morten Kringelback and colleagues, found that when adults were shown images of unfamiliar infants, there was a rapid (0.13 seconds) surge of activity in a part of the brain called the medial orbitofrontal cortex. This area of the brain is involved in our responses to rewards, indicating that just seeing infant faces may promote positive feelings. Not only that, but subsequent research found that cute images cause hormonal responses too. Dopamine and oxytocin are released, causing feelings of empathy and an urge to bond. And while it might seem obvious that we feel an instinctive urge to provide care, it wasn't until 2009 that the link to baby schema was backed up by robust science – when photos of infant faces were digitally modified so that traits fit with high (i.e. large eyes, big forehead, round face) or low (i.e. small eyes, small forehead, narrow face) baby schema models, adults not only judged the high baby schema faces as the cutest, they reported the strongest motivation to care for them too.

The same pattern of responses has been found when people view cute animals. Dog and cat faces are already cute, but in one study they were digitally tweaked to score higher or lower on baby schema: the former had even bigger eyes, set lower in an even rounder face. These higher baby schema faces were, indeed, judged as the cutest, and one study indicates that there may be other benefits from viewing cuteness, in addition to the feeling of 'aww'. In this, student volunteers were tasked with playing the game Operation (which requires good coordination and fine motor skill). Those that viewed images of puppies and kittens before playing achieved higher scores than those that saw images of adult cats and dogs, suggesting that something about cuteness improves our carefulness and attention.

The fact that juvenile features in other animals stimulate the same evolved urges as for our own babies shows the power of cute, even though such responses are completely inappropriate in an evolutionary sense. Like disgust, this indicates a fair level of over-inclusivity to *kindchenschema*. This was one of the conclusions of a light-hearted, yet scientifically sound, article published by evolutionary biologist Stephen J. Gould in 1979, in his analysis of the 'evolution' of Mickey Mouse. Created in 1928, Disney's original little mouse behaved and looked quite different to the character that is beloved today. He was a mischievous, happy-go-lucky character, with a pointy nose and big ears. But over the years, his character changed and so did his appearance. Gould measured the size and ratio between several of Mickey's facial features in the 50 years since his public debut in *Steamboat Willie* and found some significant changes: Mickey's eyes had gotten bigger compared with his overall head size; his head had gotten bigger compared with his overall body size; and his overall cranial volume had increased too. Whether consciously or not, Disney's designers had nudged Mickey towards greater juvenility, and greater public endearment. Gould noted that Mickey's return to youth also reflects our own evolutionary history, pointing out that adult chimpanzees are strikingly different in form to their babies, while adult humans progress more slowly and do not get so far.

Cuteness never really used to be a thing, in the way that it is in modern cultures, anyway. Look at medieval art. Babies aren't chubby, large-eyed, adorable little beings: they're shrunken, wizened little versions of adults. People were portrayed sternly, seriously, with most examples of rosy-cheeked joy being associated with the vices of drunken debauchery. It wasn't until the early 1900s that designers and illustrators started to draw cherubs and animals looking a little cuter, but even then, they're nothing like they are today. And it's not just cartoon characters that have capitalised on the power of cute – Japan's kawaii (cute) culture is hugely important and influences numerous aspects of day-to-day life.

While the rest of the world may not have embraced cuteness to the same extent as Japan, it has undeniably had an influence, including in our interactions with animals. Just look at social media sites to see the importance of cuteness. As of January 2025, #cute has been used 687 million times on Instagram, with #cutecat and #cutedog both having been used more than 21 million times. When Tim Berners-Lee, inventor of the World Wide Web, was asked on a 2014 Reddit chat to name one thing the internet has become used for that he had not foreseen, he famously responded with 'kittens'. They're everywhere. One is never many clicks away from finding oneself deep down a rabbit hole of cats being cute, cats being grumpy (and still adorable), or cats that look like celebrities, buildings, and more. The internet is flooded with them, and while it's (sadly) not true that cats drive about 15 per cent of all internet traffic, as claimed by a pet food company in 2013, they are undoubtedly overrepresented compared with other animals.

Cats, and especially kittens, with their big eyes, round faces and little chins, are undeniably cute, but what about other animals? In one of the largest studies of human attitudes to animals conducted to date, more than 500 volunteers were asked to rate the cuteness and moral concern (as well as other things) of animals using a publicly available bank of standardised photographs. A total of 120 different animals were included, spanning all the major animal groups, and like with beauty, the researchers found that moral concern was more strongly related to the animal's cuteness than any other factor, including their perceived intelligence and sentience. Mammals came out top for cuteness, accounting for 19 of the top 20, led by dolphin, cat and koala. Invertebrates (particularly insects) came out worst, accounting for 19 of the bottom 20, with fly, mosquito and cockroach taking the lowest spots. While mammals and birds were generally rated highly, there were a couple of clear outliers. For mammals, this was the bat, rated 73rd, and for birds it was the poor old vulture, rated 87th. Animals that were rated as cuter than vultures included the praying mantis, piranha, shark and the generic 'seagull'.

It may seem like a frivolous topic for scientific research, but cuteness is not all pastel whimsy and lovable charm. It profoundly impacts how much we value, like, and are willing to support the wild animals of this world, and in more ways than one.

★★★

We have always wanted to surround ourselves with things that we like. Because of this, we've gone out of our way to engineer our worlds not just to provide reliable sources of food, security or comfort, but to fit with our aesthetic preferences too. Take the case of European colonists in Australia or the United States – longing for the familiar, attractive species of their home country, they shipped hedgehogs, starlings and others halfway around the world, with typically disastrous consequences for native wildlife.

Today, a booming wildlife trade allows people to simply click online for an animal that tugs at their heartstrings – whether it's endangered or not. Slow lorises, for example, tick many of the baby schema boxes – with huge, brown eyes and a dinky little nose and mouth, they seem to gaze at you with an expression of the utmost solemnity. Recent years have seen a soaring demand for the little primates as pets, largely thanks to a video of one being 'tickled' that went viral in 2009.

'I often say that 2009 was the worst year in my life, because I remember where I was sitting when I saw that video.' This is Anna Nekaris, professor of ecology, conservation and environment at Anglia Ruskin University in the UK, who has been fighting for greater awareness of and protections for lorises and other nocturnal primates since 1993. In the video, which was titled 'Slow loris loves being tickled', a loris is filmed in a brightly lit bedroom, both its arms raised in the air while somebody tickles it on its chest and armpits. It was an internet sensation, with millions of shares (notably including a couple of celebrities who brought it to larger audiences), and analysis by Nekaris and colleagues of more than 12,000 comments left on this video found that the number one theme in the comments was its cuteness, and the number one comment was 'I want one'.

The animal in the video undoubtedly triggers the cute response. Tickling is, after all, something that evokes joy among humans (and some other animals, as we'll see in the next chapter), and the fact that it has its arms raised gives the impression that it must be enjoying it. That's certainly what we would do if we were enjoying being tickled. But slow lorises are not tiny humans, and their behaviour does not map to ours so predictably. The individual in the video was not at all happy. These animals are the only venomous primates, and they secrete venom from a gland on the inside of their elbow, mixing it with saliva before biting. Raising its arms up was a clear threat signal from an animal that was likely terrified. What's more, Nekaris says, the animal was severely obese, had alopecia, and was in an extremely unnatural habitat, with lights that would have been uncomfortably bright for a nocturnal mammal and no natural substrate to cling to.

Some users commented on this and similar videos that them going viral was good for loris conservation by increasing awareness of the species. It's a nice thought but one that Nekaris rejects. All that the videos did was make people think that lorises would make cute, funny little pets, spurring a trade that has been disastrous to their natural populations. The slow loris is native to south-east Asia and listed on the Convention on International Trade in Endangered Species of Wild Fauna and Flora (CITES) Appendix I (which should provide the highest level of protection), yet they are poached in their thousands and illegally sold at wildlife markets. Before they're sold their teeth are cut out, using nail clippers or pliers, to protect people from their potentially deadly venomous bite. They're then transported in dark, overcrowded, hugely stressful conditions, which results in mortality rates of anywhere between 30 to 90 per cent. Even if they make it into somebody's home, Nekaris tells me that the average lifespan of a pet loris would only be two to three years rather than 20, if it didn't have a severe infection when purchased ('if the teeth were not ripped out and infected'). These animals are being pushed to the brink of extinction, for at best a couple of years of ownership, for which somebody may have paid tens of thousands of dollars.

The tickling video was taken down in January 2012 due to welfare concerns, but after just two and a half years it had been viewed nearly ten million times. Several others have since popped up in its place, meaning that the content continues to circulate, and the demand for these animals continues to rise. YouTube has no function to mark videos of animals as illegal (compared with videos of guns, drugs or pornography), so prospects for the slow loris are depressingly grim. And members of the public are clearly still unaware of the suffering endured by the filmed animals. Nekaris tells me that she and her team have collected more than 800 images of loris tattoos that people have chosen to have inked onto their body, and that 'most of them are of tortured slow lorises from those videos.' She calls it 'decontextualization', because this image of a funny creature eating fruit in a brightly lit room has no relevance to the version of the animal that exists in the wild. It's a fictional creation that satisfies our urge for cute.

As well as wanting to own animals that are attractive, we've directly changed some of them to fit our preferences, too. Pigeons are a case in point. If you are one of the many people that despises feral pigeons, please do remember that they're only there, limping around in their own filth, because we domesticated them. Some 10,000 years ago, in the fertile lands of Mesopotamia where early farmers were toiling the earth, wild rock doves discovered spilt grain and people discovered pigeon meat. We coaxed the birds to live in lofts alongside us as livestock, ensuring a good supply of the large, plump, juicy chicks (squabs) whose meat was particularly prized. It was beneficial for human and bird alike. Then, somewhere down the line, domesticated pigeons escaped, sowing the seeds for today's feral pigeons: birds that are attracted to the artificial 'cliffs' of our towns and cities, and unfazed by the presence of humans.

In parallel, people started breeding pigeons more intensively and selecting for desirable traits. Artificial selection over several hundred years has resulted in today's 800-plus breeds of fancy pigeons – there are more pigeon breeds than any other domesticated animal, and they vary in incredible and baffling ways. Jacobins have extraordinary feathered 'hoods'; frillbacks have, well, frilly back feathers; archangels have bronze or golden metallic feathers; pouters can inflate their crops to attract mates; short-faced tumblers have barely any beak; and the German Modena looks a bit like a chicken. Fantails have peacock-like tail feathers, which makes it difficult for them to fly very high or for very long – the advice for keeping this breed includes keeping them safe from cats and other predators. The silky fantail, in particular, is famed by enthusiasts for its delicate lacelike tail feathers and exotic beauty. But its feathers are too fragile to fly properly, so it's only good for show. We've transformed them into animals that no longer really 'work' and depend entirely on us for survival.

Dogs, too, have suffered. Our desire for cuteness led us down the path of creating flat-faced dogs ('brachycephalic'), such as pugs and French bulldogs, breeds that are united by their status as both hugely popular and hugely unfit for purpose. Dog breeders homed in on certain 'appealing' features, likely because they struck the same chords as baby schema and elicited feelings of endearment, selectively breeding individuals with round and flat faces, short snouts, wide-set bulbous eyes and stubby little legs. Personally, I can't see the 'cute appeal', and it's not clear that they share any resemblance with human babies.

'No, definitely not. I know there are scientific parallels, but I have a baby and it doesn't look like that!' This is Rowena Packer, senior lecturer in companion animal behaviour and welfare science at the Royal Veterinary College in the UK, who has been studying the welfare implications of brachycephalic dogs since 2009. She explains that continued selection for these traits has led to the creation of 'hypertypes', where the traits have become so exaggerated that they're now damaging to that animal's health. Brachycephalic dogs are at high risk of developing brachycephalic obstructive airway syndrome (BOAS), which causes them to wheeze and sometimes collapse because their narrow nostrils and elongated soft palate prevent them getting enough oxygen. Pugs, for example, struggle to go for a walk around the park and are susceptible to heat-related illnesses. Their bulging eyes are prone to corneal ulcers and are even known to 'pop out', something called proptosis, which results from trauma or extreme pressure.[30] It's the same story for French and English bulldogs, and other flat-faced breeds. And all these issues contribute towards flatter-faced dogs having shorter lifespans than those with longer muzzles. Is this really the life that we want for our furry best friends?

---

[30] Packer tells me that in most proptosis episodes, the eyeball is either partially or completely out of the socket, which is painful and often results in sight loss if not treated as a medical emergency.

The number of health issues facing brachycephalic dogs has become so serious that Packer, and many other researchers and veterinarians, are calling for flat-faced breeds to be intentionally outcrossed to increase genetic diversity and reintroduce more moderate features. Some breeders are doing so, but most continue to follow the breed standard, and why would they change when public demand continues? In 2022, French bulldogs kicked Labrador retrievers off the top spot as the most popular breed of dog in the US, a crown that the labs had worn for 31 years. The same surge in popularity has been seen in the UK and numerous other countries, and in absolute terms that translates into a lot of wheezy, bug-eyed little animals being bred for sale. Sadly, when fashion and status is concerned, health concerns often don't feature in the decision-making process, either because owners aren't aware of them or they don't believe that it applies to *their* dog.

'Some owners acknowledge there's a problem in the breed,' Packer says, 'but two-thirds of owners think that their dog is better than average, and that clearly doesn't add up.' She explains that among dog owners and breeders, communications must be framed in the right way to minimise psychological discomfort, otherwise we run the risk of 'that horrible paradox where more information can harden their existing views'. That sounds familiar – it's a theme that keeps popping up, where information that doesn't fit with existing beliefs is either dismissed or met with defence. Packer tells me that a societal shift is needed, but it doesn't look like popular culture is keeping up with the science – flat-faced dogs (and cats) frequently star in cartoons, films, advertising campaigns, and celebrity social media accounts, to the exasperation of researchers and veterinary professionals, the latter of whom are increasingly having to deal with the consequences. There are glimmers of hope – one of Packer and team's recent publications (pleasingly titled 'Beauty versus the Beast') found that when given the choice between images of typical, artificially less extreme, and artificially more extreme flat-faced dogs, members of the public overwhelmingly preferred the less extreme versions. It suggests that there is an opportunity for the breed standard to shift to a more moderate version, but getting there will require a colossal, industry-wide shift and acceptance of the benefits of outcrossing. 'It's horribly frustrating,' Packer says. 'The writing's on the wall already, but it's such a shame that it's the dogs' lives that are being compromised. They deserve better.'

While we proactively try to obtain or create animals that meet with our aesthetic preferences, to the detriment of those that we decide we like, the situation faced by those at the other end of the spectrum is no less dire. That's because, as with the poor baiji, we think about and behave differently towards animals that we don't like the look of. It's a fact long recognised within the conservation sector, to the frustration of all who are trying to protect more than just large, furry mammals.

★★★

When it comes to conservation fundraising, human preferences are reasonably straightforward, really. We give more money to programmes that support large animals, animals that are more like us than not (for example mammals with forward-facing eyes), and animals that we perceive as attractive (including those that are cute, and those that have particular colourations or patterns that we consider to be beautiful). We like small, vividly coloured birds, and birds with elaborate ornamentation, while for butterflies, the presence of eyespots increases likeability. Amphibians as a group are typically perceived as disgusting, as we've heard, but some species are beautiful – namely, little frogs with large eyes, bright colours and narrow bodies. And when it comes to mammals, body shape and fur patterning are the strongest predictors of beauty ranking: in one study, zoo visitors preferred species with long tails and larger eyes and heads; specifically, big cats with spotted or striped coats, like the tiger and Amur leopard.

We don't like anything with little eyes, or that's slimy, warty, wrinkly or legless, consistent with disgust theory. Mountain gorillas and African elephants tick enough of the right boxes; rock snails and bleeding toads probably don't. But do these preferences really matter in the grand scheme of things? Surely those in charge of allocating conservation funding and conducting active work to protect wildlife aren't influenced by such biases? Sadly not.

In their analysis of the US Fish and Wildlife Service's spending decisions for 511 species listed in the Endangered Species Act (ESA) in 1990, Andrew Metrick and Martin Weitzman concluded that 'the one-line message to take away from our study of spending behaviour is "size matters a lot."' Their results showed there to be a one per cent increase in spending for a one per cent increase in body length, and overall, the data indicated that 'visceral' elements of the species (body length and taxonomic group) were more important predictors of spending than scientific elements, including actual level of endangerment. Species that were rated as more endangered were more likely to be listed on the ESA, as you would hope; however, when it came to spending, the opposite pattern emerged. The greater the level of endangerment, the less spending. It's a seemingly perverse outcome for a federal conservation organisation, but Metrick and Weitzman suggested that another factor needed to be accounted for, which was biasing the outcome of their analysis. The missing piece? Charisma. Without a satisfactory definition of the term,[31] Metrick and Weitzman

---

[31] Among the 'creative' suggestions they received were eye size, eye–body ratio, frequency of appearance in children's books or *New York Times* articles, and the amount of space devoted to the animal in zoos.

could only speculate that charisma must be important, because the bald eagle, Florida scrub jay and grizzly bear (all of which were, at the time, federally listed, but not Critically Endangered) were receiving tens of millions of dollars, while far more threatened species, like the Texas blind salamander or Alabama cave fish, received less than $10,000 each.

Thirty years later, the imbalance continues. Analysis of federal data on the $1.2 billion spent on endangered and threatened species in 2020 found that tens of millions of dollars were spent on charismatic mammals and birds, including grizzly bears, right whales, manatees and spotted owls. At the other end of the list, the tiny Virginia fringed mountain snail had $100 spent on it in 2020, and more than 200 plants and animals received nothing.

The term 'charismatic megafauna' was first termed in 1985, when conservation biologists Devra Kleiman and John Seidensticker wrote in the journal *Science* that there were likely no more than a dozen mammal species that are recognised by most people around the world, and that the giant panda 'probably tops this list of charismatic megafauna in terms of attractiveness and mass appeal'. It has become a major study focus for conservationists today, because charisma undoubtedly has a major role in influencing our attitudes to other animals.

One study combined data from public surveys, zoo websites, and Disney/Pixar film posters, to identify the 20 most charismatic species, and the results are not in the least surprising, given everything we've already seen. Large, land-based mammals came out on top, specifically the tiger, lion, elephant, giraffe and leopard, and more than half of the top 20 were species that you might see on a typical African safari. The two non-mammals were the great white shark and crocodile. Cross-reference this list against the animals you see in zoo advertising or conservation charity campaigns. We're hung up on the cute and cuddly at the expense of so much more. But the mere fact that people selected the crocodile and shark offers a glimmer of hope. It shows that there is no single dominant trait that predicts charisma; it's a concept that combines positive and negative traits about animals, including their perceived dangerousness. The implication is that animals don't have to be adorable to attract support; different, less typically cute and cuddly animals may rank highly on charisma if they are large, impressive, and endangered. Of course, animals that combine all these characteristics come out top – again, it's big cats that tick all the boxes. This is a known phenomenon – conservationists from the University of Oxford had previously written that 'big cats were so highly rated that we might think of them as one, *Felis felicis*: a globally powerful flagship for conservation.'

In creating the list of charismatic creatures, the study also provided a validated set of animals that could be used as 'flagships' to spearhead conservation campaigns, and this is another topic that elicits a lot of debate within the conservation community. Flagship species are popular, charismatic species that are used for the specific function of raising awareness and support, becoming 'the face' of a broader marketing campaign to which people can donate money. The idea is that this money can then be used to benefit other species that may not even coexist with it in nature, as has happened with WWF's giant panda logo. As one of the most recognisable and important symbols worldwide, the panda has benefitted a lot of different species, most of which have nothing to do with the species that live alongside it in China.

The use of flagships is very common, and for good reason – they work. These are animals that capture the public imagination in ways that others cannot, and consequentially forge emotional connections that lead to increased funding. In a field that is desperately crying out for money to protect even a fraction of the animals in need, why wouldn't you go with the tried-and-tested approach of using well-liked flagships? Knowing which animals elicit the highest level of charitable giving and continuing to use them is surely just common sense.

Opponents say that by doing so, the sector continues to promote the beauty bias, focusing public attention on the same handful of already-popular species while marginalising most life on Earth. As a result, conservation spending becomes a popularity contest, whereby donations are made according to likeability and not need, and the winners are the charismatic megafauna. It also means that zoo collections are biased towards species that are more popular with the public, rather than species that are most endangered. For example, Czech researchers found that perceived beauty and body length were the strongest predictors of the number of individual pythons and boas kept at zoos, rather than the level of endangerment of the snakes. They summed this up with the worrying conclusion: 'We can imagine a selective extinction of "unattractive" species as an anthropogenous macroevolutionary process forming the fauna of the future.' In other words, it is not completely crazy to think that life on this planet could end up being curated by our aesthetic preferences. With little concern for the unattractive beasts, they will be left to slip out of existence, leaving only the largest, cutest or most charismatic. What a thoroughly depressing (and ecologically disastrous) possibility.

The giant panda is a case in point – in 2016, its conservation status was downgraded by the IUCN from Endangered to Vulnerable, reflecting a 17 per cent population increase and the mountains that can move when scientific, political and public will align. So, was Packham wrong to suggest that the conservation of other species would be benefitted if these creatures were allowed to go extinct?

'I would argue that eating the last panda would be a net loss for conservation.' This is Diogo Veríssimo, senior researcher at the University of Oxford, who conducts research on the integration of marketing theory with wildlife conservation. Sitting at this historically uncomfortable intersection, Veríssimo is on a mission to reframe what marketing means in the context of conservation, arguing that its tools offer untapped potential to drive effective conservation-related behaviour change. And while he's broadly positive about the role that pandas play as global conservation flagships, he's keen to emphasise that even they won't work for everyone – the choice of flagship needs to be made around the needs and preferences of the specific audiences. 'Because of course, for some audiences, the panda will be great, and for other audiences, the panda won't be great. There is no such thing as one single species that everyone likes.'

Veríssimo was inspired to merge these interests during his biology degree, when part-time work at the local zoo revealed the lack of evidence base in their educational programmes. It was a stark contrast to the statistics-driven science that he was learning about in lectures, as he explains. 'It's funny, really, that if you want to know something like how many monkeys there are in a forest, there's all this stuff you have to do; otherwise, people will fall on you like a ton of bricks because you haven't followed proper methods. But when it comes to people, which arguably are the key thing we need to get right in conservation, then suddenly, it's 100 per cent science-free, 100 per cent evidence free. We were just hoping for the best.' He decided to focus on conservation flagships for his PhD, integrating tools from the newly established field of social marketing to develop robust ways of identifying the most effective species.

Humans don't do things in a void – all our decisions are governed by a complex interplay of genes, life experience and emotions, and when it comes to understanding how to nudge behaviour, nobody has a better handle on it than marketeers. Unfortunately, marketing is also considered a bit of a 'dark art', and conservationists have been historically uneasy about using the same tools as have allowed corporations to profit off products like cigarettes and alcohol. Nonetheless, wrote Veríssimo and Emma McKinley in a 2016 paper, 'Why should the devil have all the best tunes?' They explained that humankind's everyday choices have created lifestyles that are responsible for many of the major environmental threats, writing that: 'This makes influencing human behaviour the ultimate challenge.' Marketing theory applied to conservation emphasises the importance of understanding the audience and tailoring conservation messages to their beliefs, values and motivations; done well, this generates messages that strongly resonate with people and can drive behaviour change. Marketing principles also emphasise the importance of monitoring and evaluating campaign effectiveness – in the commercial world, this is essential to understand the return on investment. But it's essential in the conservation sector too; more so, in some respects, because the investment pot is so valuable to start with, and the consequences of getting it wrong so potentially devastating.

When it comes to improving public support for less-attractive animals, Veríssimo explains, the first step is therefore to understand your audience and their particular attitudes and emotions towards a given species. I can't help but think back to the grotesque marabou stork at the Mara River, plucking guts from a wildebeest, and wonder how anybody could have a positive emotional connection with such a beast. Marabou storks aren't endangered but I pose Veríssimo a challenge: if this member of the Ugly Five got into trouble, how would you develop a campaign for it?[32]

---

[32] They may not have the size and charisma of Africa's famed 'Big Five', but the Ugly Five are no less fascinating: spotted hyena, wildebeest, warthog, marabou stork and lappet-faced vulture.

'It's interesting that you picked the marabou stork,' says Veríssimo, 'because there's an Asian equivalent called the adjutant stork, and that *has* been the target of a community-based conservation project.' Indeed, the greater adjutant stork (known locally as the hargila) looks a lot like its African cousin, being similarly huge, bald, and with a pendulous throat pouch. One difference is that the adjutant has striking ice-blue eyes, but it's undoubtedly still not what anybody would call an attractive animal. It was once extremely abundant in the city of Calcutta and revered for keeping the city clean. But public image shifted, and reverence turned to revulsion, as it has for other scavengers. Viewing the birds as bad omens and carriers of disease, communities persecuted them and chopped down their nesting trees and this, combined with draining of the wetlands on which they rely, has decimated numbers.

The Hargila Army has stepped in to help save the adjutant, and it's doing an incredible job. Set up in 2007 by wildlife biologist Purnima Devi Barman, this all-female, grassroots conservation team (sometimes called the 'Stork Sisters') has quadrupled Assam's adjutant stork population to more than 1,800 individuals. Education about the value that these birds provide as scavengers has been key, but the group is also driven to celebrate the beauty in these oft-despised birds. As Barman said in a 2024 interview, 'While many viewed the hargila as a bad omen or even ugly, based on various perceptions, I always believed the opposite. I felt the hargila should be seen as beautiful and fashionable.' To change perceptions of the birds, the Hargila Army decided to celebrate their beauty by weaving motifs of the storks into their traditional fabric, blending their passion for conservation with fashion. People are becoming exposed to the birds as positive symbols and that has made them appreciate them more. It's a fantastic case study for the rescue of an ugly animal, and I want to cheer at Barman's take-home message: 'Our perceptions of beauty and ugliness are just mental constructs. Coexistence is fundamental. We are all interconnected threads in the tapestry of life.'

Once people learned more about the value of and the reasons to care for the adjutant stork, it was perhaps easier to view them in a more endearing light. Beauty, in these cases, may well be more than skin deep. Ultimately, improving education about unpopular animals is the best way of changing how people view them, but the Hargila Army also tapped into something far simpler – by covering their fabrics with motifs of the birds they made them more familiar to people. This taps into a cognitive bias called the 'mere exposure' effect, a term that was introduced by Robert Zajonc in the 1960s to describe how people tend to prefer familiar things. It's completely applicable to wildlife too. Simply making people aware of the existence of underappreciated animals can considerably raise their prospects, for the obvious reason that they can't support something they don't know exists.

There are other, simple, tools that can also improve prospects for nature's ugliest, and this is where marketing can offer solutions, because human choices can be governed by surprisingly straightforward factors. In an analysis of the EDGE (Evolutionarily Distinct and Globally Endangered) programme's website, Veríssimo and colleagues found that species' aesthetic appeal, order of listing on the webpage, and status as an EDGE focal species or not were the most important predictors of public donations, i.e. two of the key factors were how the species was marketed, rather than an aspect of its biology. Adjusting the marketing could make a huge difference – for example, the researchers estimated that just moving an unappealing species to the first page could increase the number of donors; in some cases by a multiple of 26. A separate research group's study of the animal adoptions made by 10,000 people at the Paris Zoological Park found something similar: the alphabetical order of listing predicted the number of adoptions more than conservation status. Aramis, a jaguar listed at the top, received 1479 adoptions, while Zyko, an arapaima (a large fish species) listed at the bottom, received just 26.

And, unsurprisingly, cuteness helps. In a recent study, Veríssimo and colleagues asked volunteers to allocate hypothetical money to photographs of endangered species – numbat, kakapo, purple frog, Indian pangolin and aye-aye – before and after the images had been digitally 'cutified'. Compared with the originals, the cuter versions all had bigger and more forward-facing eyes and, depending on the species, were also brighter, smoother-furred or declawed (or de-fingered in the case of the aye-aye). Consistent with the theory, the edited versions were rated as cuter than the originals, and also received higher donations. 'We were able to isolate aesthetics as the driving factor for increased willingness to donate,' Veríssimo says. 'That's not saying it's the only factor, but we showed that the effect is real.'

That's not to say that conservation organisations are out there, digitally manipulating images to give an unloved creature larger eyes, smaller claws or a more brightly coloured pelt. As well as being deeply unethical, these sorts of manipulations have the potential to do more harm than good. That's because they run the risk of tapping into the 'uncanny valley' response. This term, first introduced in the 1970s by Japanese roboticist Masahiro Mori, explains the phenomenon by which people's affinity with a robot increases as it begins to resemble a human, up until the point where it appears almost, but not quite, like a person. At that point, people report feeling unsettled or creeped out, and the term is now used to describe scenarios outside of robotics too – like digital image manipulation. In their study, Veríssimo's team found evidence for the uncanny valley, with some people commenting that the cuter, manipulated images were 'weird' and 'off-putting'. This is clearly not the way to go to increase positive feelings to animals; that is, unless you have the intention of making your audience laugh.

★★★

Humour is the other approach that is proving extremely helpful in raising awareness, and some animals just lend themselves to it. Take the proboscis monkey. This large primate has ashy grey limbs, a fawn body and russet cap, and a narrow, bare, wrinkled, face that looks like it's been on a sunbed a few too many times. Its narrow-set eyes are rich brown and too close to the top of its face – there is no forehead to speak of. Its mouth is too close to its little chin and on these features alone, it's lacking cute credentials. But it's what's in that disproportionately large space between the eyes and mouth that does it for these monkeys – their nose is their standout feature. In females, it is bigger than other monkeys' but not ridiculously so; it extends forwards and up into a sharp point like a caricature of a snooty butler. In male monkeys, who also have pot bellies and bright red penises, the nose is huge and it hangs down like a fleshy, pendulous growth, in many cases extending past their mouths. Males with the biggest noses are typically bigger individuals, with louder calls, larger testes and more females in their harems: the nose seems to function as a status symbol, signalling male quality.

Overall, proboscis monkeys look bizarre, and a bit mournful, and while there's nothing disgusting about them, few people would describe them as beautiful beasts. And for some reason, people in Poland have really connected with them. The monkey was relatively unknown before 2016, when an amusing meme about it appeared that compared the animal, which is termed *nosacz* in Polish (translating to 'noser'), to a 'typical *Janusz*'. A Janusz? I asked Polish zoologist Joanna Bagniewska to clarify, and she writes that this term is used to describe a 'stereotypical boomer-aged working-class male Pole.' She explains that, 'Janusz nosacz is a pretty harsh, pretty realistic, and pretty funny bit of satire (Poles love laughing at themselves).' More memes followed, drawing on this personification of the monkey and, remarkably, the proboscis monkey started to get a Polish fan club. There were knock-on effects. Shortly after the memes gained popularity, traditional media started reporting on the monkeys too, and in these articles they shared details about the monkeys' lives in Borneo and their Endangered status. As a result, six crowdfunding campaigns were organised in 2018 to raise funds for species conservation in Borneo, and while the amount raised was not a lot ($610 raised by 218 donors), it shows that social media can, in some cases, be a force for good.

What's remarkable about the Polish proboscis monkey story is how well the amusing memes connected with people compared with traditional conservation campaigns. A study analysing their impacts found that the Polish proboscis monkey memes received just as many Facebook likes as official memes released by Greenpeace and WWF Poland (which, typically, use negatively emotive images of endangered species), and more likes than the official monkey memes published on the Facebook profiles of organisations focused on conserving proboscis monkeys. 'Whether that recognition is limited to the memes of the Janusz monkey,' Bagniewska cautions, 'or people have actually began learning something about its conservation, is another matter.'

I contacted Piotr Tryjanowski, one of the authors of the study, at Poland's Poznań University of Life Sciences to find out more, starting with the question: what was it about the proboscis monkey that resonated so much with Polish people?

'No idea!' Tryjanowski says. 'To me it looks completely random, because the monkey has a big nose, it looks even ugly, but what people forget is that even some negative aspects of species can sometimes work positively for nature conservation.' He explains that there is often a focus on whether people think positively or negatively about an animal, but that the much more important question is whether or not somebody is even aware of it, harking back to Zajonc's 'mere exposure' effect. 'If I know it, and I may imagine the species, I can have some opinion about it.' Just like the Hargila Army's decoration of clothing with motifs of the storks, the Polish memes made the proboscis monkey more familiar to the general public so, Tryjanowski explains, 'if you put some information about nature conservation out there too, then both systems together can start to work.' It may be that the conservation message is only important for five per cent of people, but if enough people recognise the monkey from the memes, that can still lead to positive conservation outcomes.

Nonetheless, Tryjanowski doesn't think there has been a lasting effect. Certainly, the ephemeral nature of social media means that what resonates with people one day is old news the next. Still, it is possible that in a small proportion of users, the plight of the proboscis monkey has not been forgotten, something that would require further study.

What we do know is that humour helps. 'In very depressive times, you need something like this,' Tryjanowski says, and that undoubtedly contributed to the appeal of the proboscis monkey memes. It's also the reason behind the success of the Ugly Animal Preservation Society (UAPS), which has helped to build considerable awareness and support for creatures like the proboscis monkey and the blobfish, elevating them to almost cult status for their ugliness. Biologist and comedian Simon Watt founded the UAPS in 2012 to 'raise the profile of some of nature's most aesthetically challenged creatures.' He tells me that the motivation came after doing a book tour for a documentary series called *Inside Nature's Giants*, where he was frequently asked what his favourite animal was. 'This was a TV series all about massive creatures, a lot of the charismatic megafauna.

And I'd start telling people about ants, who've always held endless fascination for me, and I could just see the disappointment in their eyes.' We pause as his young daughter comes in asking for something and becomes distracted by this strange face on the screen. She waves and I wave back. Watt continues. 'It just hit me that these things are so overlooked. And the people who care about the elephants and the polar bears are already on my side, whereas the kind of person who thinks that the blobfish is their spirit animal didn't have somebody talking to them.'

Watt has been extremely strategic in his approach, which has been to hold comedy shows themed around different ugly animals. First, he wanted to deliberately target adults because he wanted to influence people who could go out and vote for change. Second, Watt recognised that by doing comedy shows he could get the message out to different people and in different media. 'I was able to get more column inches,' he says. 'You've got a conservation message in the review section. That was deliberate.' Third, by being satirical he could avoid treading on the toes of the big conservation organisations like WWF, because he or the comedians in his shows can say things that they can't. As he says, 'It would seem like a really weird left turn for WWF to start making fun of their mascot, whereas I can.'

In 2013, the UAPS teamed up with the British Science Association to find the world's ugliest animal and the society's new mascot. Each contender was championed by a comedian, who created a short video encouraging the public to vote for it. Thousands of votes were cast from around the world, but the overwhelming winner was a little-known, deep-sea fish called the flathead sculpin, more commonly known as the blobfish. If you've never seen one (and there must be some people out there who haven't, though it has achieved worldwide fame in the last few years), the most widely shared image is of a huge-nosed gelatinous mound, its wide mouth downturned in a comically depressed expression, an apparent rivulet of snot dribbling out of one corner of its mouth. The combination of slime, weird body shape and naked skin undeniably places this creature quite far down the disgust axis, and it beat the aforementioned proboscis monkey, axolotl, kakapo and the affectionately nicknamed 'scrotum frog' (Lake Titicaca water frog) to the crown.

This contest wasn't without controversy – for one, the kakapo's inclusion upset most of New Zealand, where the Critically Endangered bird is beloved. Nonetheless, Watt says that they came out en masse to vote for it, so pleased were they to see a New Zealand endemic getting global coverage. The kakapo is a large, flightless, nocturnal parrot, famously likened to an owl and certainly not unattractive. The axolotl, a kind of mole salamander that lives in a suspended state of neoteny (i.e. retaining all its infant features for life) would be much better placed on a list of cute animals, with its apparent perma-smile and fluffy gills. And even the blobfish's status was disputed, as the widely shared photo was of a dead individual that probably looks nothing like how it should. The difficulty is that nobody has ever seen a living blobfish so this was the best they could do. These fish have evolved to live at the oceans' depths – up to 1,200m deep where it is cold and dark and the pressure could be 100 times that at the surface. It's one of the toughest environments on the planet, but the blobfish is perfectly adapted to bob along the seabed, its gelatinous body held together by the extreme pressure. We then came along with our deep-sea trawlers and hauled it to the surface, marvelling at the hideous creature from the deep. But when you force a deep-sea specialist to ascend thousands of feet at speed, things get a bit messed up. Given that we get decompression sickness if we ascend from just 6m too quickly, just imagine the damage done to the blobfish. Even the snot isn't real – look closer and you see it's a little parasitic critter that has hitched a ride.

Nonetheless, the competition was hugely popular and got media coverage worldwide. Watt still takes the UAPS out on tour, performing evening shows with comedians aimed at adults, plus workshops for schoolchildren. He can't give me a precise number as to how many people will have seen it but says it must be well over 100,000. As one of those audience members, when the tour came to Oxford in 2017, I can testify that it hit the sweet spot of making me both laugh and learn. The children, he tells me, can be an even easier audience because he can use more puerile humour. 'Like, if you're talking about a thing which shoots snot from its face, or a fish that makes mucus sleeping bags, the gross factor is a thing that they can lean into.'

Another of Watt's key aims with the UAPS was to encourage people to think more critically about conservation, and to engage in a way that wasn't just the emotional one. 'Hooking people into the emotional relationship with nature is necessary and it works for a lot of people,' he tells me. 'Doesn't work great for me, I'm not wired quite like that. And when the problems are as bad as they are, I think we need to talk multiple languages.' He's right, of course. This was exactly the case for Charlie, and at the time I didn't know how to speak another language to him. Perhaps he'd have also enjoyed the clever, bawdy comedy of a UAPS show; perhaps he'd have even come away with a sense that there are weird and wonderful things in the world that are worthy of support.

Whether beautiful, cute or charismatic, there's undoubtedly something about physical appearance that elevates certain animals above others. We feel an instinctive urge to care for cute organisms and we ascribe greater moral standing to those that we perceive as beautiful. This is massively problematic when it comes to the ways in which we treat other people, and while having preferences between animals doesn't seem like it should be as serious, in a time of catastrophic environmental loss it's time to examine the morality of our own stance. Recognising that we have these inbuilt biases is an essential first step, and the data are unequivocal; challenging and reevaluating them in the face of a biodiversity crisis will be even more important. While the pandas, tigers and other conservation flagships do an incredible job at generating revenue for conservation, they can't continue to take centre stage in public-facing campaigns. We need to become more familiar with other kinds of creatures, because unless we know about them, we'll never step up to provide them with support. And at a time when so much feels bleak in the world, using humour to promote those unusual suspects might be one of the most effective ways to engage new audiences and encourage people to care. Surely, in today's society, where conventional beauty standards for humans are increasingly challenged and rejected, it's time to do the same for other animals too?

CHAPTER 7

Naughty neighbours

Man, as a rule, deals most cruelly with the wild creatures amongst which he has lived so long—the birds and beasts—the mystery of whose lives he is not able to fathom.
Watson, *Farm Vermin, Helpful and Hurtful*, 1894

When I was a little girl, I found a dead mouse. It was lying in an overgrown patch of our garden, and it was perfect. Probably it had died from old age or the cold; in any case, there were no obvious injuries or signs of disease. This is important, otherwise you might think that what I did next was really revolting, as well as weird. Because what I did was pick up the mouse, take it inside, put it in a little chocolate box, wrap a ribbon around it, and leave it in a drawer in my bedroom cupboard. I then promptly forgot about it. My poor mum discovered the mouse about a week later, alerted by an unpleasant smell emanating from the cupboard. She sat me down and told me what she'd found, and then she told me that dead things needed to stay outside because it wasn't nice for them to be in the house.

All I can say is that I was too young to understand. I think I knew that the little mouse was dead, but it looked so lovely and dainty, and I was sad at the idea of this cute creature being left in the garden by itself. I believed that the mouse deserved better than that.

Some 35 years later, I'm on my hands and knees scrubbing the floor of our understairs cupboard and cursing the mice. There are clumps of cat litter soaked in their urine and an unreasonable number of little brown droppings. It reeks. I've been lucky, all things considered, that this is my first real experience of having unwanted house guests. It turns out, I tell my younger self, as we strategically place traps around the house, mice do not deserve better when they're inside my home.

The global pest-control market was worth more than $24 billion in 2024 and is projected to reach almost $50 billion by 2034. In the UK alone, the industry has a market value of around £700 million, and it's growing at seven per cent each year. It's a vast industry and the bulk of it concerns agricultural pests, the control of which we can all agree is vital to safeguard global food supply. Where opinions differ is how that's done, particularly with respect to the use of broad-brush chemical insecticides, and the problem of rapidly expanding insect resistance to chemicals that were previously effective. Great advances are being made in the exploration of other forms of pest control, particularly biologically-based methods, such as the use of natural predators or pathogens, which may allow food production to be scaled up in ways that are sustainable for both yields and the environment. We'll return to this, briefly, later but my focus here is on the other kinds of pests, the unwanted house guests and neighbours who share our living spaces and sustain themselves on our food.

For these creatures, many of whom have lived alongside us for so long that they can no longer be thought of as fully wild, we tend to reject notions of coexistence, preferring instead to reach for the bug spray or rodent trap. Part of this comes down to tangible risks, such as the spread of microorganisms that can cause illness, or structural damage that can result from infestations of certain little beasts. But part of it comes down to the fact that, as a species, we're absolutely obsessed with boundaries.

Once we started keeping animals and growing crops, we started dictating where nature could be, dividing up the land into the bits for 'them' and the bits for 'us', and these boundaries have only hardened since. Environmental sociologist Colin Jerolmack has written that 'modernity posits a firm boundary between nature and culture', and that our ideal city has become a place which is 'orderly and sanitized, with nature subdued and compartmentalized'. In these environments, acceptable animals fit into certain categories. Our chosen companions are kept in our homes and gardens, while the animals that we choose to view for pleasure are either confined to a zoo or live in an exotic location that must travel to, separate from our living space. Other animals that live around us are acceptable if they are aesthetically pleasing, like songbirds or butterflies, or if they appear only transiently in our spaces, passing through on their way to another place. 'Problem' animals are labelled as such because they don't fit into these categories. They appear in our homes, gardens or public spaces, triggering our disgust sensors, and they have the nerve to stay there, flaunting their apparent disregard for our rules and desired order.

The trouble with boundaries is that they're rarely mutually agreed, even among people. And if they're not always clear to us, how do we expect wild animals to know that they're not welcome? Spiders and rats, termites and pigeons, raccoons and wasps – they don't share our fascination with portioning up pieces of land, and they don't understand that they're excluded. They might recognise their territory, but only as it relates to them and others of their species. 'Our space', our human territories, should be a meaningless concept to these creatures, but it's often even trickier than that: for not only do they not respect our spaces, they're also often attracted to them. We are all animals after all, with the same fundamental needs for food, water and shelter. But in our homes, we offer so much more than that – we've created warm, dry, protected spaces with abundant treats; while our gardens can provide enriched soils full of juicy worms, or an abundance of fruits, vegetables or tender plants. Our towns and cities provide additional habitat, in the form of waterways, sewers, undisturbed ledges, parks and many other nooks and crannies. We might not have intended it, and we certainly don't like it, but our creature comforts happen to provide perfectly comfortable living space for many other creatures.

Sadly, having built over their natural habitat, and then provided an alternative that works, we then admonish these beasts for taking advantage of it. But in many cases, we've got our priorities wrong. Understandably, most people will care more about the hornet nest in their apple tree than the encroachment of Asian hornets across the UK, one being a lot more obvious, inconvenient and emotionally salient than the other. But really, only one of these situations warrants deadly control measures, and it's not the one in your garden. Similarly, house martin droppings on the paving slabs outside your front door might be a bit annoying to clear up, but does that really justify dislodging the nests of these little summer visitors and blocking the eaves so that they can't nest at all? And while the badgers digging for grubs in your lawn are driving you mad, is deadly poison truly warranted for this crime? It's very easy for us in to sit back in our safe, comfy homes and tut at the wildlife destruction going on in other parts of the world, thinking that things are much better in our higher-income nations. They're not much better. In many ways, they're much worse, because our increasing disconnect with nature means that when it does pop up in our back yard, we're a lot less comfortable.

'Not us!' say Mr and Mrs Mann, as they unwrap their brand-new snap traps. 'We love nature! We take our kids to the zoo, we go on safari holidays, we adore our two dogs. We aren't the animal haters that you need to worry about. It's just ...' They pause as they go outside, and Mr Mann sticks a trap down the hole in a mole hill. 'We don't really want it here, making a mess of our garden.'

Pests, you see, are extremely tricky.

They're a broad and varied cast of characters, but they all share a few key characteristics, as Natalie Bungay of the British Pest Control Association explains: 'In the eyes of the law, a pest is any animal that can cause harm to public health, safety and welfare, and damage to the economy as well.' A rat or mouse that's nibbling through grain stores on farms is clearly a pest, she says, whereas 'a rat in the woods that's living its best life on berries is not.' The difference is that the latter is not harming anybody, 'So just because it's a rat doesn't make it a pest by default.' Although, she adds, it clearly is for many people.

In essence, pests are animals that are in places we don't want them to be, doing things we don't want them to do. They're the animal version of weeds, those wildflowers that pop up where they're not wanted, like the dandelion, which, were it not unfairly labelled this way, could plausibly be sold in garden centres as a cheery, bee-friendly, early-flowering staple. Unlike big predators like tigers, pests aren't usually acutely harmful if bumped into, although severe allergic reactions to bee or wasp stings are a notable exception. That means we tend to experience a mix of annoyance, disgust and fear towards pest creatures, although even when it's the latter it's not the same kind of heart-thumping terror as we might feel towards a grizzly bear. The emotions are valid in some cases: bed bugs can suck our blood, cockroaches can trigger allergies, and rats and mice can spread disease. Termites, rabbits and moles can damage property and livelihoods. And yet, compared with a tiger on the rampage, we'd surely prefer to have a wasp nest or a few moles in the garden? Why, then, is the tiger a much-loved symbol of power and status, a flagship creature for conservation that is revered around the world, whereas wasps and moles are systematically destroyed wherever they show their heads? A lot of it comes down to the language we use – when we apply the terms 'pest' or 'vermin' to other animals (and indeed other people), it becomes that much easier to persecute them guilt-free. But what if we introduced some nuance to our mental models of 'pest' – what if we were open to the idea that these creatures can also have a good side?

There's no better way to try and answer this than to examine our relationship with one of the most loathed of our neighbours, those little creatures that people love to hate every summer: wasps.

★★★

Watching the ducks, I almost stand on her. A hornet, curled on her side, lifeless on the wooden floor. I bend down, poke with my pen, watch her slowly slide through the dust. Take a moment to look closely at her shrivelled, though still impressively large, corpse; to admire her warm chestnut and yellow hues. Then I spot another, curled in the cobwebs and mud. Then a third, under the huge glass windows. A fourth a little further away. And a fifth.

A hornet massacre! Or so it appears. But it's October, so foul play is unlikely. At the end of summer, the queen of these social insects switches from laying eggs to make new workers to eggs that will make new queens and males, and during autumn these gentle giants cruise the woodlands looking for food and love. Once mated, the males (and workers) die and the new queens look for somewhere to hibernate over winter, ready to start building a new nest of workers in spring. The hornets on the floor of this large hide at the Wildfowl and Wetlands Trust (WWT) Llanelli reserve were likely female workers who had naturally come to the end of their lives.

Be that as it may, there was something about the way that their bodies were littering the room that I found sad. I think it was the realisation that nobody else cared. Worse, that people had probably come in here, spotted them and thought 'oh good'.

In the UK, the European hornet is just one of an estimated 9,000 species of wasp, which in turn is a small fraction of the 100,000 or so species found worldwide. Before writing this, I would have struggled to name more than a handful, and I'm guessing that for most people only 'wasp/yellowjacket' and 'hornet' would come to mind. But while these are certainly among the most visible, and therefore hated, kinds of wasps, they are far from representative of the entire group. That's because they're in the minority of species that are social, meaning that they work together as a colony to build and maintain their papery nests and rear the queen's offspring. Sociality is only seen in about five per cent of wasps but, importantly, is a feature of all the wasps that we don't like. These are the yellow-striped 'waspy' wasps, and the conflict with us stems from their sociality – the individuals we encounter are either foraging to bring back food for the queen's babies, or they're actively defending their nest from potential threats. Us lumbering, naked apes unfortunately fall into the category of potential threat, and even more so when we start randomly flailing and trying to swat them – you'd do the same, I suspect. The European hornet is the largest of any European social wasp, and I think also the most beautiful. Alas, for most people, their size makes them even more hated and feared than the rest of the family, despite them being known for their docility.

The bad feelings go back a long way. Aristotle wrote that hornets and wasps are 'devoid of the extraordinary features which characterize bees; this we should expect, for they have nothing divine about them as the bees have.' Pliny the Elder, in Book XI of his *Natural History*, which covered insects, wrote one chapter about wasps and hornets (suffixed with 'animals which appropriate what belongs to others'), in contrast to 20 chapters about bees – one of which was the whimsically titled, 'Happy omens sometimes afforded by a swarm of bees'. Pliny had little to say on wasps or hornets, other than the slightly disparaging, 'they are all of them carnivorous, while on the other hand bees will touch no animal substance whatever.'

And yet, as wasp expert Seirian Sumner, professor at University College London, argues, a bee is 'just a wasp that has forgotten how to hunt.' Ancestral wasps with the characteristic 'wasp waist' evolved around 226 million years ago, and were a very successful group, giving rise to several key lineages. Some 80 million years ago, coinciding with the spread of flowering plants around the planet, a group of wasps evolved to be 'phytophagous' (plant eaters).[33] These, the ancestors to bees, formed a partnership with flowering plants that spurred the evolution of an incredible array of different bees, including, it should be noted, social species that will vigorously defend their nests with painful stings. From this perspective, bees are just upstart wasps and according to Sumner, writing in *Endless Forms: The Secret World of Wasps*, the ancestral insects are 'much older, cleverer and more diverse' than their more popular descendants.

---

[33] A separate lineage evolved around the same time within the wasps, likely also benefitting from the evolution of flowering plants. This gave rise to ants.

Sumner wasn't always a wasp fan: she fell in love with the insects while studying them for her PhD and discovered the heated soap operas that go on inside each nest. As well as still conducting cutting-edge research into wasp genetics and the use of wasps for pest control (more shortly), Sumner has become a dedicated wasp champion, on a crusade to raise their public profile. Her social media handle of @waspwoman was, she tells me, set up by her husband as a joke when he created her Twitter account (now X), but it now fits perfectly.

In a study of public attitudes towards bees and wasps, Sumner and team found that bees were largely perceived in terms that reflected their useful ecosystem function: 'honey' was the top word associated with them, and 'flowers', 'pollination', 'pollen' and 'hive' were also commonly used. In contrast, the top word associated with wasps was 'sting', while 'annoying', 'pain', 'nest', 'dangerous' and 'angry' were also frequently used. There was a similar difference in people's understanding of the insects' importance in ecosystem functioning – the role of bees as pollinators was well understood, but the role of wasps was not.

Sumner's study provided evidence to support what everyone already knew – everybody loves and sees the value of bees, but few people like or see the value of wasps. The bias wasn't confined to the general public either: an audit of scientific papers published in recent decades found that far fewer had been published on wasps than bees. This was particularly notable for the topic of ecosystem functioning, where, of the 908 papers published since 1980, those on bees outnumbered those on wasps by 40:1. This isn't because wasps aren't ecologically valuable – as we'll see, they fulfil several important roles. It comes down to cultural prejudice, which is clearly extremely important in shaping public opinions, but surprisingly influences scientists too.

In a follow-up study, Sumner and colleagues looked at the role of the media in shaping negative perceptions towards wasps. It's fair to say that the media aren't, in general, very balanced when it comes to reporting on these insects. In 2018, for example, after a consistently cold UK winter, more wasp queens made it through to spring and formed colonies, meaning there were more of the insects around. Some good news from the natural world for once! But no, this was reported as wasp numbers being the 'worst on record'. Sumner's study showed that there are consistent differences in the interactions that bee and wasp scientists have had with media outlets, and these are seen through the whole journalistic process. Seventy per cent of initial enquiries made to wasp researchers, for example, already had a negative slant compared with 18 per cent for bees (and these were only mildly negative). Once it got to the interview stage, 50 per cent of interviews with wasp researchers were about the negative aspects of wasps, compared with only 2 per cent for bee researchers (and again, these were reported as only mildly negative). As we'll see, this isn't because there's nothing good or interesting to say about wasps.

I have a personal stake in trying to nudge people away from villainising wasps, because both my brothers hate them. Both have asked, 'What's the point of wasps?' It was this question that prompted Sumner to write *Endless Forms* and, as she says in the book, what people really mean when they ask that question is, 'What can wasps do for me? Why should I value them?' It's a very transactional view of nature, a very 'Charlie' view of nature. What's the point in these creatures being alive? They're annoying and I don't appear to be benefitting from their presence, so why are they here?

My second-oldest brother's take is essentially, 'there's no point to wasps and they should all die.' On a video call, he showed me the wasp traps hanging from the fence of his California garden. 'They can get in, but they can't get out,' he said gleefully. 'I'm attracting all the wasps and then I'm going to kill them.' My oldest brother shares the same philosophy but takes a different approach. 'Hairspray,' he

NAUGHTY NEIGHBOURS

says. 'It's a useful way to finish them off before they get a chance to release their evil pheromones and attract other wasps.'

This chapter is all about how to coexist with the space-invading creatures that we don't really want around. And wasps play complex characters in this story. On the one hand, they're widely cast as one of the most annoying pests to be in or near your homes. On the other, if you had the power to enact your wish of ridding the world of wasps, you'd be throwing a lot of babies out with the bathwater. The evidence has been lacking, probably because of cultural bias against them, but study after study is now showing the benefits of wasps. They are chronically overlooked for their role in pollination, which seems even more surprising when we consider that they gave rise to bees, and, as we heard in Chapter 3, wasp venom offers the potential for life-saving medical advances. Most compellingly, they are master pest controllers.

This isn't a novel finding. The American naturalist, Margaret Morley, in her 1900 book *Wasps and Their Ways*, wrote that, 'To most people the wasp, like the fly and the grasshopper, is a nuisance, a mere pest that the world would well be rid of. Yet the world could not afford to lose its wasps.' My oldest brother (the hairspray wielder) is open to this and accepts that wasps kill garden pests, like aphids. Nonetheless, he'd still rather they weren't in *his* garden. 'There are other things that kill aphids,' he said. 'Ladybirds kill aphids, and they're nice.'

He's got a point. Ladybirds are small, shiny, attractive little beetles with a voracious appetite for aphids. What's more, they rarely fly at your face, rarely try and steal from your picnics, and never sting your lip while you're taking a sip of beer. If ladybirds can do the job of keeping pest populations down, then is there really any point to wasps? 'Well', frowns Sumner, 'a ladybird might be more effective at completely getting rid of your aphids, but aphids aren't the only pests.'

She explains that as generalist predators, yellowjacket wasps will hunt all sorts of things, while ladybirds are aphid specialists, making the wasps more useful if another kind of pest multiplies out of control. Wasps will cream off what's abundant – that might be aphids, but if there's a huge outbreak of flies or caterpillars once the aphids are under control, they will switch to feed on them. A ladybird, in contrast, cannot help to protect your garden from an infestation of cabbage white caterpillars or armyworms.

More than 30,000 species of solitary and social wasps hunt invertebrate prey, including caterpillars, spiders, flies, cockroaches and more. They're spectacularly good at it too – thought to be at least as good, if not more effective than insect-eating birds, mammals and amphibians. Sumner says that a big advantage of wasps is that more of them can be made quickly, which, when you're dealing with something like an aphid, which can be born already pregnant, is essential to stop them multiplying out of control.

Around half of all known wasp species, and most of the hunting wasps, are parasitoids. And honestly, if I was a caterpillar or spider I would much rather that a predatory hornet got me than one of these. Parasitoid wasps have a very simple, very effective and very gruesome strategy. Females lay their eggs on or in the bodies of other arthropod 'hosts' and when the eggs hatch, the tiny larval wasps feed on the haemolymph (insect 'blood') and other juicy parts of their host, who is still alive but doomed (and in some cases unable to move). Once they've sucked their host dry and are ready to enter the world, they burst forth, alien-like, to go and start the whole cycle again. Needless to say, the host isn't coming along too.

Unlike social predatory species, parasitoid wasps are picky about their hosts – many target the caterpillars of specific moth and butterfly species, while others parasitise spiders, lice, beetles and more. The tiniest of all are the fairyfly wasps, which sound cute and dainty but are miniature baby killers, parasitising not the adult insect or spider, but its eggs. The fairyfly wasps include the smallest insects in the world, *Dicopomorpha echmepterygis*, the wingless males of which are just 0.13mm long, and *Kikiki huna* (made from Hawaiian words for 'tiny bit'), females of which measure 0.15–0.19mm long; for these miniature beasts, even a single fly or beetle egg could provide enough sustenance for tens of baby wasp larvae.

One group of more than 130 species of parasitoid wasps (belonging to the genus *Ampulex*) have evolved as cockroach specialists. The best studied is *Ampulex compressa*, the emerald cockroach wasp, which is also known as the 'jewel wasp' for its stunning shades of metallic indigo, emerald and teal. What it, and other *Ampulex* species, do to cockroaches is nothing short of mind-blowing. For the cockroach, quite literally.

One of the jewel wasp's favourite hosts is that common pest, the American cockroach. As we've heard, these insects are not all bad, but it's still the case that we don't want them and their faecal smears in our homes. So, if you're a cockroach hater, you might feel some schadenfreude at what the jewel wasp does to them.

Once she's found a cockroach, the female wasp (males lack a stinger) makes a quick, targeted sting to its chest, which temporarily knocks out communication to its legs, leaving it collapsed and unable to escape. She then goes off and finds a good nest spot, before coming back to her prey and stinging it again. This time, with the precision of a surgeon, she jabs her stinger right into the animal's brain, delivering venom directly to the target ganglia (nerve-cell clusters). Studies have shown that the wasp's stinger has specialised sensors on it that can detect the location of the ganglia, helping her to achieve this phenomenal level of accuracy. We've already heard about venom complexity, in particular snake venoms, but the diversity does not stop there. In the *Ampulex* wasps, unlike in snakes, spiders or scorpions, the venom isn't designed to kill. Instead, the cocktail of neurotoxic compounds messes with the cockroach's brain, causing changes to its behaviour that last for up to 10 days. That's all it takes. The cockroach is transformed into a placid, compliant participant in its own demise, allowing the wasp to guide it into her nest, lay a single egg on one of its legs, then seal up the burrow and head off to start the whole sequence again. The cockroach is not paralysed but it does not have the will to leave the burrow; upon hatching, the wasp larva therefore has ample fresh food. It starts by drinking the haemolymph from the leg it is on, and then moves inside the still-living cockroach, feeding on its internal organs to prepare it for pupation. After about eight days, the larva spins a silken cocoon in the cockroach, and after several weeks it emerges from the now desiccated husk of its host, ready to enter the world. It's enough to make you feel sorry for the cockroach, and that's quite an unusual feeling.

Charles Darwin was famously troubled by the existence of parasitoid wasps, specifically the family Ichneumonidae, one of the largest and most diverse families, with about 25,000 known species. Darwin wrote to Asa Gray in 1860 that the presence of these little creatures, with a lifecycle that is so grisly, had contributed to his belief that not all of creation could have been made by a benevolent god.[34]

> I cannot see, as plainly as others do, & as I sh^d wish to do, evidence of design & beneficence on all sides of us. There seems to me too much misery in the world. I cannot persuade myself that a beneficent & omnipotent God would have designedly created the Ichneumonidae with the express intention of their feeding within the living bodies of caterpillars.

---

[34] So important were the ichneumonid wasps to Darwin's thinking, that some have advocated changing the name of the group to 'Darwin wasps'.

Gruesome their lifecycle may be, but these tiny insects are incredibly important. Not only are parasitoids harmless to us, since they don't defend a communal nest, like social wasps, nor use us as hosts for their offspring, but they do a huge amount of heavy lifting when it comes to regulating pests. Chemicals, while offering powerful ways to kill insects, can only take us so far, in large part because, just as the overuse of antibiotics has favoured the evolution of resistant bacterial strains, the excessive use of a handful of chemicals has created an environment in which genetically resistant organisms can thrive. There's an ongoing arms race between insect pests and chemical companies, and continuing to try and get the upper hand is not a sustainable solution. Even if the chemicals were guaranteed to work, they're both less good than natural pest control and they come with other costs, including killing all sorts of other, non-harmful insects and having worrying impacts on human health. But, as the world loses its natural pest-controllers, farmers may feel that they need to compensate with more chemical control.

This was the sobering conclusion of a pivotal study by economist Eyal Frank, who analysed what happened after insect-eating bats were hit by white nose syndrome, a deadly disease caused by an invasive fungus that has spread across North America in recent decades. He found that in counties that have experienced bat declines, farmers have compensated by upping their use of insecticides: by an average of 31 per cent. That's bad enough, from an environmental perspective, but it was financially costly too – not only did farmers have to buy more insecticides, but they made less money from these crops. And Frank identified another, concerning, pattern in the data: rates of infant mortality in the affected counties, where more pesticides were being used, were almost 8 per cent greater than in counties without bat declines. It's not proof of direct causation but it highlights how species interactions can extend well beyond an ecosystem, and how biodiversity loss can have a variety of knock-on effects. And it's these kinds of analyses that might resonate most with the Charlies of the world, who might otherwise wonder why people care about losing a few bats.

When it comes to natural pest control, parasitoid wasps have been used in agriculture for decades and are well established as highly effective controllers of sugarcane and maize crop pests. Social wasps, on the other hand, have been overlooked as pest controllers, but Sumner and colleagues are determined to change this.

In 2019, Robin Southon, working with Sumner and Brazilian colleagues, published the first study to show experimentally that social wasps could work for pest control. Their focus was on the Brazilian paper wasp, *Polistes satan*, a striking, slender all-black wasp belonging to a widespread group of about 200 predatory, social species. The experiment was simple – the researchers placed pest larvae onto the leaves and hidden in the stems of crop plants and then tested how good the wasps were at hunting them. They found that the predators snaffled up almost all of the larvae when they had been positioned on the leaf's surface. This was as expected. Even better was that *P. satan* also detected larvae that had been hidden in the stem of the plants, albeit not quite as proficiently. Overall, *P. satan* significantly reduced crop damage from both the sugarcane borer and fall armyworm, clearly showing the value of these animals for pest control.

Sumner has described how US entomologists had already found good evidence for the predatory capacity of northern paper wasps, *P. fuscatus*, which removed enough caterpillars of cabbage white butterflies (genus *Pieris*) to improve crop yield in a study run in the 1980s. I'm baffled as to why this work wasn't followed up, but Sumner puts it down to fewer researchers studying wasps, and the fact that the year after the promising results, things didn't go quite so well.

One of the things that makes social wasps fantastic apex predators in the garden is that they will fixate upon the most abundant prey species. That means that if cabbage white butterflies have had a bumper year and laid eggs all over your plants, the wasps will notice and they will focus on seeking out cabbage white caterpillars. Once they've caught all of those, their attention will shift to the next most abundant, and they'll cream off the crop of those too. In the US study, the year after the wasps did such a good job against the cabbage whites, they were attracted to a neighbouring crop field, where there was an abundance of other pests; by fixating on those, their predation on the cabbage white caterpillars fell, and the researchers concluded the previous year's findings were a fluke.

Nonetheless, the evidence is there, it's accumulating, and it suggests that wasps may offer an untapped potential for pest control. By combining the specialist skills of parasitoids with the opportunistic, generalist approach of social wasps, we may reap the rewards offered by two of nature's finest pest-control agents. And without a chemical in sight. For this alone, we should be celebrating these much maligned little beasts.

★★★

Another thing that Morley cottoned onto was the potential sophistication of wasp brains. One of the things that she claimed was that, 'Wasps, like bees, learn to know individuals.' For a book that was written 120 years ago, this was remarkably prescient.

Morley's reasoning was based on anecdotal reports of nesting wasps discriminating between humans, preferentially stinging some people and not others. It's the sort of inference that scientists are used to dismissing, particularly when it concerns such an unlikely group of animals – insects, with their tiny brains, are not likely candidates for such abilities. But her conclusion was correct, for in the last 25 years, scientific studies have indeed found that wasps can recognise faces, not just those of other wasps but humans too.

Elizabeth Tibbetts, professor of ecology and evolutionary biology at the University of Michigan, was the first to show facial recognition in wasps, with her studies of the northern paper wasp, *P. fuscatus*. Rather than one queen founding a colony, as is typical for many other social wasps, *P. fuscatus* colonies are typically founded by several queens (foundresses) in early spring. With each vying for dominance, these foundresses must resort to violence to work it out. The dust settles after a few days, and they settle into a stable dominance hierarchy, and as worker wasps emerge, they too integrate into this. A wasp's place in the hierarchy influences her lot in life: more dominant individuals have a greater share of the colony's reproduction and food, do less work and receive less aggression from other individuals. Since wasps don't fight to establish dominance every time they meet, Tibbetts wondered how they were assessing the ranks of their colony mates. Was it possible that they could recognise each other?

P. fuscatus wasps have extremely variable facial markings, so Tibbets focused on this as a potential method for individual recognition. Against a backdrop of dark chestnut or black, individuals have an array of yellow splashes and squiggles, some resembling 'eyebrows', others with funky eyeliner along either the inner or outer edge of the eye, some on their 'clypeus' (the lower part of the face). Individuals may have some or all these markings, and in varying sizes and shapes. Collecting 259 wasps from nests on the eaves of houses and barns in upstate New York, Tibbetts documented the variability, and then she tested what happened when she changed it. She painted the wasps' faces, covering yellow markings in individuals that naturally had them, adding yellow markings to individuals that didn't, and painting around their yellow markings in a control group. She found that when an individual with visibly changed face markings was returned to the colony, she was more likely to receive aggression from her colony mates compared with control individuals, suggesting that they didn't recognise her. However, the aggression was 'mild', consisting of lunges and 'mounts' (where a lower-ranked wasp lowers her antennae and allows the more dominant individual to climb on her head), which are the types of interactions individuals use when establishing dominance, rather than the full-blown aggression shown to unrelated intruders. As Tibbets explains to me: 'Each wasp has a unique face, and when they meet each other [and fight, as they're prone to do], they learn each other's face. So, the next time they meet, they don't need to fight again. They can just be like, "Oh hey, Susie, I remember you."'

This, Tibbets tells me, was not what people had expected. First, people assumed that insects communicated via chemical, not visual, signals, largely because their eyes are so different from ours. But the deeper surprise was what the findings suggested about wasp cognition. 'People were surprised that it was individual recognition, because that's supposed to be a relatively sophisticated form of recognition.' Other kinds of recognition, Tibbets explains, may simply require the organism to have a template that tells it what kind of object or organism it is. 'So I could just look at you and be like, you're a person, and I have this template that says this is what a person looks like. And every time I meet a person I can just say, "that's a person". But individual recognition requires that you learn and remember individuals.' This suggested a previously unheard-of level of cognitive complexity for these insects.

Since then, Tibbetts' lab has been at the forefront of research into the social smarts of *Polistes* wasps. And it's all showing that these little insects, whose brains are about the size of a grain of rice, are far more interesting than anybody had thought. So interesting, in fact, that 20 years after the face recognition study, Tibbetts is still conducting pioneering research with wasps. 'Early on, I kept thinking I should study something else. But there just kept being new, amazing things to do. So I've never switched.'

One of those amazing things is that as well as recognising others, the wasps also keep track of what their colony mates are doing. They will actively watch fights, and when subsequently placed together with either the winner or loser of that fight, they respond appropriately, behaving more aggressively to the loser wasp than to the winner. This eavesdropping behaviour helps them to learn and keep track of their relative status in the colony. 'And that is interesting,' Tibbets says, 'because it tells you they're living in a really complicated social world. So they're not only paying attention to themselves, they're paying attention to how others interact too.' This is behaviour more typically associated with 'brainier' social animals, like chimpanzees, ravens or hyenas.

The wasps are also capable of a cognitive feat called transitive inference, a form of deductive reasoning whereby an individual can infer a novel relationship between two items based on how each relates to other, known items. For the wasps, it's all in the context of dominance – so if Paula watched Susie beat Julie in a fight, and also separately watched Julie beat Jane, then transitive inference would allow her to deduce that Susie should also beat Jane. This is what Tibbets' lab found, and it was a pivotal result, being the first demonstration of the ability in an invertebrate. There was another reason to be delighted by the results too, Tibbets tells me: 'I was particularly thrilled because bees cannot do transitive inference, or at least the test that they tried to use, the bees failed. So I felt really happy that wasps went up one on bees. I like to be proud of the wasps when I can be!'

This research isn't just about working out whether wasps can recognise others. It's also providing an alternative way to think about the evolution of intelligence. These are creatures with fewer than one million brain cells, compared with our 86 billion, and yet they can form abstract concepts, remember individuals, remember relationships and more. Does that mean we can say that wasps are intelligent?

'Wasps are very smart,' says Tibbets. 'But I think they're just smart in the one, very specific, way that they need to be. They're just little face geniuses, because it's so important for their life.' Wasps aren't going to be writing poems, or making fire, because doing those things is irrelevant to the challenges they face in their day-to-day lives. But recognising and responding appropriately to their colony mates? Their little brains are all over that.

Tibbets points out that humans are also extremely specialised for face recognition because it's essential for the functioning of our societies, but we take it for granted because it comes so easily. Many of our assumptions about human minds are built on something called the social intelligence hypothesis, which proposes that the mental challenges of remembering who's who in a group, including their respective ranks and relationships, drove the evolution of intelligence in many species, including primates and humans. But as Tibbets points out, 'Wasps independently evolved this specialisation, and they're smarter at learning faces. They learn faces more accurately. And they remember them longer than they remember other information.'

Unlike the northern paper wasp, our European common wasps don't seem to recognise other individuals within their colonies, but why would they? These are colonies ruled by a single queen, with workers knowing their place in the pecking order from birth. They don't need to learn about and respond appropriately to all their colony mates. Intriguingly, however, they do seem to be capable of recognising the faces of another species: us.

At Monash University in Melbourne, Adrian Dyer and team have been studying visual discrimination in European wasps and honeybees, and in one study they evaluated whether both species could learn to recognise human faces. Individual wasps were collected in late summer, when they no longer needed to hunt for prey and were in wasp party mode. Luring them to a sugar solution feeder, the researchers followed satiated wasps back to their nest, where they could collect individuals for use in the experiment. Initially, the wasps were trained to discriminate between two faces (both were black and white photographs of young men, but with quite different features). When they landed on a platform next to the 'target' face a dispenser released a drop of sugar solution, whereas when they landed on a platform next to the incorrect face, a drop of bitter quinine solution was released, which wasps do not like at all. Dyer said that the wasps were 'highly motivated' to participate in the task: they would complete several trials before heading back to the nest to deliver the sugar and then quickly fly back to do more. Each wasp made a total of 90 choices, and the whole training took about three hours, which is astoundingly fast. I can say this as someone who once spent several weeks trying to train one crow to hold a tool the right way round.

Once they were reliably picking the correct face, each wasp was presented with test options, in which the target face was paired against different 'distractor' images: one was a simple line drawing of a face, while two others were men's faces that were either similar to the target or very different. The wasps were unfazed and continued picking the target at well above chance levels. Only when the images were presented upside down did their performance fall, suggesting that the insects were no longer able to process the configuration accurately. This is also true of honeybees when tested on the same procedure.

I mentioned this study to a friend who isn't a big fan of wasps, hoping to impress him with how interesting they are: *wasps can tell the difference between human faces – isn't that cool?* 'Nope,' he said. 'That just makes them scarier!' I ran this past Dyer – is this the typical reaction? Does learning about these sorts of abilities improve people's attitudes towards wasps or does it just feed into the myth of the 'intelligent monster' (as *Jaws* did for sharks)? 'My general feeling from feedback about our work is that the better people understand different species, the more people appreciate their capabilities, and this lowers the scare factor.'

My brothers are not easily convinced, but I'm hoping that the more they hear about the good sides of wasps, the less easily they'll reach for the hairspray and wasp traps. In other places, tolerance has increased for these insects, particularly where effective options exist for non-destructive wasp nest removal. Bungay tells me that pest controllers no longer automatically recommend nest destruction, if it is not located in a problematic place.

What's not known is whether wasps are adapting to live alongside people. Certainly, the structures that we build provide social wasps with excellent sites for their nests, and on a summer's day there's an abundance of sweet treats to tempt them. It's possible that social wasps are doing well from urbanisation, though further research is needed to know for sure. For other animals, the evidence is far clearer.

★★★

There's a common belief that in London you are never more than six feet away from a rat.[35] It's a saying that does the rounds so often that it's accepted as gospel. It's not true, of course. Nor is it true that there's one rat for every human in the UK: that would equate to around 67 million rats, which is quite different to the 10 million estimated by experts. Nonetheless, rats are Pest #1 for most people. In the UK, rat control is the biggest segment of the pest control market.

---

[35] Throughout this chapter, 'rat' refers to the most common species in the UK, the brown rat (aka Norway or sewer rat, *Rattus norvegicus*). The smaller, less aggressive black rat (aka ship or house rat, *R. rattus*), the UK's original rat species that arrived in Roman times, has not been seen in many cities for decades, and is thought to have been outcompeted by the brown rat and exterminated by pest control.

Rats, small mammals belonging to the largest mammal group, Rodentia, have been a feature of human life for millennia. These opportunistic, highly adaptable little animals learned a long time ago that in human settlements the streets are paved with gold. Admittedly, a rat's version of gold is human waste, but they're not picky. They originated in central Asia and have been living alongside people since at least the early Neolithic (7,000 to 9,000 years ago): archaeological evidence from this time in China found rat remains in human refuse middens, showing that their love of our waste is by no means a modern phenomenon. Since then, rats have followed us all around the world, sticking close by like a loyal puppy. Albeit a loyal puppy that can gnaw through wood, brick and electrical wires, and spread an impressive array of dangerous pathogens. Despite this, rats have what's known as a commensal relationship with us, a term used to describe an association between two organisms in which one derives benefit from the other without providing any benefit or harm.[36]

Rats haven't always been so widely despised. In ancient Egypt, for example, rats were revered for their association with the goddess Wadjet, protector of the pharaohs. In the Chinese zodiac calendar, the rat is the first animal, and it symbolises fresh beginnings. It is also associated with intelligence and resourcefulness, since as the calendar's origin story goes, the rat used its brains to win the Great Race set by the Jade Emperor. Rats also symbolise wealth, prosperity and fertility, thanks to their extremely fast reproductive rate and survival abilities.

In Europe, on the other hand, rats have long been depicted as our shadows; scurrying at our feet, embodying our worst

---

[36] Commensalism contrasts with parasitism, in which one derives benefit from another but to the detriment of the host, and mutualism, where both derive benefits from each other.

tendencies of thievery, uncleanliness, destructiveness and vice. The European plagues didn't help. The fourteenth-century Black Death killed more than 25 million people across the continent, and fingers were pointed very firmly at the rats. They remain firmly pointed at them today: go to any European city and ask 100 people what caused the plague and I will bet that 'rats' is the most common answer. The truth is that for many people, the words 'plague' and 'rat' have become irrevocably entwined.

Plague is an infectious disease caused by a species of bacteria called *Yersinia pestis*. It predominantly infects rodents, but rodents don't usually develop the disease; because of this, they are what's known as a reservoir for the pathogens. Rats, therefore, don't directly infect people. What they do is transport little blood-sucking fleas, like a nimble, erratic bus, allowing the true disease-causers to hop on and off at will and bite humans (who are susceptible to developing the disease).

It's the smaller, native black rat that's implicated in spreading the plague across Europe – brown rats didn't arrive until the eighteenth century. But recently, doubts have been cast over the rats' role of super-spreader – some researchers argue that the speed of the outbreaks and the pattern of infection is more consistent with the disease spreading via human parasites, rather than rats. That is, the pattern of transmission caused by fleas and human lice hopping between people is a better match for what was seen than that of rat-to-human transfer. Could it be that we owe rats an apology?

Rats' reputations went out of the window after the plagues, and that perceived connection will be very tough to sever. But even if it is the case that rats weren't the major causal agents of the Black Death, that doesn't really matter today. They're still legitimate pests and still not an animal that anybody should have to live in proximity to. That's because, like the German cockroach, their love of all things human means they have no qualms about flitting from rubbish tips and sewers to restaurants, homes and hospitals, and that presents a serious problem. We don't want a creature that's been hanging out in filth tramping in germs and gnawing at our worktops.

That said, the common perception that rats are dirty, and that this is why fleas travelled on them, couldn't be further from the truth, as Charlotte Burn, associate professor in animal welfare and behaviour science at the Royal Veterinary College, explains. 'They're actually very clean animals; they groom themselves a lot and they've often got lovely, shiny, clean fur.' That's a far cry from the common depiction of rats in popular culture – in films, cartoons or books they are often depicted as dirty, oily, and yellow-fanged. Burn explains that it takes some effort to make real rats look the part on the screen, describing how hair gel is often used to make a rat's fur look greasy. No wonder that people assume that's what rats look like, and that stereotype continues to be reinforced. 'People almost want that image of the rat with this greasy, clumped together fur, often a little bit bald in places.' She pauses and sighs. 'And then you've got the bald tail. And that's a weird thing because it's often pictured as being segmented like a worm, but they're not like that. A rat's tail is just skin, like most of our body.'

The generic 'rat' that Burn is describing bothers us for good reason – it ticks many of the boxes that trigger our disgust response. Greasiness suggests a lack of cleanliness or the secretion of bodily substances; patchiness in the fur suggests infection; the bald, wormlike tail may trigger responses to other animals we evolved to avoid. It's no wonder that they're reviled. The trouble is, this rat is not based in fact.

What's more, says Burn, there's no evidence that rats seek out dirty places to live. Some of her early research with lab rats has shown that they'll quite happily go for a nice, clean cage if given the choice between that and their old, soiled one. It's likely that, all things being equal, rats would prefer to live on a lush riverbank, but in our towns and cities, the sewers offer a perfectly good alternative: they provide shelter, protection, food and an unrivalled network by which the animals can efficiently and safely travel around a city. Rats don't understand that sewers are our purpose-built waste removal networks, and therefore lack the cultural baggage that accompanies any association with these places. That's quite different to the popular image of them seeking out sewers because they're attracted to filth.

Admittedly, I don't want to share my home with wild rats (pet rats, on the other hand, are said to make wonderful companions). But I also don't want to share my home with hedgehogs, sparrows or frogs. Or anything that will poo and pee at will and potentially in places that are difficult to reach. That's just basic hygiene and common sense. Clearly, for the rat, there's more to it — people don't cringe at the sight of frogs or sparrows in the park, nor would they put out poison bait if they saw hedgehogs scurrying around in their garden. At least, I hope that most people wouldn't. The boundaries we construct around our spaces are a little more blurred for some animals than others. And when it comes to rats, it's a hard 'Keep Out'.

That's a shame, because as much as we don't want to live alongside rats, they really want to be around us. They are the ultimate 'synanthrope', meaning that they have evolved to live in proximity to people and benefit from the environments we create. Synanthropes are the creatures that are doing well out of humanity's spread across the planet, and theoretically, therefore they should be the species that we celebrate. Sadly, the qualities that have made them well-adapted to live alongside us are exactly why we despise them. And when that happens, it's all too easy to reach for the poison or call out a pest-control firm.

The most common way to kill rodents is to leave out food baited with rodenticide — typically, an anticoagulant such as warfarin, which kills the animals by stopping blood clotting, causing massive internal bleeding. It doesn't work straight away, and that's by design — rats are cautious about strange new foods in their environment, so tend to nibble a little and see if it makes them feel sick before eating their fill. The delayed onset of poison baits means that rats don't learn to avoid them, making these horribly efficient options. Nonetheless, if we know anything about rats it's that they are survivors, with remarkable abilities to adapt, and incredibly, they are adapting to poison. Rats started developing resistance to warfarin and other first-generation anticoagulation rodenticides in the late 1950s, driving the creation of more potent and persistent second-generation options. These are extremely effective at killing rats, but they're also extremely good at killing all sorts of other creatures. It's an issue that didn't get a huge amount of public attention until early in 2024, when Flaco the eagle owl, liberated from Central Park Zoo after vandals cut open his enclosure, crashed into a Manhattan tower block and died. As well as a severe case of pigeon herpesvirus, the post-mortem revealed that Flaco had four different types of rodenticides in his system. And it's interesting that Flaco's death, as well as increasing reports of birds of prey and pets dying from secondary rodenticide poisoning, captured public attention, because while people are right to be horrified by the potential suffering in these non-targeted animals, they should also be horrified that this is what happens to poisoned rats and mice, too.

 I'll leave it to you to decide whether death by slow internal haemorrhage is better or worse than another cheap and easy method of rat control: glue boards. These are exactly what they sound like, and remind me of Roald Dahl's classic story, *The Twits*, where every week, Mr Twit put a ladder against the Big Dead Tree and smeared the branches with 'Hugtight' sticky glue to catch birds for the next day's pie. In the UK, Bungay explains that glue boards can now only be used under license by professional pest controllers, and that generally this method of rat catching is only used in exceptional circumstances, where public health and safety is at risk. I'm glad to hear that they are regulated, but not that such a method is still deemed acceptable. Even without the devastating impact that anticoagulants and glue have on native wildlife (many non-target animals get stuck to the boards as well as rodents), these are cruel ways to kill sentient beings. And there is no doubt that rodents are sentient beings, when sentience is defined as the ability to experience positive and negative emotions, such as joy, pleasure, pain and fear.

Rats live in colonies of 100 or more, and within these they are extremely social and highly bonded: they groom each other, share food, play and babysit each other's pups. As we've heard, they're fastidiously clean and will spend many hours of each day licking their fur, and the fur of their ratty friends. They also, without question, experience emotions. Much of the evidence, as for most animals, comes from research into negative emotional states, particularly pain and fear, which can be objectively measured by sampling stress hormones, facial expressions or behavioural responses. It's easier to get research funding for investigating negative emotions, because of the obvious application for human psychiatric disorders such as post-traumatic stress disorder (PTSD). When it comes to rat control methods, it was research from studies of rat facial expressions, writhing and other indicators of pain that led to a consumer ban on glue traps, and greater awareness that the internal haemorrhaging caused by anticoagulant rodenticides causes a huge amount of suffering to these little animals.

Research on positive emotions has lagged, although it has been gaining traction with the rise of the positive psychology movement and greater awareness of the importance of mental health for human well-being. Nonetheless, it's clear that rats experience positive mental states, and when you hear about the evidence you may even experience the same.

In the 1990s, the pioneering, late neuroscientist Jaak Panksepp and his team were engaged in researching the neurobiology of rat play, and part of this involved recording the noises made by playing rats. Panksepp found that when the animals were engaged in rough-and-tumble play they emitted high-frequency chirps – a bat detector revealed these to be at a frequency of 50kHz. He noted in an interview with *Discover* magazine, that one morning in 1996 he woke up and said, 'What if that sound is laughter?' Since the simplest way to induce laughter in children is tickling, this led Panksepp down what, at first glance, seems like a very bizarre research question: could rats be tickled? Together with then-student Jeffery Burgdorf, he decided to find out.

To study something scientifically, you need a repeatable, standardised method, something that might not, at first glance, seem possible for tickling. Panksepp and Burgdorf initially investigated getting 'tickle machines', but they were a non-starter because they were apparently, 'nothing like the human hand'. Instead, they spent much time honing the optimum method, which turned out to be using their right (gloved) hand to make rapid finger movements over the back of a tame rat's neck, before quickly flipping the animal on its back and making the same movements on their belly.

The rats loved it. They erupted into ultrasonic 'giggles' when tickled on their backs or bellies and actively chased the experimenter's hand for more tickles when they stopped, sometimes giving little play bites to start the tickling again. Burgdorf and Panksepp wrote in their initial publication that more than 95 per cent of the animals studied by that point had unambiguously exhibited the response, although (like humans) there were some rats that weren't so keen. Drawing parallels with the joyful laughter of human children during play, they summarised that 'although we would be surprised if rats have a sense of humor, they certainly do appear to have a sense of fun.'

It was a groundbreaking discovery, and yet their original write-up of the study was rejected by the prestigious journal *Nature* in 1997. One reviewer completely disparaged the work, and the editor seemed to agree. The research community was not ready for rats having fun. Reflecting on that decision a couple of years later, after the results had been published elsewhere and picked up by the popular press, the pair wrote that they 'remain saddened that many of our colleagues in the prevailing scientific establishment are not more open to entertaining such possibilities.' Nonetheless, Panksepp and Burgdorf went on to investigate the neurobiology of tickling and rat laughter in a series of studies, and the work today is recognised as a pivotal step towards understanding rat emotions. It also inspired many other researchers to investigate different aspects of the phenomenon.

One of those is neuroscientist Michael Brecht, at Humboldt University in Berlin, whose research focuses on the neuroscience of rat emotions, particularly positive emotions. With colleagues, Brecht has replicated Panksepp and Burgdorf's findings, confirming that the animals really do love tickling. They've also found that rats' responses to being tickled were contagious: simply watching another rat being tickled induced the same chirps, as well as little jumps (which Brecht and team call *Freudensprunge*, i.e. joy jumps).

In one delightful study, Brecht and his student, Annika Reinhold, used tickling to teach the rats to play hide-and-seek. When the rat was the 'seeker', it was enclosed in a box while Reinhold hid somewhere in the room, and then opened the box using a remote control. When the rat found the hidden researcher, she rewarded it with a tickle. The animals also learned to hide while Reinhold searched for them. The rats loved it. Brecht and Reinhold recorded high-pitched chirps and squeaks (rat giggles) when the game began and when they either found or were found by the experimenter and received a belly tickle. In a remarkable development, the rats started to prolong the game – when Reinhold found them, they didn't wait for their tickle but ran off and hid again. The researchers wrote that the animals 'looked like they are having fun', and I can only imagine that the researchers did too.

It's a remarkable study, not just for the findings that rats can learn to play what is a cognitively complex game – the rat needs to learn the rules, switch strategies depending on its role, and consider what their opponent is doing and seeing – but also for the departure from the typical, strictly controlled, food- or drink-motivated studies that tend to define studies of animal minds. These rats eagerly participated and for the sole reason that they found it enjoyable, and that provides an alternative way to study their mental processes in a way that is far closer to their natural abilities.

Communicating emotions, like happiness, is important for highly social species, us included. It's hard to conceive of a world in which we keep a poker face at all times, and still maintain strong social relationships. But we don't just project how we're feeling into the ether, to be picked up willy-nilly by anybody in the vicinity. We typically reserve sharing our deepest emotional states for close friends or family, and the communication isn't one-way. When a friend is sharing something upsetting with me, the same parts of my brain fire up as if I was experiencing her pain. I feel sad for her, because her emotional state has been replicated in me. Similarly, if I've had a bit of a 'meh' day and then meet a friend who is projecting joy and positivity, I'm likely to become a bit more joyful and positive too. Emotions are contagious, and the capacity we have for emotional contagion is considered a foundational component of our ability to empathise.

Rats also pick up on others' emotions, as do several other animals. As we've seen, when they see another rat being tickled, they seem to similarly experience joy. They can also learn to fear something when they see another rat being fearful of it. Rats, therefore, seem to possess the same capacity for emotional contagion, but that on its own is not enough to demonstrate empathy. An empathetic individual must also be motivated to help another in need, and that's where things get really interesting.

The first studies suggesting empathy in rats date to the 1950s and 1960s, where in one study the animals chose *not* to press a lever for a treat when they learned that doing so also administered an electric shock to another rat. In another study, the rats would press a lever to lower another rat that was dangling in distress in mid-air. Rats seem to look out for other rats, and since then several studies have looked into this in more depth, including, in 2011, a seminal study which showed that the little rodents would spontaneously release a companion who was trapped in a small tube.

Subsequent research has probed this behaviour further and revealed two key things about when and why the rats help others. First, it's much more likely when the other rat is showing signs of distress – dangling in mid-air, for example, or trapped in a small box. Second, rats don't help any old rat – they are much more likely to help a friend than a stranger. They will help strangers in distress, but only if they belong to a familiar strain – either the same strain as themselves or, remarkably, a different strain if they have had time to get to know them. Rats will even help robots, but only if that robot has previously helped them, which is a tit-for-tat form of helping.

Overall, neuroscientific research is showing that rats have brains that are not too dissimilar to our own, providing them with the capacity to laugh and have fun, pick up on others' pain and help those in distress, and to even play with us. And on the problem-solving side of things, rats also excel. This shouldn't be surprising given how quickly they can learn and adapt to changing environments – this is why they're so good at living alongside us.

The following anecdote will give you an idea of how smart and resourceful rats can be. In 2004, a team of New Zealand researchers released a single male rat onto the small, rat-free island of Motuhoropapa. While that sounds like quite an irresponsible thing to do, given the destruction to native ground-nesting birds wreaked by rats, they had a legitimate aim – to document the behaviour of a solitary, 'invading' rat and to test different methods of detection and elimination. Given that the island is less than 1km^2, and that the rat had been fitted with a radio collar so it could be tracked around the clock, that seemed reasonable. Unfortunately, they completely underestimated this rat. It took more than four months to catch him, despite deploying nine different kinds of detection methods, including a total of 30 live traps, 20 snap traps, 20 peanut-butter baits, 5 poison baits and 2 trained sniffer dogs. Ratty threw them a curveball at 10 weeks, when his radio signal died. Assuming this also meant the end of the rat, the researchers were in for a shock when the signal suddenly pinged back into action, this time on the different island of Otata, which lies 400m across open water. It wasn't until week 18 that he was caught and killed, demonstrating just how easily these animals can spread to and colonise new environments, when given the chance.

For these clever, quick little learners, no challenge is too great. That's apparent from a study conducted by Kelly Lambert and colleagues at the University of Richmond in Virginia, which had the relatively innocuous aim of investigating whether their home environment impacted rats' ability to learn a novel, complex skill. Some rats were kept in pairs in standard lab conditions, while others were kept in larger social groups in enriched environments, meaning the cage had extra levels to explore and extra toys to play with. Around five months of age, the rats then embarked on learning the complex skill – driving a car! These 'rodent-operated vehicles' (ROVs) were quite basic in their original incarnation, comprising little more than a plastic cereal container mounted to four wheels. The rat voluntarily entered the container and learned, through gradual reinforcement involving many (highly prized) Froot Loops, to operate it by touching one of three copper wires: the central one made the car move forward, while the left and right wires were for direction. Incredibly, all rats learned to drive the car and to steer it around an arena to get a treat, although the rats in the enriched group learned faster and showed higher motivation to interact with the ROV. In a fantastic development, even after testing had finished and no Froot Loops were available, these rats continued to drive their little cars around, suggesting that they found the activity pleasurable. The rats were quite literally joyriding.

In a follow-up study, Lambert and team got more serious. The homemade *Blue Peter*-style ROVs were upgraded to feature rat-proof wiring, indestructible tires and ergonomic driving levers. As Lambert has commented, they were more 'akin to rodent versions of Tesla's Cybertruck'. And the rats were just as keen to drive them. 'Unexpectedly, we found that the rats had an intense motivation for their driving training, often jumping into the car and revving the "lever engine" before their vehicle hit the road.' Lambert has commented that when she came into the lab in the morning the rats ran to the sides of their cages and seemed to be anticipating the testing. Could it be that they were excited about doing something that they found fun?

Having revealed that rats have thoughts and feelings, these studies are having another impact – they're prompting people to question the ethics of studying rats. Some researchers are uneasy with the apparent disconnect between, on the one hand, finding out remarkable things that show them to be sentient, and on the other, euthanising them to study their brains, or subjecting them to pain and suffering. Jeffrey Mogil, a neuroscientist at McGill University in Canada, commented in an interview with *Science* magazine in 2015 that, 'The more we do experiments like this, the more we wonder if we should do experiments like this.' Mogil was commenting on another team's study, which showed that rats were sensitive to other rats' facial expressions of pain. The study utilised a tool originally developed by his lab with rodents, called the pain grimace scale, which combines scores for eye narrowing, nose position, ear position, cheek bulging and whisker changes to provide an overall score on the degree of pain being experienced (none, some, or clear evidence for pain). The score has since been applied to a range of other animals, allowing researchers or veterinary workers to make reliable judgements about the animal's emotional state in order to reduce distress.

Rats, very clearly, experience pain. And yet, current legislation for the welfare of these animals not only appears to ignore their sentience, but in some cases dismisses that they are even animals at all. This is the case for the US Animal Welfare Act, which states that the term 'animal' specifically excludes 'birds, rats of the genus *Rattus*, and mice of the genus *Mus*, bred for use in research.' As philosophers Kristin Andrews and Susana Monsó pointed out in an essay entitled 'Rats are us' for the online journal Aeon in 2020, there's a clear paradox here, in that it's considered justifiable to use rats in medical research due to their physiological similarity to humans (including for mental health research), but they aren't considered similar enough to warrant any legal protection from harm. Andrews and Monsó explain how greater recognition of ape and monkey cognition and emotion led to greater protections around their use, because the apparent moral costs were too great. They write, 'These moral costs exist in the case of rats too. It is only our moral short-sightedness and relentless anthropocentrism that have prevented us from taking them into account.'

Given all that we are learning about rats, this leaves me in a bit of a quandary. These little mammals wear several different hats in their relationship with us, and that can make thinking about how to behave towards them challenging. They can clearly be damaging to crops, property and health, so we're justified in wanting to remove them from our homes, businesses and health centres. But how do we square the use of cruel killing methods with the fact that rats are sentient little animals who experience pain and suffering, jump for joy when they're having fun, and go out of their way to help other members of their group? I put this to Burn — how does she balance all the fascinating things that science is revealing about rats with the fact that they can also be monumental pests? 'Well.' She pauses. 'When you say they're monumental pests, I would say that they're monumental animals as well.' Burn says that she is horrified by the levels of cruelty inflicted on rats by some people, particularly when the person seems to take pleasure in the animal's suffering. 'They're doing their "pest" behaviours in all innocence,' she says. 'All they're doing is going about their lives and trying to survive using their natural curiosity. In many ways, they're a lot like us.' One of Burn's recent studies emphasises this point — laboratory rats who were faced with doing the same, monotonous task on repeat were more likely to hop onto an 'exit platform', signalling that they'd had enough, compared with rats for whom the tasks varied each time. Like us, Burn writes to me, 'rats seek to escape monotony, possibly due to boredom.'

The difficulty we have in thinking about rats likely comes back to affective reasoning and the way that we process affect. We struggle to weigh up risks and benefits in isolation, preferring instead to label something as either positive or negative. The truth is that rats are both. But society seems to have fixated on the negatives, even when the animals don't directly impact us, and that means we overlook all their positive traits. Burn says she would like our conception of rats to broaden, for us to create space in our minds to even allow enjoyment of the animals. 'They are wildlife, and they can be appreciated like you would appreciate any other species of wildlife,' she says. 'Also, they're fun to watch.' I can only agree with this, having spent many a happy moment watching the plump rats that scurry along the brook in our local park.

One thing is certain. In our cities, we created the conditions for them to thrive alongside us, and we must take some responsibility for the fact that we maintain an environment with abundant opportunities for cosy living quarters and high-calorie food. Urban life has also undoubtedly exerted selection pressures on them, and a whole cast of other city slickers.

★★★

In 2011, a red fox was discovered living on the 72nd floor of the unfinished Shard building in central London. The animal, a young male named Romeo by the animal centre where he was taken after his capture, used the central stairwell to climb to the top of the 288m-tall building, where he became trapped. He lived off scraps of food left by workers at the site for two weeks before the pest-control services were called in. The centre's founder commented in a subsequent interview: 'We explained to him that if foxes were meant to be 72 storeys off the ground, they would have evolved wings.' But foxes don't need wings. These resourceful mammals take their opportunities where they can, using their incredible senses and agility to get wherever they need. And, overwhelmingly tall buildings aside, it has paid off for them. In the UK, red foxes started colonising our towns and cities close to a century ago, and today they're everywhere.

While it's unknown whether Romeo had the sense of beauty necessary to appreciate the view from his 72nd-floor lodgings, foxes are highly adaptable, opportunistic problem-solvers, and these inbuilt cognitive traits have enabled urban foxes to thrive in the city. What's more, given this history of living alongside us, the red fox is a fantastic animal to ask questions about how the urban environment might be influencing them. And initial results are intriguing.

In a study of fox skulls that were collected in and around London in the 1970s, those belonging to the city foxes had shorter, wider snouts compared with their rural counterparts and, somewhat surprisingly, *smaller* braincases. It's a result that flies in the face of the idea that urban animals are necessarily more cunning and street-smart than their rural relatives, but it reflects two very different lifestyles and needs. Squatter snouts may provide an advantage for crunching down on leftover bones or getting inside food packaging, helping urban foxes to make the most of their waste-filled world, while the smaller braincase may simply reflect the difference in mental effort required to forage in these two environments. Urban foxes can get a lot of their calories from human leftovers and rubbish, and this is cognitively far easier than catching prey, in that a discarded kebab doesn't try and run away or hide.

The findings are also consistent with another, fascinating possibility. These morphological changes to foxes' skulls are strikingly similar to the changes that have occurred in domesticated animals compared with their wild relatives, which additionally include floppy ears, curly tails and white-patched coats, together with behavioural changes like increased docility and friendliness, and decreased fear and stress towards people. Collectively, these changes have been termed 'domestication syndrome,' and it raises an intriguing question: could it be that by living in such proximity to humans, urban foxes are treading the path towards self-domestication? It's too soon to know, and it may be that this is as far as it goes for foxes, but as the study's coauthor, Andrew Kitchener, has commented, 'Adapting to life around humans actually primes some animals for domestication.' Since the skulls were collected more than 50 years ago, it would be fascinating to know whether the same trend has since intensified.

We also don't yet know how, or indeed if, these changes are manifesting themselves in fox behaviour – it is not possible to simply match up what a fox does with its skull shape, or even its brain size. Fox intelligence is not something that has been extensively studied compared with other animals, but the evidence is starting to appear. In one study, foxes from a range of different habitats across the UK were presented with 'puzzle boxes' containing treats. To get the food, the animal needed to open the box by biting, pulling, pushing or lifting it, and while city foxes were more likely to approach and interact with the boxes than country foxes, there was no difference in their likelihood of actually getting the food. Rather than selecting for a super-smart new breed of foxes, city life may be doing the opposite, consistent with the skull changes – when food is so abundant, the most successful foxes may not be the ones that can use their wits as much as the ones that can overcome their shyness and fear of humans. In our human landscapes, boldness might be a better bet than brainpower, which has the unfortunate consequence that as city-dwellers become generally less comfortable around wild creatures in our spaces, our environments are selecting for individuals that are *more* comfortable around us.

In North America, the same difference in boldness and exploratory tendencies is seen in coyotes. And raccoons have moved into towns and cities with gusto, their dextrous little hands making light work of garbage bins or car doors. But the opposite pattern of bigger brain size has been reported for some species of small mammals, showing that the fox story is not a universal one, and that living among us may well exert a selection pressure to be smarter. It might be different for different species, and it might also be different for different timepoints – being clever might be more useful in the early, unpredictable, days of human disturbance, whereas after several decades the environment might have become much more predictable. Either way, the evidence is there to show that animals can and are adapting to human environments – what remains to be seen is how humanity will respond to our uninvited neighbours. Is coexistence possible?

As I said, pests are tricky. Accept them all and we undoubtedly have to accept some kind of cost – the risk of disease, the potential for damage to our property, or the sheer annoyance of having them around. But on the flipside, for those who don't have good opportunities to access nature, these animals might be their main way of experiencing wildlife. For many people, the presence of wild animals in towns and cities, especially large, charismatic wild animals, can be a rewarding and joyful experience. That means there is no one-size-fits-all approach to pests, just as there is no hard-and-fast categorisation of animals that are and are not pests. The only defining trait is that these animals are doing something that causes harm, but even agreeing on this is a challenge – opinions can differ at the level of a nation, a city, a street and even within the same house. Mountain gorillas, for example, are thought of as gentle giants by much of the world, but they are very real pests for the people whose crops they raid outside Bwindi National Park. Closer to home, some people will not give the molehill in their garden a second thought, while others will call in pest control at the merest sign of disturbed soil. It comes down to individual perceptions of harm, which I think we urgently need to reconsider.

When it comes to controlling the typical pest species, we've dug ourselves a hole. As for so many things, nature already had the solution, in the form of predators and parasites, and it's a solution that has been fine-tuned over millions of years of intertwined evolution. Then humans came along and messed up the natural balance, not just persecuting many of these predators to extinction but also creating the perfect habitats for the 'pests' to thrive. To rectify the situation, we've tried to create novel solutions in the form of chemicals or high-tech gadgets that promise to exterminate the nuisance beasts. These represent many years and billions of dollars of investment, and ultimately they're both less effective and more harmful than nature's original solution. Put like that, we perhaps need to have a few words with ourselves about our pride in human 'intelligence' and 'progress'.

Nonetheless, here we are, and there's no point dwelling on all we've lost. But we can take stock and think about our ongoing attitudes to these misplaced beasts in our homes, gardens and towns. One option is to continue trying to fight them, constructing our barriers and our boundaries and being outraged that they refuse to stay in their 'proper place'. The other is to reframe our attitudes, stop thinking about these creatures as 'invaders' and 'vermin' and see them for what they really are: other animals that are, like us, simply trying to live their best lives.

Spoiler alert, option one doesn't work. We've already seen this with household arthropods – no matter how clean you believe your home to be, you will always be sharing it with other little creatures. Going down the route of trying to exterminate all these will only lead to more anger, fear and annoyance towards wildlife – and in your home I think you would be driven mad, unless you could live in a hermetically sealed building and never open a window again. Or have any pets. And think about it. Even if you could create a completely sterile home environment, the chances are that every time you left the house, you'd become more bothered by the nature you encountered. That same negative feedback loop we heard about for insects would come into play, only magnified and expanded to include all wild animals. Taken to its extreme, this route leads to future cities of concrete sterility, bedecked with fakery and devoid of wildlife, with crack troops of pest controllers on hand to exterminate any wild creature that dares show its face. For me, that is a future that doesn't bear thinking about.

Option two shows more promise but it requires a seismic shift in our understanding of the importance of nature, and an acceptance of increasing the mental permeability of our borders to allow a bit more of it through. It requires us to reconnect with the natural world, and to recognise that we, as animals, are part of it too. Given how quickly we're changing the world and destroying so many creatures' homes, we cannot continue to expect that cities exist only for people; we must recognise that by sharing some of this space we can make a real difference to wildlife. Each and every one of us. We must learn to coexist. As Pavol Prokop writes to me: 'Every animal on this planet has the right to exist here, regardless of whether the species is deemed useful to humans. Unfortunately, this philosophy is still unfamiliar to many people.'

That doesn't mean flinging our doors wide to all other life forms: as we've already heard, that will never be appropriate for all. Instead, I advocate for a little more tolerance in the situations where tolerance is possible, and if it isn't possible, then the most humane method of removal. Let's start with the spider in your bath: does it truly need to die, or can it be relocated outside? How about the wasp nest in the scrubby corner of your garden: is it uncomfortably close to the house, or could it be left alone? Do the aphids on your plants warrant the whole lot being sprayed with poison or can you experiment with leaving them to natural pest control (like the newly relocated spider and the newly tolerated wasps, or the ladybird and lacewing larvae that have voracious appetites for such pests?). There are other ways to deal with pests, and if we can break the habit of reaching for the poison spray, we will be making progress. Some businesses have embraced natural techniques even more fully, such as that of the Vergenoegd Löw Wine Estate in South Africa, where pest control has been outsourced to more than 1,600 Indian runner ducks. These 'soldiers of the vineyards' are let out twice a day to roam through the vines where they eat aphids, snails and worms. This might not be so appropriate in your back garden, especially in a fox-frequented area, but hedgehogs, toads, and foraging birds will happily get to work on these unwanted visitors, if they're given the chance.

★★★

Back at the WWT reserve, I continue my walk from the hide of hornet horrors. It's a still and hazy autumn morning, and the sounds of traffic compete with the 'me-me-me-me' of long-tailed tits in the yellowing foliage. I'm lost in my thoughts as I walk down the track, mentally preparing a to-do list for the rest of the day. And then I spot her, gliding past a stand of willow. A female hornet, and she is magnificent. Bigger than her shrivelled sisters, of course. Vibrant. Purposeful. I marvel as she passes, immersed in her own vespine world of sights and smells. In this, I do not feature. I am irrelevant. And that, I think, is a very good thing.

CHAPTER 8

The good, the bad and the animal

But not all animals were regarded as diabolical incarnations; on the contrary, many were revered as embodiments and emblems of divine perfections.
       Evans, *The Criminal Prosecution and Capital Punishment of Animals,* 1906

When I was a child, I had a framed photographic print of a bottlenose dolphin hanging on my bedroom wall. The dolphin was mid-leap above a deep blue ocean, sparkling in the sun and generally looking fantastic. I'd seen the print at a stall at our local summer fair and begged my parents for it. And I loved that picture. To me, the dolphin represented the best of all animals – beautiful, athletic, intelligent, playful.

Permanently smiling, radiating benevolence, I had no doubt that it was a thoroughly Good animal.

Young me had no idea what dolphins are actually like.

In August 2023, dolphin watchers on a boat trip with SeaMôr Dolphin Watching, just off the coast of the pretty little Welsh harbour town of New Quay, had front-row seats to a horrific spectacle. The group had already spent a little time watching a pod of about eight bottlenose dolphins, and as the boat made its way back to the headland, they spotted a porpoise. 'We thought "this could get interesting" – half joking initially.' This is tour guide Josh Pedley, speaking to BBC News after the event. But things did get interesting, and brutal, because as soon as the dolphins spotted the porpoise, all hell broke loose. And SeaMôr Dolphin Watching's boat was in exactly the right place. The dolphins were relentless in their pursuit of the smaller cetacean, which at one point tried to hide underneath the boat. But there was no escape. The dolphins rammed the animal hard, flipping it up into the air and repeatedly smashing into it, breaking its body and ultimately killing it. Company owner Brett Stones told the BBC that he was stunned by the experience. 'It looked so vulnerable lying there, it shocks you to the core. I'm pretty unshakeable and it was almost too much for me to watch.'

Harbour porpoises are the second smallest members of the cetacean family, measuring up to 2m in length and weighing up to 75kg. That's the size of a tall man, so might not sound very little, but compared with bottlenose dolphins, which are typically 2.5m–3.5m in length and around 300kg, they're dinky. They have shorter, blunter heads than dolphins (they're all melon, no beak), and they're much shyer than their larger relatives. Endearingly, they're nicknamed 'puffing pigs' for the sound they make when they come up to breathe. And they're under attack. Porpicide is not a commonly recorded behaviour, but it is being increasingly documented. New Quay sits in the wide expanse of Cardigan Bay, a well-known location for dolphin and whale spotting, and between 1991 and 2011, 137 harbour porpoises were killed in bottlenose dolphin attacks here. It's not just a Welsh phenomenon. Off the California coast, tens of dead porpoises have washed up since 2005, their bodies betraying the telltale injuries of dolphin attack. And in 2020, German-based researchers documented similar injuries to the bodies of six harbour porpoises off the Schleswig-Holstein coast, which appeared around the same time that a solitary male bottlenose dolphin was recorded in the area.

Bottlenose dolphins are not the only perpetrators of porpicide. Orcas (the largest dolphins), particularly members of the Southern Resident population living off the northwest Pacific coast of North America, have been documented tossing baby porpoises between each other as if the little animals were beach balls. Between 1962 and 2020, researchers identified and analysed 78 episodes in which Southern Resident orcas harassed porpoises, 28 of which resulted in the porpoise's death. The Southern Residents are an endangered group of Chinook salmon specialists – unlike other orca populations, they're not generalists, so can't switch to feed on seals or other prey when salmon aren't abundant. And since overfishing has decimated salmon populations, the Southern Resident population has been declining since the 1970s. It's therefore possible that the behaviour may be a form of hunting practice, since the orcas preferentially targeted young porpoises of a similar size to adult Chinook salmon. But it's also possible that they are just mean bullies.

There are more reports, and undoubtedly far more violence is being inflicted by dolphins against their porpoise brethren. The key thing about these findings, as well as the Welsh attack, is that the porpoises aren't being eaten. Dolphins aren't hunting the little cetaceans, they seem to be playing with them, killing for the fun of it. And that's not something that we expect to see in other animals – particularly in other animals that are beloved.

Porpicide is not the only violent crime committed by dolphins. From 1999 to 2020, researchers recorded 10 occasions in which bottlenose dolphins attacked baby Antillean manatees off the coast of Belize. Since manatee calves are not eaten by the dolphins, the reasons for the behaviour are unknown but in an interview for the website LiveScience following publication of the reports, senior researcher Jeremy Kiszka summed it up when he said, 'Around the world we see bottlenose dolphins literally acting like jerks and being violent with other species.' They're not all sweetness and light to other dolphins, either. Males are sexual predators and bullies, and will work in small groups to isolate a female from her pod and then take turns to forcibly mate with her.

It even extends to us: between 2022 and 2024, 29 people have been injured by dolphin interactions off beaches in the Fukui prefecture, on the Sea of Japan coast. Injuries range from bites on the hand to broken bones, and researchers believe it has all been caused by a single, lonely male. Why he's doing so is impossible to say – some experts have commented that biting is a common form of communication between social partners in a pod, and so it may be that this male has been ostracised from his pod and is now seeking social interactions with people. Reports that the dolphin has been trying to press his genitals against victims point to a different explanation. Certainly, if this large, powerful animal intended harm, he would be ramming them at speed and that would result in injuries more typical of a high-speed car crash.

The key thing to remember, as the National Oceanic and Atmospheric Administration (NOAA) Fisheries points out on its website, is that 'Dolphins are not water toys or pets. The "Flipper myth" of a friendly wild dolphin has given us the wrong idea.' Flipper indeed. Decades of friendly, helpful dolphins in stories and films have painted dolphins as 'nice' animals, and that has done them a disservice. Dolphins are

THE GOOD, THE BAD AND THE ANIMAL

wild, intelligent and extremely powerful beasts, and even if they see us as nothing more than playthings, the force with which they might interact (which would be normal between dolphins) is more than we might expect or that our bodies can cope with. For our sake and theirs, we need to be respectful of these animals and give them their space. In fairness, that's a good rule to follow for all wild animals, but particularly for the ones that could legitimately and unexpectedly cause you injury and death.

Sharks are the marine predators that we all fear, though hopefully Chapter 2 alleviated some of these concerns, but most researchers of marine animal behaviour would say that we've got our fears the wrong way round. While sharks might be able to learn to anticipate a fishy treat at the right time and place, and to tell apart a red square from a blue circle, they've got nothing on the dolphin family when it comes to sheer, frightening intelligence, and especially in the social domain. The ways that orcas, for example, have learned to work together and devise creative new strategies to hunt is both incredible and terrifying. The fact that some of these animals have been on a spree of hunting great white sharks and ripping out their livers is testament to their status as innovative, apex predators – there's a new king in town, and it's a smarter, scarier one. When orcas turned their attention to us and started ramming yachts and fishing boats, we got a taste of how powerful and potentially dangerous these animals can be. So far, they've shown no interest in hunting humans, but if they did the oceans would become a far more frightening place. For now, we can take comfort in the conclusion by marine biologists that the 'attacks' reflect nothing more than bored adolescents playing with the rudders. Far from trying to enact revenge on us, it seems that these curious, highly intelligent predators are simply entertained by our marine vessels.

It's not just dolphins that go out of their way to hurt other animals, excluding humans of course – there's no question that we're the worst of all species when it comes to inflicting unnecessary suffering on others. And random acts of violence are not the only crimes committed. Murdering babies, gang rape, tribal wars, necrophilia, feasting on faeces – the animal kingdom has it all. The difficulty, when it comes to thinking about these 'true' crimes, is that many of these seemingly depraved acts are committed by precisely the animals that are culturally most popular, and therefore the ones that we hold in highest moral regard. It begs the question: how should we think about the good animals gone bad?

★★★

Dr George Murray Levick, surgeon and officer on the 1910 British Antarctic Expedition, studied the world's largest colony of Adélie penguins for three months between October and December 1911. He became the first person to witness a complete breeding season of these birds, and his meticulous records revealed previously unknown glimpses into their social lives. His 1914 publication, *Antarctic Penguins – A Study of Their Social Habits*, and 1915 scientific report, 'The Natural History of the Adélie Penguin', also made several references to the behaviour of 'hooligan cocks':

> *Many of the colonies, especially those nearer the water, are plagued by little knots of 'hooligans' who hang about their outskirts, and should a chick go astray it stands a good chance of losing its life at their hands. The crimes which they commit are such as to find no place in this book, but it is interesting indeed to note that, when nature intends them to find employment, these birds, like men, degenerate in idleness.*

Levick did not elaborate on the aforementioned 'crimes' in these publications, and it was not for another 40 or so years that the breeding biology of these birds was described more fully by others, but unbeknownst to these researchers, Levick had already done the work. Senior curator of birds at the Natural History Museum, Douglas Russell, happened upon a four-page printed paper entitled 'The Sexual Habits of the Adélie Penguin' while he was going through Levick's file at the museum. 'As it was boldly headed "Not for Publication" it immediately caught my eye,' Russell told LiveScience in 2012. Printed in 1915, it had been intended for inclusion in Levick's report, but was subsequently removed from the final publication because what was included was deemed too challenging for the times. Levick himself had clearly recognized this, since some of the more risqué elements in his field notebooks had either been pasted over with Greek text or were simply written in Greek. These included penguin necrophilia, penguin rape and sexual and physical violence towards chicks. Levick's distress at what he'd observed is also apparent; underneath one of the entries in his notebook he wrote, 'There seems to be no crime too low for these Penguins.'

Levick's hesitation, and the decision not to publish these observations, which he bracketed under the term 'depraved', are well-aligned with societal expectations and scientific thought at that time. Indeed, as Russell and colleagues wrote in their 2012 publication on the newly discovered paper, the decision not to publish them suggests 'an inability of the science of the period to either acknowledge or interpret the behaviour.' In a subsequent interview, Russell said of Levick's shock: 'He, to a certain extent, falls into the same trap as an awful lot of people in seeing penguins as little people. They're not. They are birds and should be interpreted as such.'

This, it must be acknowledged, is jarring for most people. We all think that we know these comical, upright, waddling birds, who huddle together for warmth and whose babies are adorable balls of fluff. We grew up on *Pingu*, *Happy Feet* and *March of the Penguins*, while nature documentaries highlighted the strength of their pair bonds and their resilience against the polar winters. Penguins were loyal, industrious, stoic characters, not these sexual deviants. The trouble, as Jon Green, senior lecturer in marine biology at the University of Liverpool, tells me, is that 'When people think about penguins, they think about emperor penguins.' And all the cultural references above are, indeed, emperors. These, the largest penguin species, do indeed huddle together on the ice and cooperate to protect their chicks, helping to ensure their survival during the harshest winter of any environment. Which they do and they do very well. But, says Green, 'that's not how most penguins live.'

Take macaroni penguins. Sporting vivid mango-yellow crests (which are either excitedly erect or foppish), they're charismatic birds, and nest in huge colonies. But if you take a closer look at the spacing, you'll see they never get that close to their neighbours. 'They're fighting distance apart,' says Green. 'Penguins fight all the time. They are scrappy, angry animals in many circumstances.' He points to an image of a macaroni penguin's beak on his screen. 'See that? They have massive beaks. They aim for a soft bit behind the eye and will wrench that until it bleeds, and then they will batter the intruder with their flippers and drag them through the guano, still beating them up.' That sounds painful and Green confirms it. 'I've been bitten hundreds of times and when one of these bad boys bites you it really hurts. It is quite a piece of equipment that they've got.'

Even emperor penguins aren't free from flaws. It has long been known that some birds will kidnap other chicks, and when they do they tend to abandon the infants after just a few hours, which usually results in death. But even if we put 'kidnapping and manslaughter' next to their name, when you compare them against the Adélies, they're saintly. And on that, it seems that Levick was right about these birds, because there's more. 'Of course, there's the prostitution stuff too,' says Green. 'Do you know about that?'

Adélie penguins build raised nests out of pebbles on the Antarctic beaches where they breed; a strategy for keeping their eggs away from meltwater floods that may happen when the ice melts too quickly and too soon. Pebbles, therefore, are important, but there are only so many to go around, and that means they become extremely valuable during the breeding season. This pressure has led to the penguins becoming a bit sneaky: when they get the opportunity, they nab another bird's pebbles while it's off searching for more. You may well have seen documentary clips of this, and it's usually accompanied with some musical accompaniment that makes it seem mischievous and cheeky. The sort that makes people laugh and say, 'Oh, those funny little penguins, aren't they cute?' What's less typically shown, although the BBC did capture it in their 2001 series, *Deep into the Wild*, is that female penguins will also prostitute themselves for pebbles.

In the mid-1990s, researchers Fiona Hunter and Lloyd Spencer Davis witnessed 10 instances of female Adélie penguin prostitution while studying breeding behaviour at a colony on Ross Island, Antarctica. On each occasion, the female left her partner at the nest and approached an unpaired male on his nest site, doing the penguin equivalent of fluttering her eyelashes at him. The male needed little convincing and incredibly, after each copulation the female then picked up a stone from the male's nest and went back to her nest and partner. That wasn't the end of it. In five of the cases, the female went back again and took another stone, without offering any more sex. One female went back 10 times and took a stone every time. And the male being robbed didn't seem to mind – a far cry from the way that a male would usually behave to any other bird getting close to his nest or, heaven forbid, trying to steal his stones. In fact, just flirting with a male did it. Hunter and Davis observed 10 females going up to unpaired males at their nests and engaging them in mutual courtship behaviour.

They then just took a stone and left before having sex. One female made the most that she could of this opportunity, taking a whopping 62 stones from a single male in the space of an hour, with no aggression from the male. The researchers also noted that although males also solicited sex from females at their nests, on no occasion did a male take a stone from a female's nest site. On the surface, this might suggest that males either possess morals or lack brains. But from an evolutionary perspective, it boils down to the fact that if, by tolerating females' thievery, a singleton male increases his chances of fathering a chick or two, that more than outweighs his loss of a few pebbles.

In fairness, we should also acknowledge that penguins are on the receiving end of bad behaviour too. On the sub-Antarctic Marion Island, male Antarctic fur seals have forced themselves on king penguins on four separate occasions, starting in 2008. Witnesses to the subsequent incidents described the seals' behaviour in detail – researchers' photographs show the mammals' erect penises, and one unfortunate penguin was seen with blood-stained feathers between its legs.

Not all the 'bad' behaviour happens in the sea, although there does seem to be quite a high frequency of apparent immorality under the waves. But land animals are certainly no saints either. And in between the sea and the land are some of the worst offenders, beasts that one researcher has called 'pure evil'. They look cute but they're necrophiliac, murderous sexual predators, who'll kill your dogs and bite your face given the slimmest chance. When it comes to 'good' animals doing 'bad' things, we need to talk about otters.

★★★

Remember how research has shown that people tend to rate beautiful and cute animals as higher on moral standing than ugly animals? Well, otters provide one good reason to treat that instinct with a pinch of salt. No other animal demonstrates quite so clearly that cuteness does not equal goodness. They have sweet, whiskery round faces, with inquisitive eyes and a shiny black dog's nose, and when they're swimming they are models of agility and grace. Sea otters are even cuter, thanks to their habit of bobbing around on their back, grooming themselves with their adorable little paws and holding hands while they drift off to sleep. Their pelt is so thick and soft it is just crying out for you to rub your face in it. Except if you did, you probably wouldn't see your nose again.

Examples abound of river otters attacking people, although on the grand scheme of things it should still be acknowledged as a rare event. That doesn't make it any less scary for those involved, though. Like Mariasella Harun, who on the morning of 11th September 2024, was jogging in a park in Kota Kinabalu, Malaysia, when a group of eight otters rushed at her from a drain and bit her arms, legs and head. She was helped by other joggers, who were also bitten, and the deep gashes she sustained required hospital treatment. Or, when in November 2023, a swimmer in a California lake suffered around 40 puncture wounds after otters attacked him in the water. In an interview with NBC News, the man said, 'I felt like they wanted to kill me … It is by far the most terrifying experience I've ever had in my life.' Even in Singapore, where otters have moved into the city and are widely treated as a positive example of human–wildlife coexistence, the slinky water weasels have attacked people.

Otters are sometimes mixed up with beavers and assumed to eat a similarly plant-based diet. In fact, they're not at all closely related: beavers are huge rodents while otters are carnivores, belonging to the weasel family. The order Carnivora includes cats, dogs, bears, mongooses, seals and more; all are in possession of sharp canines and carnassial teeth, and otters are no exception. You don't often see them unless they're eating something, but when they bare those teeth you can see they have an impressive set of weaponry. These are not animals that anybody should be trying to pet. And on the subject of pets, you also don't want to let your dogs near them, because otters will try to get them too. Several owners have had to save their dogs after otters tried to drag them to a watery demise.

Attacking us and our pets is one thing, but the way that otters behave towards members of their own, and other, wild species is also shocking. And this isn't new knowledge. In an article for *New Scientist* in 1994, for example, writer Rosie Mestel beautifully summarised the depravity of sea otter behaviour when she wrote that, 'If sea otters had newspapers, their pages would be packed with stories of rampant thievery, child kidnapping, rough sex and even murder.'

It is male sea otters that commit most of the crimes, starting with sexual violence towards females. To keep hold of a female while mating, a male will often bite down on her nose, gouging deep cuts and sometimes ripping off chunks of flesh. Sometimes the males are so intent on subduing females that they hold them underwater for too long and drown them. And when they're not trying to violently mate with a female, they're likely stealing her food – observations of Californian sea otters in the 1980s and 1990s found that males obtain up to one-third of their food this way. Sometimes they even kidnap a female's pup, keeping it hostage while she's underwater, only giving it back once they have got the food.

If that's not bad enough, male sea otters also commit sexual violence to other species. Namely, they rape baby harbour seals. Between 2000 and 2002, researchers reported 19 occasions in Monterey Bay where male sea otters forcibly mated with infant seals, showing the same aggression as to females of their species and causing the same kinds of injuries and fatalities. All but four of these resulted in the seal's death, and postmortem examinations of nine of the bodies revealed they had suffered major sexual trauma – specifically, they exhibited perforations in the vaginal and/or colorectal walls to about 15 cm depth, which correlates well with the length of a sea otter penis. The researchers also reported that attacks were not restricted to live seals – on several occasions the otter would drag the seal carcass through the water, guard it and continue trying to mate with it for up to seven days after death. Sea otter necrophilia has also been observed with a dead dog and a dead cormorant, and undoubtedly these are not the only examples.

So now you know. Next time you're browsing social media and see an adorable reel of #OttersHoldingHands or #CuteOtters or the like, remember that appearances can be deceiving. Otters aren't your friends, and you shouldn't want them to be. Now let's get out of their territory and move further onto land.

★★★

It must have been around 2011 when I first saw *that* video of a chimpanzee and a frog. If you know you know. And if you don't, well that's probably a good thing too. My then-friend and now-partner (and no, it wasn't the video) had stumbled upon it somewhere on social media and couldn't help sending it to a few of his biologically minded friends. In it, a young male chimpanzee at Honolulu Zoo grabs a live frog or toad from his enclosure and proceeds to use it as a sex toy. He lies on his back, then gets up and leans one arm onto the floor, resting his head on his arm, all the while gripping the frog and thrusting into its mouth. The frog did not survive the ordeal, which allegedly lasted for several hours, and the video obviously went viral – to be met by stunned silences, howls of disbelief, and a group of social media commentators ready with appropriate puns. 'Ribbited for your pleasure,' surely deserves a mention.

We've known since Jane Goodall's research that chimpanzees have a dark side, although it took many years before Goodall and her team documented anything to challenge the notion that chimpanzees were peaceful apes. Indeed, before this it was commonly assumed that humans were the 'rogue' apes – we were the only ones that went to war and killed each other, and it was all down to the corrupting influence of modern civilisation. Goodall and her team were the first to show that this was nonsense, largely in their documentation of the Gombe Chimpanzee War.

This marked a period when Goodall's focal group at Gombe underwent a fission event, splitting into two as they naturally sometimes do. But nobody was prepared for what happened next, because what had started as a group of closely bonded individuals ended up as two warring tribes, each prepared to commit horrific levels of violence on the 'other' group. Two of the males that Goodall had studied, Goliath and Junio, were friends in the original group, and yet when old, toothless Goliath became the target for the intruding faction, Junio was there, helping to beat his previous ally to death. Coexistence in neighbouring territories didn't seem to be an option – the group that took the more northerly territory wanted total domination, and they achieved it by systematically killing all six of the southern group's males, before moving on to attacking and killing several of the females and infants too. It's not an isolated incident – a little later a group of Japanese researchers studying chimpanzees at a different site documented something eerily similar. A troop with six adult males was attacked, with each male picked off and killed individually. In this case the attackers did allow the females and their infants to join their troop, apart from the adolescent males. This proved to be a death sentence for them as, with no adults to feed and care for them, they simply stayed put in their home territory and wasted away.

Why are chimpanzees so violent to others of their kind? When Goodall first shared her observations, many people found them too hard to accept, instead blaming Goodall for 'corrupting' the animals' natural behaviour by handing out bananas to the troop. The implication was that the extra resource had caused the group to split into two and fight over the bananas. We now know that everything Goodall reported is typical of our closest relatives, whether they've had much contact with humans or not. And that shouldn't be surprising really – as our closest relatives, it makes sense that we find traces of ourselves in them. For one, they're hostile to 'different' chimpanzees – as evidenced by the apparent fear and subsequent brutal killing of an albino baby born in one troop. For another, they're highly territorial animals, so when troops meet it's almost always hostile, leading to lots of whooping and posturing. But it's when one group meets a lone male from another troop that things get ugly. They will chase him, pin him down and repeatedly beat him until he's too battered to put up any kind of fight. They're not just randomly being violent – all the observations indicate that when a gang of males went to attack another troop's male, they seemed purposeful and intentional in their behaviour.

Chimpanzees are violent by nature, and not just to other chimps. In 2019, on two separate occasions, scientists studying a troop of 27 chimpanzees in Loango National Park, Gabon, witnessed groups encountering gorillas. On both occasions, the chimpanzees formed coalitions and attacked their ape cousins, stealing an infant gorilla from its mother. On both occasions, the baby gorilla was killed. The paper makes for difficult reading, providing a blow-by-blow account of the violence inflicted and the squeaks and whimpers made by the infant gorilla after being struck. It should be acknowledged that most interactions between chimps and gorillas (and they're not uncommon, given that both species are found in the same habitats) are peaceful, and youngsters of both species have been seen playing together too, showing chasing, wrestling and play-biting behaviours. Some chimpanzees have even been seen beating their chests, which is a characteristic gorilla behaviour. Scientists are still puzzling over the reasons behind the fatal attacks seen in Loango.

Chimpanzees aren't the only primates to show violence to another species. In a small forest fragment in Colombia, a male spider monkey went on a violent spree through 2010 and 2011. His victims were babies belonging to red howler monkeys or white-fronted capuchins, both of which live in the same forest habitat (and typically coexist peacefully). But this male was different. On seven occasions, he attacked mothers who were carrying infants, and on two of these the baby monkey died. The first attack was of a mother in a tree who had recently given birth, as the umbilical cord was still attached to her infant. She dropped the baby and it fell to the forest floor, and although it was still alive when she retrieved it, once she'd climbed back into the tree, the spider monkey attacked again and again the baby fell. It died later that day, and researchers noticed several bite marks on its body.

It's undeniably difficult to watch an adult animal actively inflicting harm upon a baby, and it's very hard for us to get our heads around why such a thing would happen. And while killing babies of other species is not that common, and may well reflect a single individual, infanticide towards babies of one's own species happens a lot.

'I like teaching about infanticide very much,' Pavol Prokop writes to me, explaining that many people find it very surprising. 'My feeling is that the public consider aggressive behaviour of parents toward offspring immoral and given that we are designed to protect small, helpless and vulnerable subjects, people are sad when they see infanticide by lions or storks.' This ties in with what we've already heard about the cuteness of baby animals stimulating urges to provide care and protection. I'm not sure that we can help but feel sad.

Infanticide happens a lot in mammals, and in females as well as males. The classic example comes from the African savannah, where roving coalitions of desperate, horny, murdering male lions have the single goal of taking over a pride so that they can mate with its females. When a coalition succeeds in seizing control, their number one priority is having sex, lots of it, to give themselves the best chance of passing on their genes. That's fine for receptive females who have no cubs, but females who have cubs sired by the previous pride-holders present a problem – they have absolutely no interest in sex while they're in mother mode. And they make this abundantly clear through aggression. The new pride-holders have no interest in protecting a group of cubs that don't bear their genes, and particularly when it means that their mothers are off the market. The only sensible option is to kill the cubs. It brings the lionesses back into heat in days, ready for the males to start trying to sire their own offspring. At least, until the next coalition comes in and starts all over again. The same behaviour has been documented in numerous other species, including baboons, chimpanzees, red squirrels, orcas and bottlenose dolphins. Indeed, when researchers witnessed the first bottlenose dolphin wild birth in 2013, their initial delight rapidly turned to concern when two males attacked the newborn – the duo seemed to have been trailing the mother and so immediate was their attack after the birth that the placenta was still visible. Bottlenose dolphin infanticide has even been suggested to explain why they're so aggressive towards porpoises – the smaller cetaceans may simply trigger infanticidal behaviour by males that are on a mission for sex.

Killing unrelated babies is quite straightforward to explain from an evolutionary standpoint, though that doesn't make it easier to see. But things get worse when the murderer is the infant's parent. In human society, parents who murder their babies are vilified, condemned and punished for being wicked, evil, or mentally ill. We would be disgusted to see such a thing take place. Animals, not so much. White storks, for example, are known to kill their smallest chicks and this so-called 'filial infanticide' may affect up to 20 per cent of breeding pairs. Mother moustached tamarins in the Peruvian Amazon have been observed killing their offspring, with one particularly gruesome example where the mother killed the baby by biting its head, before eating its brain and part of its upper body.

When the murderer turns cannibal and eats its own offspring, that's off-the-scale bad. Or it would be for us. But it's quite normal in fish. Scientists have quantified how frequently this occurs using a species of mouthbrooding cichlid fish called Burton's mouthbrooder. Most fish reproduce in spawning events, meaning that the female releases eggs and the male releases sperm and it all mixes up in the water and sparks new life, and that's the end of it for the parents – they've done their job, and now it's up to the tiny larval fish to make it in the world alone. An experienced older female Atlantic sturgeon may release two million eggs in one spawning event, and really who is going to notice if she's tempted by a bit of her own black gold to top up energy levels before she goes on her way? Burton's mouthbrooder, as you can probably guess from its name, goes the extra mile on parental care. The mother fish carries her fertilised eggs in her mouth for around two weeks to protect them from predators, and even once they've hatched, she allows the tiny larval fish to return to the shelter of her mouth to avoid danger. From this perspective, she's an extremely diligent and caring mother, especially because she can't eat or really breathe properly while she's carrying her babies around. Who can blame this exhausted mum for snacking on one or two to get her strength back? Experimental evidence from 31 mothers found that 29 of them ate at least some of their young, and on average, they ate around 40 per cent of their brood.

Eating your own babies may seem like it should be an oddity and evolutionary dead-end, but that's only because we don't like it. It's a specific form of cannibalism, which is a behaviour that is taboo in most human societies. And yet, cannibalism is 'wildly common across the animal kingdom,' according to biologist Bill Schutt, author of *Cannibalism: A Perfectly Natural History*, in an interview with *National Geographic* magazine in 2023. It's most often observed in invertebrates and fish, he says, but species in every major animal group have been documented eating others of their kind, including their genetic offspring.

That includes primates, and that's where things start to feel a lot more uncomfortable. Take the case of Evalyne, a Tonkean macaque whose baby died at four days old. This species is known for suffering high infant mortality, and it's not unheard of for mothers to carry the bodies of their dead infants around for hours and even days. But Evalyne carried hers around for so long that it became mummified, and its head fell off. She started nibbling at small bits of it on day 19 and had consumed the entire corpse down to a single bone by day 25. The same has been observed in a captive Japanese macaque, who carried two consecutive dead infants for four weeks before eating the mummified remains. Other observations of mother-infant cannibalism include Sumatran orangutan mothers, rhesus macaques and wild bonobos – in the latter, a dead infant was consumed by several members of the troop, including its mother.

Snacking on baby biltong might seem like an aberration of normal behaviour, and historically, that's how biologists interpreted it too. The animals must be desperate for food, or psychologically damaged due to unnatural conditions or other forms of stress. *It can't be normal*. This, of course, reflected our own, strict, taboo about eating members of our own species. As should be abundantly clear by now, that's not how other animals work. Mother mammals may eat their offspring if their infants' health is compromised and the chances of it surviving are already reduced — this was thought to be why Khali, a female sloth bear living at Smithsonian's National Zoo, ate her first and second cubs and distanced herself from her third. Or, they may kill and eat their offspring if they perceive their own condition as too poor to bear the intense energetic cost of suckling their brood — evolutionarily, it makes sense to cut your losses at that point, take advantage of the nutrient boost, and build up strength to try again with a later brood.

We should acknowledge that even if other creatures aren't assaulting, killing or raping others, their natural behaviour might not always line up with what we consider to be 'good.' Butterflies, as we've heard, are rated highly for beauty and perceived 'goodness,' and I imagine that most people would be happier to have a butterfly land on their arm than a fly. But, like otters, appearances can be deceiving — these insects can be viciously territorial, engaging in violent mid-air brawls, and several species shun feeding on flowers in favour of blood, sweat, tears, rotting corpses, urine and even poo.

Then there are hedgehogs. Much-loved in the UK, largely thanks to Beatrix Potter's 1905 book, *The Tale of Mrs Tiggy Winkle*, these prickly little beasts have undergone severe population declines over the last few decades, so it's important and welcoming that people care about them.[37] But that doesn't mean they're without fault. Hedgehogs are partial to birds' eggs and chicks, and in some parts of the UK they are munching their way through the precious offspring of endangered ground-nesting birds, single-handedly ruining entire breeding seasons. They can be a conservationist's nightmare and nowhere is this more apparent than in New Zealand, where hedgehogs were deliberately shipped in the

---

[37] And care they do. In 2021, 108,000 people petitioned the UK government to update the legal status of hedgehogs and provide greater protection. Parliament debated it but the government ultimately said no.

1870s at the request of British colonists who wanted the 'gardener's friend' to control slugs, snails and grubs. Today, the New Zealand Department of Conservation (DoC) refers to them as 'our most underrated predator,' outlining a dizzying array of native wildlife that the hedgehog will happily tuck into, including kakī (Critically Endangered black stilts), wētā (rare giant native arthropods), banded dotterels, black-fronted terns and pied oystercatchers, native snails, lizards, frogs and more. And yet, despite the clear evidence of hedgehog predation on endemic, rare wildlife, 'many people still believe hedgehogs do not fit into the same category as stoats, possums, rats and feral cats.' That's an issue for the DoC, because their position is very clear: hedgehogs cannot coexist with New Zealand's endemic wildlife. The only long-term solution is to eradicate them from the environment.

★★★

Examples of 'good' animals doing 'bad' things abound in the animal kingdom, and it's hard not to interpret them in humanistic, anthropomorphised ways. These beasts must be depraved, immoral, evil. As we discussed already, the question of animal morals is a tricky one, but the one thing that's for sure is that human standards shouldn't be applied to them. Killing babies, committing rape, eating other people and having sex with dead bodies are all behaviours that we criminally police and which trigger deep-rooted disgust responses in us, because in human society we have moral expectations of what people should do that carry significantly more weight than the payoffs of doing such things might be for those individuals. Most other animals have no such expectations of how they, their family or their social group should behave. They commit these 'crimes' because by doing so they maximise their own fitness, without any penalty for violating societal rules. That means that the moral unacceptability of these acts for *H. sapiens* don't have any relevance to the rest of the animal kingdom, just as the rest of our laws don't either.

Thinking about the nuances involved in our attitudes towards animals is challenging, and rightly so. Much as we desire information to be neatly parcelled into dichotomous categories, it's rarely that simple. But we need to let the water get muddy, because some things are worth the extra mental gymnastics. Indeed, not just worth it but essential. And our views towards animals are one of those things.

I don't want you to start persecuting penguins or hating hedgehogs. That would be the worst outcome! But I strongly believe in an evidence-based approach to inform our thinking towards all animals. Pingu and Mrs Tiggywinkle are endearing and make wonderful stories, but the living animals they represent are not 'good'. We created stories and cultural references about them that fit a narrative we wanted. And it stuck. We know that stories can be incredibly powerful ways of sharing information, and throughout our history, getting together to share stories was probably a fundamental way in which we created bonds with other individuals and shared information with them. Certainly, a fundamental way by which we educate our children.

The problem comes when we put the hedgehog, dolphin or penguin up on a pedestal and believe them incapable of aberrant behaviour. Because no matter how beautiful, smart or endearing they are, they're fundamentally not good. They're not bad either, which should be abundantly clear from previous chapters. They are animal and, unlike us, they have stayed true to their animal natures. It just so happens that as they go about their daily lives, doing the things that they have evolved to do and using the tools that natural selection equipped them with, they sometimes overlap with us. And it's the outcomes of those overlapping moments in time that inform our judgements of them, both bad and good.

THE GOOD, THE BAD AND THE ANIMAL

The key message, I guess, is that there's no tight correlation between what an animal *does* and what an animal *is*. A bear can do something that is bad for a person (such as attack them or steal their produce), but that doesn't make the bear bad. A cat can provide you with affection that makes you feel good, but that doesn't make the cat good. Even an otter, as much as it pains me to say this, abusing the lifeless body of a baby seal that it drowned while sexually assaulting it, is not evil. Animal is animal, and we need to take the highs with the lows when it comes to living alongside them. Because the alternative is a world that is neither easy for us to live in, nor rich enough in diversity for us to want to.

Epilogue

Nature is constantly enforcing the lesson, that when man interferes too greatly with the nice balance of forces she sets up, he may expect to pay the penalty, sometimes in ways little anticipated by him.
Watson, *Farm Vermin, Helpful and Hurtful,* 1894

This has been a whistlestop tour of some of the less commonly examined parts of the animal kingdom and I wish I could tell you more. About how hyenas are devoted mothers, bats have friends and spiders may dream. And how all of them have their place in the natural way of things, that ultimately makes the world a better place for us.

In researching this book, one thing that is apparent is how one-dimensional our perceptions of many animals are. When people think of a 'shark' they tend to think of a great white (the 'prototype', in the words of João Neves), and that does such a disservice to the other species. Not only does it dismiss the reality of their own, remarkable qualities, but it also, unintentionally, shunts the label of villain on to them, too. As we've seen, even great whites don't deserve this, let alone all the other shark species that feed on plankton or fish and pose us absolutely no threat. And it's the same story for crocodiles, wasps, cockroaches, snakes and mosquitoes – our brains tend to pull up one version to represent the whole group, and it's usually the version that's most problematic. It makes sense from a survival perspective to have greater awareness of the most dangerous animals but, as we've heard, in modern times our risk in many parts of the world is so much lower than in our past. We're overlooking so much of interest by our mental unwillingness to progress past the minority. That's not to say that there are no problems with any of these creatures, because there are. But what a shame for our minds to get stuck on these few, when there's so much more out there that's worth celebrating.

The other thing that's struck me is that the animals we demonise are very often Earth's greatest survivors. Many of these creatures have evolved over hundreds of millions of years and some of them have survived multiple mass extinction events. We should be celebrating them for being so good at surviving on this planet. But no. We are newcomers to this race, evolutionarily speaking, and we seem intent on removing our most venerable beasts, purging the world of the ancient wisdoms preserved in their genetic code, and replacing them with the mere striplings of domesticated, compliant beasts, or the most attractive wild mammals. Think of how much evolutionary diversity we would be wiping out if we did this.

How do we turn things around?

The world is in bad shape. We've channelled so much into separating ourselves from nature, embracing the promises of technology as we strive for wealth, growth and power, that we've turned our backs on what got us here. Yes, incredible advances have and are being made, many of which offer previously unimaginable solutions to the major issues in our lives, but technology creates a whole host of problems too. One of those is the unparalleled speed and reach by which information can spread.

When it comes to the natural world, there's no doubt that the internet helps to propagate myths and misinformation, since anybody can make claims that have no factual basis, and these can both have a global reach and greatly influence others. We've seen the devastating impacts of this for conservation, such as with the slow loris, and it's the case for many other creatures too. When I spoke to Neves about sharks, he told me that people championing these animals can work for years to challenge the stereotypes and raise their public profile. 'And then along comes a set of people that will just crash the argument with nonsense.'

We might think that newspaper articles would be better, since they aren't the work of a single voice, but sadly they can be just as affected by bias and errors. An analysis conducted by researcher Stefano Mammola and colleagues of online newspaper stories about spiders published between 2010 and 2020, for example, concluded that 'the quality of global articles on spiders was exceedingly poor.' Of the more than 5,000 articles, 47 per cent of them contained errors, and 43 per cent were sensationalist. For an animal that is already unfairly persecuted, this is a serious issue, and not just because of what human readers will take away from it. Artificial Intelligence models are trained on existing internet content, and if that content is fundamentally flawed, then those models will also be flawed. We're already seeing this with race, gender and identity and unless things change, AI models will also have a 'speciesist bias,' which will continue to perpetuate misinformation, discrimination and the unfair treatment of animals.

Modern technology offers solutions too, and that's where we need to focus attention. By connecting with others from around the world and taking control of the narrative, we can help to combat the spread of misinformation. Sticking with spiders, Mammola and colleagues have created a list of 99 fact-based 'spider world records', hosted on a global arachnology website, for educators to use to encourage interest and intrigue about the group. We need to ensure that the public have access to such resources, providing credible yet engaging facts about a diversity of different creatures.

Given its global reach, the internet also offers possibilities to glean insights into public perception and understanding of different species; this kind of data is of the utmost value for policymakers and conservation charities. Historically, measuring public attitudes towards animals involved surveys, which were both resource-intensive and limited in scope. The internet, in contrast, provides vast amounts of data, offering new possibilities to understand how people engage with information about the natural world.

Ultimately, coexistence with other animals requires a perceptual shift. To be nudged away from exceptionalism and the dominionistic views by which we only see what animals can do for us. They're not on this planet to serve us, so we need to move away from asking about their 'point'. We'd also do well to recognise that the world is not a theme park, with animals put here for our entertainment. We can't make them perform for us as if they were trained in a circus, and we can't admonish them for doing things that we don't like.

Doing these things also means appreciating that species do not live in isolation, and that we can't just pick and choose the animals that we want to live alongside, like we're selecting from a menu. We can't say, 'Well, I'll have the hedgehog and the robin for the garden, but I'm going to pass on the aphids and the slugs.' Nature doesn't work like that – you've got to have it all, or risk having none, for the hedgehogs and robins won't stick around for long if you've blitzed the shrubs of all insect life and replaced the grass with plastic.

As I've tried to make clear in the book, we depend on many species for the services they provide, but we also depend on the functioning of much wider ecosystems – for food, products, waste disposal, economies and so on. There's another, huge, area that I've not talked about, and that's our health and wellbeing. I first started thinking about the interconnectedness of human health and nature after reading Richard Mabey's wonderful 2005 book, *Nature Cure*, which focused on his relationship with the natural world during a period of depression. Since then, evidence has accumulated in an extraordinarily broad range of health outcomes, and it all points in one direction – contact with nature is good for us. From reduced stress, anxiety, depression, blood pressure, and aggression, to improved sleep, eyesight, social

EPILOGUE

connectedness, life satisfaction, and even postoperative recovery times, nature offers a powerful antidote to the stresses of modern life, and it's one that we can all take advantage of. But to harness its power, we need to both preserve it and be comfortable in it. Preserving nature is only partly in our control, in that we can only directly influence the land that we each own, although we can also campaign and demand that politicians do more for wider nature preservation. We have more control over how comfortable we feel in nature, and how we choose to respond to its many components. A potential, troubling, consequence of society's growing disconnect with nature is that people's anxieties about wild creatures may either deter them from spending time in anything but the most manicured park, or may overshadow the experience to the extent that the benefits of nature are no longer felt.

The ecological, and often economical, reasons for tolerating nature as a whole, rather than little pieces of it, are conclusive enough, but I didn't want to just write about what wildlife can do for us. I also wanted to convince you that these animals are fascinating in their own right. I want you to go away and tell people that wasps, cockroaches, and mosquitos have important roles in the web of life, but also that crocodiles are thoughtful parents, sharks seek out company, and rats love being tickled. In doing so, I'm trying to give these creatures another side; I want to pad them out in the mind, transform them from two-dimensional characters ('villain', 'pest') to complex living entities, many of whom have their own thoughts, feelings, motivations and fears. It will take time but the more that we understand about these beasts, especially about why they do things and how they are similar to us, the more likely we are to tolerate, if not care, about them.

When conflict arises with other animals, it might be because we're in the wrong place. Or it might be because they're in the wrong place. Or we might both be in what we consider to be the right place, but we don't yet know how to coexist. This is the most problematic option, and it's the space that we desperately need to be better at occupying. By which, I mean we need to be better at understanding the needs and true natures of the creatures vying for space, better at understanding how many Indigenous cultures have already learned how to occupy this space, and better, ultimately, at learning to tolerate and coexist with wildlife in all its forms.

I find my thoughts turning back to Charlie, with whom I've long since lost touch. Would any of this be enough to nudge him towards seeing greater value in wildlife? I don't know. Things were bad back in 2010, when that brief conversation altered my worldview, and they're so much worse now. I can only hope that he, and so many like him, start to appreciate the beauty in all the beasts. Before it's too late for us all.

Acknowledgements

I know it's a cliché, but it still deserves to be said: writing looks like a solo activity but it's not. I literally could not have produced this book without the input of so many others over the past couple of years.

To my agent, Jane Turnbull – thank you for being a constant champion of this work, and for your expert thoughts, guidance and reassurance throughout this process.

At Bloomsbury Wildlife, I'm indebted to the stellar editing duo of Julie Bailey and Amy Hodkin. Julie – thank you for seeing the early potential in this and for giving my embryonic Beasts wings, and Amy – thank you for your unwavering enthusiasm, thoughtful edits and patience in tolerating my many additional changes. It has been a wonderfully collaborative editing process, and a pleasure to work on this with you both.

The wider team at Bloomsbury deserve heartfelt thanks for bringing this to life, as do Liz Peters and Marianne Taylor, for scrutinising, querying and improving the text, and Abby Cook for the stunning cover and illustrations.

Writing takes time, and time spent writing is time not earning. I'm therefore incredibly grateful to the Society of Authors for granting me an Authors' Foundation award for my work-in-progress. News of this came at a time when I was struggling with both cashflow and feelings of self-doubt, and it provided a much-needed boost.

A huge amount of research goes into a book like this, the majority desk-based, but it's also been my pleasure to talk with numerous experts. I am indebted to the following people who took the time to host me and show me their animals: Adam Bloch and Holly Cale of The Horstmann Trust; Cassie Modahl, Edd Crittenden and Paul Rowley of the CSRI at the University of Liverpool; Colin Stevenson of Crocodiles of the World; and Beulah Garner at the NHM in London. Many thanks also to the following experts for chatting with me virtually or emailing responses to my questions: Melissa Amarello, Joanna Bagniewska, Judith Benz-Schwarzburg, Brian Briggs, Natalie Bungay, Gordon Burghardt, Charlotte Burn, Rajan Chaudhary, Kai Collins, Arjun Dheer, Vladimir Dinets, Adrian Dyer, Stella Egbe, Niall Gallagher, Beulah Garner, Jonathan Green, Harry Green, Hal Herzog, Kay Holekamp, Lily Johnson-Ulrich, Yuri Kawaguchi, Christoph Klebl, Peter Klimley, Vanessa LoBue, Jorg Massen, Niall McCann, Holly McKinlay, Cassie Modahl, Susana Monsó, Christine Nalepa, Anna Nekaris, João Neves, Yamni Nigam, Rowena Packer, Pavol Prokop, Lawrence Reeves, Cécile Sarabian, Coby Schal, Rick Shine, Brandon Sideleau, Morgan Skinner, Seirian Sumner, Elisabeth Tibbets, Piotr Tryjanowski, Eva van Dijk, Mathijs van Overveld, Diogo Verissimo, Simon Watt. Several of you also took the time to read through and sense check chapter drafts or sections, for which I am especially appreciative, while numerous others shared or directed me towards useful information. Thank you all for your generosity of time and spirit, and thank you to all who gave permission for their words to be used here.

I'm grateful to JV Chamary, my mentor in the ABSW pilot scheme, for always providing the perfect balance of honest feedback and encouragement. And to Stephen Moss, surely one of the most generous writers out there when it comes to providing encouragement and writing wisdom.

I've been lucky to have a wonderful support network of family and friends, some of whom enthusiastically also signed up to read chapter drafts – Annie, Michael, Josh, thank you in particular for reading my ramblings and providing helpful comments. Outside of that, it's fair to say that I couldn't have done this without the support and love of friends and family. I'm grateful that every one of you is in my life.

And to John and Hattie, of course.

Selected bibliography

Chapter 1: All animals aren't equal
Correia, R. C. & Mammola, S. 2023. The searchscape of fear: A global analysis of internet search trends for biophobias. *People and Nature* 00: 1–15.

Evans, E. P. 1906. *The Criminal Prosecution and Capital Punishment of Animals*. W. Heinemann, London.

Girgen, J. 2003. The Historical and Contemporary Prosecution and Punishment of Animals. *Animal Law Review* 9: 97–133.

Herzog, H. & Burghardt, G. M. 1988. Attitudes Towards Animals: Origins and Diversity. *Anthrozoös* 1: 214–222.

Kim, J. et al. 2023. Conceptualizing Human–Nature Relationships: Implications of Human Exceptionalist Thinking for Sustainability and Conservation. *Topics in Cognitive Science* 15: 357–387.

Monsó, S. 2019. Humans are superior — by human standards. *Animal Sentience* 23(17).

Soga, M. & Evans, M. J. 2024. Biophobia: What it is, how it works and why it matters. *People and Nature* 6: 922–931.

Soga, M. & Gaston, K. J. 2016. Extinction of experience: the loss of human–nature interactions. *Frontiers in Ecology and the Environment* 14: 94–101.

Chapter 2: An awfulness of teeth and claws
Andermann, T. et al. 2020. The past and future human impact on mammalian diversity. *Science Advances* 6: eabb2313.

Braczkowski, A. R. et al. 2018. Leopards provide public health benefits in Mumbai, India. *Frontiers in Ecology and the Environment* 16: 176–182.

Brown, C. & Schluessel, V. 2023. Smart sharks: a review of chondrichthyan cognition. *Animal Cognition* 26: 175–188.

Dinets, V. 2010. Nocturnal behaviour of American Alligator (*Alligator mississippiensis*) in the wild during the mating season. *Herpetological Bulletin* 111: 4–11.

Doody, J. S., Dinets, V., Burghardt, G. M. 2021. *The Secret Social Lives of Reptiles*. Johns Hopkins University Press.

Gilbert, S. L. et al. 2016. Socioeconomic Benefits of Large Carnivore Recolonization Through Reduced Wildlife-Vehicle Collisions. *Conservation Letters* 10: 431–439.

Midway, T. R. et al. 2019. Trends in global shark attacks. *PLoS ONE* 14(2): e0211049.

Neves, J. et al. 2022. Changing trends: Beliefs and attitudes toward sharks and implications for conservation. *Ethnobiology and Conservation* 11: 11.

Neves, J. et al. 2023. Focusing on Social Behaviors: Improving the Perceived Warmth of Sharks in an Aquarium Setting. *Animals* 13: 2455.

Pepin-Neff, C. 2014. The Jaws Effect: How movie narratives are used to influence policy responses to shark bites in Western Australia. *Australian Journal of Political Science* 50: 114–127.

Plumwood, V. 1995. Human vulnerability and the experience of being prey. *Quadrant* 39(3): 29–34.

Rex, P. T. et al. 2023. Patterns of overlapping habitat use of juvenile white shark and human recreational water users along southern California beaches. *PLoS ONE* 18(6): e0286575.

Smith, F. A. et al. 2018. Body size downgrading of mammals over the late Quaternary. *Science* 360: 310–313.

Wolf, C. & Ripple, W. J. 2018. Rewilding the world's large carnivores. *R. Soc. open sci.* 5: 172235.

Chapter 3: Snake in the grass

Burghardt, GM. et al. 2021. Chemically mediated self-recognition in sibling juvenile common gartersnakes (*Thamnophis sirtalis*) reared on same or different diets. *Behaviour*. 158: 1169-1191.

Gutiérrez, J.M. et al. 2017. Snakebite envenoming. *Nature Reviews Disease Primers*. 3: 17079.

Freiburger, T. et al. 2024. Olfactory self-recognition in two species of snake. *Proc. R. Soc. B* 291: 20240125.

Hall, S.S. 2025. *Slither: How Nature's Most Maligned Creatures Illuminate Our World*. Grand Central Publishing, New York.

Headland, T.N. & Greene, H.W. 2011. Hunter-gatherers and other primates as prey, predators, and competitors of snakes. *Proc Natl Acad Sci U S A*. 108(52): E1470-4.

Isbell, L.A. 2006. Snakes as agents of evolutionary change in primate brains. *Journal of Human Evolution*. 51: 1–35.

LoBue, V. et al. 2013. Young children's interest in live animals. *British Journal of Developmental Psychology*. 31: 57–69.

Oliveira, A.L. et al. 2022. The chemistry of snake venom and its medicinal potential. *Nature Reviews.* 6: 451–469.

Shine, R. et al. 2023. Why Australian farmers should not kill venomous snakes. *Animal Conservation.* 27: 415–425.

World Health Organization. 2023. Fact sheet: Snakebite envenoming.

Chapter 4: To make flesh creep

Bell, W.J., Roth, L.M. & Nalepa, C.A. 2007. *Cockroaches: Ecology, Behaviour, and Natural History.* The Johns Hopkins University Press, Baltimore.

Cardoso, P. et al. 2020. Scientists' warning to humanity on insect extinctions. *Biological Conservation.* 242: 108426.

Case, T.I. et al. 2020. The Animal Origins of Disgust: Reports of Basic Disgust in Nonhuman Great Apes. *Evolutionary Behavioral Sciences.* 14: 231–260.

Davey, G.C.L. 2011. Disgust: the disease-avoidance emotion and its dysfunctions. *Phil. Trans. R. Soc. B.* 366: 3453–3465.

Fukano, Y. & Soga, M. 2023. Evolutionary psychology of entomophobia and its implications for insect conservation. *Current Opinion in Insect Science.* 59: 101100.

Goulson, D. 2021. *Silent Earth: Averting the Insect Apocalypse.* Jonathan Cape.

Nigam, Y. et al. 2022. An exploration of public perceptions and attitudes towards maggot therapy. *J Wound Care.* 31(9): 756–770.

Rozin, P., Haidt, J., & McCauley, C.R. 2000. Disgust. Entry in: D. Levinson, J. Ponzetti, & P. Jorgenson (eds.) *Encyclopedia of human emotions. Volume 1* (second edition) (pp. 188–193). Macmillan, New York.

Sarabian, C., Curtis, V. & McMullan, R. 2018. Evolution of pathogen and parasite avoidance behaviours. *Phil. Trans. R. Soc. B.* 373: 20170256.

Schal, C., Gautier, J-Y., and Bell, W. 1984. Behavioral ecology of cockroaches. *Biol Rev.* 59: 209–254.

Staňková, H. et al. 2021. The Ultimate List of the Most Frightening and Disgusting Animals: Negative Emotions Elicited by Animals in Central European Respondents. *Animals.* 11(3): 747.

Winegard, T.C. 2019. *The Mosquito: A Human History of Our Deadliest Predator.* E.P. Dutton.

World Health Organization. 2024. World malaria report 2024: addressing inequity in the global malaria response. Geneva: World Health Organization.

Chapter 5: Keep calm and carrion

Bildstein, K.L. 2022. *Vultures of the World: Essential Ecology and Conservation*. Comstock Publishing Associates, Ithaca, New York, USA.

Cook, S.E. et al. 2024. Current policies in Europe and South Asia do not prevent veterinary use of drugs toxic to vultures. *Ecological Solutions and Evidence*. 5: e12357.

Ellison, A.M., Watson, J., Demers, E. 2015. Testing problem solving in turkey vultures (*Cathartes aura*) using the string-pulling test. *Animal Cognition*. 18: 111–118.

Frank, E.G. & Sudarshan, A. 2024. The Social Costs of Keystone Species Collapse: Evidence From The Decline of Vultures in India. *American Economic Review*. 114(10): 3007–3040.

Greenspoon, L. et al. 2023. The global biomass of wild mammals. *Proceedings of the National Academy of Sciences* 120: e2204892120.

Ogada, D. et al. 2016. Another Continental Vulture Crisis: Africa's Vultures Collapsing toward Extinction. *Conservation Letters*. 9(2): 89–97.

Prakash, V. et al. 2003. Catastrophic collapse of Indian white-backed *Gyps bengalensis* and long-billed *Gyps indicus* vulture populations. *Biological Conservation*. 109: 381–390.

Subalusky, A.L. et al. 2017. Annual mass drownings of the Serengeti wildebeest migration influence nutrient cycling and storage in the Mara River. *Proceedings of the National Academy of Sciences*. 114: 7647–7652.

Van Overveld, T. et al. 2021. Vultures as an overlooked model in cognitive ecology. *Animal Cognition*. 25(3):495–507.

Chapter 6: Easy on the aye-aye

Albert, C., Luque, G.M. and Courchamp, F. 2018. The twenty most charismatic species. *PLoS ONE*. 13(7): e0199149.

Jarić, I. et al. 2024. Flagship individuals in biodiversity conservation. *Frontiers in Ecology and the Environment*. 22(1): e2599.

Klebl, C. et al. 2021. Beauty of the Beast: Beauty as an important dimension in the moral standing of animals. *Journal of Environmental Psychology* 75: 101624.

Kringelbach, M.L. et al. 2016. On cuteness: unlocking the parental brain and beyond. *Trends in Cognitive Sciences*. 20(7): 545–558.

Nekaris K.A. et al. 2013. Tickled to Death: Analysing Public Perceptions of 'Cute' Videos of Threatened Species (Slow Lorises – *Nycticebus* spp.) on Web 2.0 Sites. *PLoS ONE*. 8(7): e69215.

Nittono, H. et al. 2012. The Power of *Kawaii*: Viewing Cute Images Promotes a Careful Behavior and Narrows Attentional Focus. *PLoS ONE*. 7(9): e46362.

Shaw, M. et al. 2024. Using photo editing to understand the impact of species aesthetics on support for conservation. *People and Nature*. 6: 660–675.

Smith, R.J. et al. 2012. Identifying Cinderella species: uncovering mammals with conservation flagship appeal. *Conservation Letters*. 5: 205–212.

Turvey, S. 2009. *Witness to Extinction: How We Failed to Save the Yangtze River Dolphin*. Oxford University Press, Oxford, UK.

Wei, F. et al. 2018. The Value of Ecosystem Services from Giant Panda Reserves. *Current Biology*. 28: 2174–2180.

Chapter 7: Naughty neighbours

Andrews, K. and Monsó, S. 2020. *Rats are us*. Aeon.

Bartal, I.B-A. 2024. The complex affective and cognitive capacities of rats. *Science*. 385: 1298–1305.

Bertone, M.A. et al. 2016. Arthropods of the great indoors: characterizing diversity inside urban and suburban homes. *PeerJ*. 4:e1582.

Boldorini, G.X. et al. 2024 Predators control pests and increase yield across crop types and climates: a meta-analysis. *Proc. R. Soc. B*. 291: 20232522.

Brock, R.E., Cini, A. and Sumner, S. 2021. Ecosystem services provided by aculeate wasps. *Biological Reviews*. 96: 1645–1675.

Crawford, L.E. et al. 2020. Enriched environment exposure accelerates rodent driving skills. *Behavioural Brain Research*. 378: 112309.

Frank, E. 2024. The economic impacts of ecosystem disruptions: Costs from substituting biological pest control. *Science*. 385(6713): eadg0344.

Morton, F.B. et al. 2023. Urban foxes are bolder but not more innovative than their rural conspecifics. *Animal Behaviour*. 203: 101–113.

Parsons, K.J. et al. 2020. Skull morphology diverges between urban and rural populations of red foxes mirroring patterns of domestication and macroevolution. *Proc. R. Soc. B*. 287: 20200763.

Reinhold, A.S. et al. 2019. Behavioral and neural correlates of hide-and-seek in rats. *Science*. 365: 1180–1183.

Southon, R.J. et al. 2019. Social wasps are effective biocontrol agents of key lepidopteran crop pests. *Proc. R. Soc. B* 286: 20191676.

Sumner, S. 2022. *Endless Forms: The Secret World of Wasps*. William Collins, London, UK.

Tibbetts, E.A. 2002. Visual signals of individual identity in the wasp *Polistes fuscatus*. *Proc. R. Soc. Lond.* B. 269: 1423–1428.

Tibbetts, E.A. et al. 2019 Transitive inference in *Polistes* paper wasps. *Biology Letters*. 15: 20190015.

Chapter 8: The good, the bad and the animal

Giles, D.A. et al. 2023. Harassment and killing of porpoises ("phocoenacide") by fish-eating Southern Resident killer whales (*Orcinus orca*). *Marine Mammal Science*. 40: e13073.

Harris, H.S. et al. 2010. Lesions and Behavior Associated with Forced Copulation of Juvenile Pacific Harbor Seals (*Phoca vitulina richardsi*) by Southern Sea Otters (*Enhydra lutris nereis*). *Aquatic Mammals*. 36: 331–341.

Hunter, F.M. & Davis, L.S. 1998. Female Adélie Penguins Acquire Nest Material from Extrapair Males after Engaging in Extrapair Copulations. *The Auk*. 115: 526–528.

Lukas, D. and Huchard, E. 2019. The evolution of infanticide by females in mammals. *Phil. Trans. R. Soc. B*. 374(1780): 20180075.

Rimbach, R. et al. 2012. Interspecific Infanticide and Infant-Directed Aggression by Spider Monkeys (*Ateles hybridus*) in a Fragmented Forest in Colombia. *American Journal of Primatology* 74: 990–997.

Russell, D.G.D., Sladen, W.J.L., and Ainley, D.G. 2012. Dr. George Murray Levick (1876–1956): unpublished notes on the sexual habits of the Adélie penguin. *Polar Record*. 1–7.

Schutt, B. 2017. *Cannibalism: A Perfectly Natural History*. Algonquin Books.

Southern, L.M. Deschner, T, and Pika, S. 2021. Lethal coalitionary attacks of chimpanzees (*Pan troglodytes troglodytes*) on gorillas (*Gorilla gorilla gorilla*) in the wild. *Scientific Reports*. 11: 14673.

Towner, A.V. et al. 2023. Direct observation of killer whales predating on white sharks and evidence of a flight response. *Ecology*. 104: e3875.

Index

Advocates for Snake Preservation (ASP) 111
affective reasoning 24
Africa
   crocodiles 41, 42
   great migration 42, 157–159, 160–161
   lions 37, 60, 171, 293
   megafauna extinctions 59
   vultures 163, 164, 173–177, 181
Agta hunter-gatherers, Philippines 92
Andrews, Kristin 268–269
animal criminal trials 15–18
animal self-recognition 103–105
animal villainisation 22–28
animism 14, 15, 70
anthropocentrism 18
anthropomorphism 18, 25–27
antibiotics 132, 138
anticoagulants 152, 259–260, 261
antivenoms 78, 84, 86, 97, 110
Asian vulture crisis 178–180
attractiveness *see* physical attractiveness
Australia
   crocodiles 33–34, 68–69
   megafauna extinctions 59–60
   sharks 32, 48, 49, 63–64, 69
   snakes 85, 90–91, 96–98

baby schema 205–207, 213
baiji 198–199
bats 247
bears 18, 61, 64, 296
beauty *see* physical attractiveness
bees 240, 241, 252
behavioural immune system 116, 144–146, 202–203
Bildstein, Keith 159, 187
biological preparedness theory 92–95
biophilia theory 22–23
biophobia 22–24
   see also fear and phobias
BirdLife International 176, 177
Blair Witch Project, The (film) 37
blatticomposting 131
Bloch, Adam 162, 165, 167, 172, 174, 178, 184–185, 191–193

brachycephalic dogs 212–215
brain
   size in urban animals 271, 272–273
   human fear response 36
   nucleus accumbens 106–107
   'reptile brain' concept 46, 100
   snakes 106–107
   see also cognition
Brown, Culum 52–53, 55–56, 57–58
Burghardt, Gordon 45–47, 101, 102–104, 105, 108, 110–111
Burn, Charlotte 258–259, 269, 270

Cale, Holly 162, 164, 165, 175–176, 177, 185, 189, 193
cannibalism 294–296
carbofuran 172–173
cats, pet 121, 206, 208
cave art 13–14
Centre for Snakebite Research & Interventions (CSRI), Liverpool 78–79, 82–83, 85–88, 99–100
'charismatic megafauna' 195–199, 217–220
Chaudhary, Rajan 31–32, 70
chimpanzees 103, 118–119, 289–292
China 197–199, 256
cockroaches 122–133
   benefits to humans 130–132
   courtship behaviour 132
   cyborg 131
   disgust towards 122–125
   diversity 126–129
   medical uses 131–132
   and parasitoid wasps 245–246
   parental care 132
   pest species 123, 124–126, 129–130, 133, 143–144, 145
   physical feats 130
cognition
   and animal villainisation 26, 27, 28
   crocodiles 43–48
   dolphins 281
   foxes 271, 272
   rats 261–267
   and 'reptile brain' concept 46, 100

cognition (*continued*)
    sharks 51–52, 55–57, 281
    snakes 100–108
    vultures 185–192
    wasps 249–255
condor
    Andean 162–163, 165–168, 171–173, 191–192
    California 166
conservation funding
    for attractive vs unattractive animals 196–199, 215–230
    for insects 155
    for vultures 192
courtship behaviour
    cockroaches 132
    crocodiles 44–45
    sea snakes 97–98
criminal trials of animals 15–18
Crittenden, Edd 78, 82–83, 86–88, 96, 99–100
crocodiles 40–48
    American alligator 44, 47
    attacks on humans 32, 33–34, 41
    conservation 68–69, 71–73
    courtship behaviour 44–45
    ecotourism 72–73
    extinction threats 62
    farming 71–72
    gharials 46–47
    hunting and persecution of 62
    in natural history documentaries 41–42
    Nile crocodile 41, 42, 158
    parental care 45–47
    saltwater crocodile 41, 68–69
    tool use 44
Crocodiles of the World zoo 40, 43, 44–45, 47

Darwin, Charles 63, 113, 114–115, 165–166, 246
dengue fever 89–90, 146, 150
diclofenac 178–181
Dinets, Vladimir 42–44, 47
diseases and pathogens
    antibiotics 132, 138
    behavioural immune system 116, 144–146, 202–203
    and cockroaches 125–126, 132
    dengue fever 89–90, 146, 150
    and disgust response 115–116, 144–146, 202–203

and loss of vultures 182–183
    malaria 146–148, 150
    and meat 169
    mosquito-transmitted 89–90, 146–149, 150
    plague 257
    rabies 68, 182
    and rats 257–258
    sickle cell disorder 147
    tickborne 65–66
disgust response 113–146
    behavioural immune system 116, 144–146, 202–203
    cockroaches 122–133, 143–144, 145, 156
    and disease avoidance 115–116, 144–146, 202–203
    evolution of 114–117
    maggots 136–141
    most disgusting animals 119–122
    oral contamination hypothesis 114–115, 116
    slime and mucus 133–135
    and ugliness 202–203, 204
    urbanisation-disgust hypothesis 141–146
dogs
    cuteness 206
    feral 67–68, 182
    flat-faced breeds 212–215
    self-awareness 105
dolphins
    'bad' behaviour 277–281, 293
    Yangtze River dolphin 198–199
domestication syndrome 271–272
Dyer, Adrian 253–255

ecotourism 72–73
Egbe, Stella 175, 176, 177
Egypt, ancient 171, 256
elephants 17–18, 160, 174
emotional contagion 264–265
emotions 35–36
    in rats 261–265
    see also disgust response; fear and phobias
empathy 264–265
Evans, Edmund 15, 16, 17
exceptionalist thinking 18–21, 25
'extinction of experience' 22, 95
extinction threats
    insects 146, 153–155
    predators 60–62

INDEX

vultures 163, 172–181
extinctions
　five mass extinction events 21–22, 53, 79–80, 302
　megafauna extinctions 58–60
　sixth mass extinction 22, 58
　Yangtze River dolphin 198–199

facial recognition by wasps 249–255
fear and phobias
　of insects 144–146
　of predators 32–33, 35–39, 48, 50–51, 64–65
　of snakes 91–95
　of spiders 10–11, 23, 24, 91, 93–95
fight-or-flight response 36
fish
　blobfish 228–229
　Burton's mouthbrooder 294
　hagfish 134–135
flagship species 218–220
fox, red 270–272
Frank, Eyal 182–183, 247
frogs 121, 135, 289
Fukano, Yuya 141, 144, 145

Garner, Beulah 125, 127–128, 129
'good' animals with 'bad' behaviour 277–299
　butterflies 296
　cannibalism 294–296
　chimpanzees 289–292
　dolphins 277–281, 293
　hedgehogs 296–297
　infanticide 291–296
　monkeys 292, 294, 295
　otters 286–289
　penguins 282–286
Goodall, Jane 290–291
gorillas 273, 291–292
great migration 42, 157–159, 160–161
Greene, Harry 92, 96, 99, 108, 111

Hargila Army 222–223
health and wellbeing 304–305
hedgehogs 296–297
Hegel, G. W. F. 195, 201
Horstmann Vulture Conservation Trust 162–167, 175–176, 177–178, 184–185, 189, 191–193
human deaths and injury
　crocodiles 32, 33–34, 41
　deer-vehicle collisions 66
　dolphins 280–281
　due to loss of vultures 182
　feral dogs 68, 182
　malaria 146–147
　otters 287–288
　plague 257
　sharks 48–50
　snakes 78, 82–85, 92, 97, 98, 109–110
　tigers 31–32
human diseases *see* diseases and pathogens
human exceptionalism 18–21, 25
hyenas 161, 164, 171

immune system, behavioural 116, 144–146, 202–203
India
　adjutant stork 222–223
　leopards and feral dogs 67–68
　snakes 84, 109–110
　vultures 178–180, 182–183
Indonesia 13, 41
infanticide 291–296
insecticides 89–90, 234, 247
insects 141–156
　butterflies 296
　diversity 153–154
　ecological importance 90, 150–151, 154, 241, 243–249
　fear of 144–146
　global insect apocalypse 146, 153–155
　ladybirds 243–244
　maggots 136–141
　medical uses 131–132, 136–140, 152
　mosquitoes 89–90, 146–153, 156
　urbanisation-disgust hypothesis 141–146
　weevils 17
　see also cockroaches; wasps
intelligence *see* cognition

Jaws (film) 38–39, 58, 61–62
jellyfish 19

kakapo 229
keystone species 63–64
Klebl, Chris 121, 202–204

ladybirds 243–244
leeches 152

leopards 67–68
Leopold, Aldo 63, 65
Levick, George Murray 282–283, 284
lions 37, 60, 171, 293
livestock 14–15, 16, 179, 182–184
LoBue, Vanessa 93–95
loris, slow 209–211
Lyme disease 65–66

maggots 136–141
malaria 146–148, 150
manatees 280
medical uses
  cockroaches 131–132
  leeches 152
  maggots 136–140
  mosquitoes 152
  venom 88–89
  see also traditional medicine
megafauna extinctions 58–60
'mere exposure' effect 223, 227
Modahl, Cassie 85–88, 89–90
mole rat, naked 121
moles 15, 16
monkeys
  disgust response 117–118
  infanticide 292, 294, 295
  proboscis monkey memes 225–227
Monsó, Susana 19, 268–269
mosquitoes 89–90, 146–153, 156
mucus 133–135

nature, definitions of 20
Nekaris, Anna 209–211
Nepal 31–32, 70–71, 179, 180
neurotoxic chemicals 88, 109, 173, 246
Neves, João 50–51, 73, 301, 302
New Zealand 229, 265, 296–297
Nigam, Yamni 136, 137, 138, 139, 140
Nigeria 175–177

orca 279
otters 286–289

Packer, Rowena 213–215
Packham, Chris 196–197, 198
pain grimace scale 268
panda, giant 196–198, 217, 219
parasites 115–116, 118, 119–120, 147–148, 257
parasitoid wasps 244–248
parental care
  cockroaches 132

crocodiles 45–47
snakes 108
vultures 173
pathogens *see* diseases and pathogens
penguins 282–286
  Adélie penguin 282–283, 284–286
  emperor penguin 284
  king penguin 286
  macaroni penguin 284
Pepin-Neff, Chris 38, 39
pest control 234
  insecticides 89–90, 234, 247
  of rats 259–261
  by snakes 90
  by spiders 90
  by wasps 90, 243–249
pests 233–238, 270–276
  see also cockroaches; rats; wasps
phobias *see* fear and phobias
physical attractiveness 195–231
  'charismatic megafauna' 195–199, 217–220
  and conservation funding 215–230
  cuteness 205–209, 224
  and disease avoidance 202–203
  evolution of appreciation for beauty 201–204
  flat-faced dogs 212–215
  humour and positive feelings for ugly animals 225–230
  and moral concern 203–204, 208
  slow loris pet trade 209–211
  ugliness and disgust response 202–203, 204
pigeon breeding 212
Plasmodium parasites 147–148
Plumwood, Val 33–34, 38
Poland 225–227
pollination 151, 154, 241
Poltergeist (film) 113–114
porpoise, harbour 278–279
Prakash, Vibhu 178, 179
predators
  attacks on humans 31–32, 33–34, 41, 48–50
  bears 18, 61, 64, 296
  benefits to humans 65–68
  conservation 68–73
  ecological importance 62–65
  ecotourism 72–73
  extinction threats 60–62
  fear of 32–33, 35–39, 48, 50–51, 64–65

INDEX

leopards 67–68
lions 37, 60, 171, 293
megafauna extinctions 58–60
tigers 9–10, 31–32, 60–61, 70–71
wolves 61, 63, 64, 66
see also crocodiles; sharks
Prokop, Pavol 114, 116, 120, 156, 292

raccoons 64–65, 272
rats 237, 255–270
    cleanliness of 258–259, 261
    cognition 261–267
    disease transmission 257–258
    emotions 261–265
    empathy and helping other rats 265
    ethics of experimenting on 267–269
    in human culture 256
    laughter 262–264
    learning to drive 267
    and plague 257
    playing hide-and-seek 263–264
    poison baits 259–260, 261
    tickling 262–264
rays 51–52, 56, 61–62
religions 14, 15, 70, 184
robots 130, 224, 265
rodent-operated vehicles (ROVs) 267
Rowley, Paul 78, 86–87

scavengers 157–161
    cockroaches 127–128
    early humans 171
    see also vultures
Schal, Coby 125–126, 132, 133
seals 286, 288–289
self-recognition by animals 103–105
sharks 48–58
    attacks on humans 48–50
    cognition 51–52, 55–57, 281
    conservation 69, 73
    diversity 51
    ecological importance 63–64
    ecotourism 73
    evolution 52–53
    extinction threats 62
    fear of 32, 38–39, 48, 50–51
    Galapagos shark 73
    great white shark 38, 49–50, 51, 57, 281, 301
    hammerhead sharks 53, 54–55, 73
    hunting and persecution of 61–62
    lemon shark 56, 57
    magnetic orientation 54–55

    nurse shark 57
    Port Jackson shark 53
    reef sharks 56–57, 73
    social behaviour 56–57
    tiger sharks 51, 63–64
Shine, Rick 90–91, 96–98
Skinner, Morgan 100, 104–107, 108
slugs and snails 120, 135
'smoke detector principle' 144–145
snakes 75–112
    adder 76, 85
    African egg-eating snake 78–79
    aggression 96–99
    antivenoms 78, 84, 86, 97, 110
    brown snake 85, 90, 96–97
    brown tree snake 91
    cobras 84, 87, 88, 99
    cognition 100–108
    constrictor snakes 82
    diversity 79–80
    evolution 79–80, 99
    fear of 91–95
    garter snakes 100, 101, 103–104, 106, 107
    human deaths and injury 78, 82–85, 92, 97, 98, 109–110
    kraits 84, 88, 109
    milking 86–88
    parental care 108
    persecution of 76–77
    pest control by 90
    pythons 79, 82, 91, 92, 102, 104, 106, 107
    rattlesnakes 75–77, 96, 106, 108, 111
    sea snakes 97–98
    self-recognition 103–105
    senses 101–102
    social behaviour 105–107
    spitting 99
    venom 78, 80–82, 85–90
    vipers 82–83, 84, 88, 102
social intelligence hypothesis 253
Soga, Masashi 22, 141, 144, 145
Spain 180–181, 183, 185–187
spiders 10–11, 23, 24, 80–81, 90, 91, 93–95, 120, 303
Stevenson, Colin 40–42, 44–45, 47–48, 72
stork
    adjutant 222–223
    marabou 158–159, 221
    white 294
Sudarshan, Anant 182–183

Sumner, Seirian 240–242, 243–244, 248
Survival of the Cutest (Who Gets on the Ark?) art installation 195–196
symmetry, facial 202
synanthropes 259

tardigrades 19
Tibbetts, Elizabeth 250–253
ticks 65–66
tigers 9–10, 31–32, 60–61, 70–71
tool use
   alligators 44
   vultures 188–189
traditional medicine 110, 131, 174–177
transitive inference 252
trophic cascades 63–64

Ugly Animal Preservation Society (UAPS) 227–230
'uncanny valley' response 224
urbanisation-disgust hypothesis 141–146
US
   deer-vehicle collisions 66
   fear of predators 39
   rattlesnake roundups 76–77, 111
   starfish and mollusc diversity 63–64

van Overveld, Mathjis 185–188
venom
   antivenoms 78, 84, 86, 97, 110
   cytotoxic components 88
   evolution of 81
   haemotoxic components 88
   medical uses 88–89
   milking 86–88
   neurotoxic components 88, 109, 246
   slow loris 210
   snakes 78, 80–82, 85–90
   spiders 80–81
   use as insecticides 89–90
   wasps 245–246
venomics 86
Veríssimo, Diogo 219–220, 221–222, 223, 224
villainisation of animals 22–28
vultures 121, 158, 161–194
   Andean condor 162–163, 165–168, 171–173, 191–192
   bearded vulture 162–163, 170
   black vulture 191
   California condor 166
   cognition 185–192
   and diclofenac 178–181
   dominance hierarchies 186, 187
   Egyptian vulture 162–163, 168, 171, 180, 181, 184–187, 188–189, 193
   extinction threats 163, 172–181
   griffon vultures 162, 163, 164, 167, 168
   hooded vulture 162–163, 164, 165, 175, 177
   and human culture 171–172, 184
   impacts of loss of 182–184
   Indian vulture 168, 178, 180
   king vulture 164
   mud bathing 186–187
   palm nut vulture 175–176
   physiology 168–170
   poisoning 172–174, 175, 178–181
   preening 186
   Rüppell's vulture 167, 189–190
   and sky burials 184
   slender-billed vulture 178, 180
   social behaviour 185–188
   tool use 188–189
   in traditional medicine 174–177
   turkey vulture 168, 190–191
   white-backed vulture 164, 174, 175
   white-rumped vulture 178, 180

warfarin 259–260
wasps 238–255
   Brazilian paper wasp 248
   cognition 249–255
   ecological importance 90, 241, 243–249
   facial recognition 249–255
   fairyfly wasps 244–245
   hornets 236, 238–240, 276
   jewel wasp 245–246
   negative attitudes towards 240–243
   northern paper wasp 248, 250–253
   parasitoid wasps 244–248
   pest control by 90, 243–249
   social wasps 238–240, 248–249, 250–255
   venom 88, 245–246
weevils 17
wildebeest 42, 158–159
wildlife trade 68–69, 175–177, 209–211
wolves 61, 63, 64, 66
World Health Organization (the WHO) 83–84, 109, 146
Worldwide Fund for Nature (WWF) 196, 198, 228